TOPICAL   ENILCONAZOLE - (0.2%)
        ↳ CLINAFARM (SCHERING) - USE IN POULTRY HOUSES
                        - NOT EPA APPROVED FOR TOPICAL USE
- 14.5 mL DILUTED W/
  1 L H₂O   - CHEAP E·coum
- SPONGE ON COAT (100 cc/CAT); AIR DRY; 2x WEEKLY FOR @ LEAST 1 mo
                                                      (VOMITING, SALIV.

Terbenafine - anti-fungal (RINGWORM)
        - 10-20 mg/kg SID
        - MONITOR W/ CBC, PROF. (SIDE EFFECTS NOT
          DOCUMENTED YET)

Skin and Coat Care for Your Dog

Compiled by Lowell Ackerman, DVM, PhD,
Diplomate, American College of Veterinary Dermatology

TS–249

Title page: Great coat on Mystique, the world's premiere show dog: Ch. Altana's Mystique, owned by Jane Firestone and handled by Mr. James Moses. This German Shepherd has won Best in Show in over 275 American Kennel Club dog shows, more than any other dog in history. Photograph by Isabelle Francais.

Publisher's Note: *The portrayal of pet products in this book is strictly for instructive value only; the appearance of such products does not necessarily constitute an endorsement by the editor, authors, the publisher or the owners of the dogs portrayed in this book.*

Distributed in the UNITED STATES to the Pet Trade by T.F.H. Publications, Inc., One T.F.H. Plaza, Neptune City, NJ 07753; distributed in the UNITED STATES to the Bookstore and Library Trade by National Book Network, Inc. 4720 Boston Way, Lanham MD 20706; in CANADA to the Pet Trade by H & L Pet Supplies Inc., 27 Kingston Crescent, Kitchener, Ontario N2B 2T6; Rolf C. Hagen Ltd., 3225 Sartelon Street, Montreal 382 Quebec; in CANADA to the Book Trade by Vanwell Publishing Ltd., 1 Northrup Crescent, St. Catharines, Ontario L2M 6P5 ; in ENGLAND by T.F.H. Publications, PO Box 15, Waterlooville PO7 6BQ; in AUSTRALIA AND THE SOUTH PACIFIC by T.F.H. (Australia), Pty. Ltd., Box 149, Brookvale 2100 N.S.W., Australia; in NEW ZEALAND by Brooklands Aquarium Ltd. 5 McGiven Drive, New Plymouth, RD1 New Zealand; in Japan by T.F.H. Publications, Japan—Jiro Tsuda, 10-12-3 Ohjidai, Sakura, Chiba 285, Japan; in SOUTH AFRICA by Lopis (Pty) Ltd., P.O. Box 39127, Booysens, 2016, Johannesburg, South Africa. Published by T.F.H. Publications, Inc.
MANUFACTURED IN THE UNITED STATES OF AMERICA
BY T.F.H. PUBLICATIONS, INC.

Contents

About the Editor

Lowell Ackerman, DVM, PhD is a board-certified veterinary dermatologist and a consultant in the fields of dermatology and nutrition. He is the author of nine books and over 130 articles and book chapters. Dr. Ackerman has lectured extensively on an international basis, including the United States, Canada, Europe and South Africa.

Preface

Skin problems represent a large proportion of veterinary visits. They are also some of the most frustrating cases to diagnose and treat. However, help is on the way! Over the past 20 years, veterinary dermatology has emerged as a major veterinary specialty and breakthroughs are being made on a regular basis. Because we understand skin diseases much better now, diagnoses are being made more routinely, and therapies are often very specific in their actions.

With all the new developments in veterinary dermatology, it is becoming exceedingly difficult for veterinarians to remain current. Fortunately, the American College of Veterinary Dermatology certifies new diplomates each year to help meet this challenge. Veterinary dermatologists work with general veterinary practitioners in a team approach to best manage stubborn skin problems. There are now dermatology specialists available in most geographic areas.

The goal of this book is straightforward—to provide individuals with information about the most common skin ailments, and for that information to be relayed by internationally renowned experts. All of the chapters on skin problems have been written by board-certified veterinary dermatologists. The chapter entitled "Lumps and Bumps" was written by a board-certified veterinary oncologist, a cancer specialist. Finally, the chapter on "grooming and maintenance" was written by a highly qualified professional groomer.

My thanks to all the contributors. They have done a remarkable job in distilling the important aspects of dermatologic conditions into a very readable and informative text.

Lowell Ackerman, DVM, PhD

A standing ovation for Scottish Terrier, Ch. Gaelforce Post Script, Best in Show at the 1995 Westminster Kennel Club Dog Show, is owned by Vandra Huber and Dr. Joe Kinnarney and handled by Maripi Wooldridge. Photograph by Holloway Studios.

Introduction

By Lowell Ackerman, DVM
Diplomate, American College of
  Veterinary Dermatology
Mesa Veterinary Hospital, Ltd.
858 N. Country Club Drive
Mesa, AZ 85201

The skin is the largest organ of the body and serves many functions, including protection from the environment, heat regulation and water balance. It accomplishes these important functions in a variety of ways. The dead surface covering of the skin (the stratum corneum) is composed of shingle-like skin cells known as keratinocytes. These cells migrate upwards from deeper skin layers, eventually dying to fulfill their destiny. This whole layer (the epidermis) has no blood supply of its own; it depends on the deeper fibrous layer (the dermis) for all its nutritive needs. And, below the dermis is the subcutis, a collection of fat that provides a cushioning effect to the wear and tear of everyday life.

The haircoat (more correctly termed fur) is a joint project of the dermis and epidermis. Specialized cells of the epidermis extend down into the dermis where they meet with the dermal papilla and a blood supply to form a hair follicle. After birth, no new hair follicles are produced. There are two main types of hair, the long bristly guard hairs and the downy vellus hairs. Whiskers (vibrissae) are specialized sensory hairs that have an elaborate blood and nerve supply.

But, the skin is much more than just epidermis and hair follicles. It is also an important immunologic defense mechanism that helps ward off microorganisms (bacteria, parasites, fungi) and produces antibodies against many other invaders, especially viruses. In fact, the skin immunologic system (SIS) is one of the most important defenses we have against many life-threatening infections.

Because the skin and its protective mechanisms are so complex and far-reaching, accurate diagnosis and proper management of skin problems is not always straightforward.

Karla Addington-Smith is a Certified Master Groomer from Cincinnati, Ohio. She has spent 18 years in the world of professional dog grooming. Karla is an international contest judge, grooming contest winner, noted speaker and writer. After a two-year veterinary technician program and then apprentice position, Karla opened the first of the chain of three grooming/retail shops in 1978. Karla was a member of both the 1988 and 1989 Groom Team USA and the winner of the 1988 creative grooming competition and the 1989 national groomer title at Intergroom. Karla has also collected three Cardinal Crystal Achievement Awards for the 1988 American Groomer of the Year, the 1990 Congeniality Award and the 1991 Grooming Journalist of the Year. She is well versed in business relations as well, being named the 1988 Outstanding Young Entrepreneur in America by the United States Association of Small Business and Entrepreneurship. Karla writes for various publications and is a regular contributor to Today's Breeder, *and* Groomer to Groomer *magazines. She was the grooming columnist and regular feature writer for* Pets Supplies Marketing *magazine from 1989-1992. Karla has appeared on numerous television programs promoting pet care and education, both locally and nationally. Karla now works as an independent manufacturer's representative in the pet industry as she continues to write, speak and judge.*

Professional Grooming Techniques for Optimum Coat and Skin Care

By Karla Addington-Smith
1358 Avalon Drive
Maineville, OH 45039

INTRODUCTION

The professional groomer plays an important role in the care and good health of our clients' pets. Professional grooming services applied routinely will not only enhance the dog's looks but improve his comfort, health and social acceptance. Professional grooming services can be divided into two separate categories.

MAINTENANCE AND ART

Maintenance grooming consists of brushing, combing, dematting, bathing, conditioning, external parasite control, drying, nail trimming and ear cleaning. All dogs regardless of breed or coat type benefit from general grooming maintenance. How often the dog needs professional grooming will depend on the length and texture of coat, his activity and how much home grooming he receives.

The art of grooming is just that: an art. Considering changes in styles, trends and technique in grooming associated with dog exhi-bition, it's no doubt an endless struggle to stay up to date. It can take many years to learn the correct breed profile and comprehend the standard for all breeds recognized by the American Kennel Club. Add the myriad of possible mix-breed styles and the professional groomer has quite a challenge in making their client's dog the best possible presentation.

A HEALTH VISIT

Regular visits to the professional grooming shop gives the groomer an opportunity to detect any potential health problems and changes in the dog's coat, skin and behavior. A professional groomer may see a client four to eight times a year for grooming. A veterinarian may see that same client once a year unless the dog needs monitoring for a certain problem. The professional groomer has an important responsibility to the overall good health of our clients' beloved pets. An important aspect in properly caring for a client's pet is to spend a few mo-

Professional groomers usually see a client four to eight times a year.

ments carefully examining the dog. Evaluate the condition of the coat and which tools, products and techniques would best serve this particular animal. Run your hands over his skin. Are there any new growths, lesions, irritations or lumps that need to be brought to the attention of the owner and avoided by brushes and other grooming tools? Look closely at the skin. Are there signs of external parasites? Are the ears free of redness, discharge and odor? Are the teeth white and secure in the gums or inflamed and the mouth a source of odor? The eyes should be bright and clear without discharge. Check the pads of the feet for foreign objects and the nails for splitting or fungal infections. Rusty coat discoloration occurs from licking representing injury, pain or allergy. Early detection and referral to a veterinarian for treatment can greatly reduce the seriousness of a manifesting problem. Your client's pet is best served when owner, veterinarian and professional groomer work together.

GROOMING TOOLS AND TECHNIQUES

Brushing

Perhaps brushing is the single most important service rendered by the professional groomer. A dog's skin is its largest organ. Routine brushing helps to keep this organ healthy and shiny and is the first step in the grooming process. Choosing the proper brush and using it correctly can make the grooming visit more effective and pleasant.

A bristle brush is used on short-

or smooth-coated dogs only. Even the most firm bristle brush will not penetrate coats longer than the short- or smooth-coated breeds. This brush does not remove undercoat but does a fine job massaging the skin and distributing the natural oils keeping the skin healthy and the hair shiny.

A pin brush has long straight metal pins attached to a rubber backing. Most are oval shaped and used by exhibitors on long-coated breeds. This brush is not practical for pet owners or as a multi-purpose brush for the professional groomer as it does not remove undercoat, which is the culprit for matting. It does, however, work well for finishing or fluff drying on long-haired breeds free of tangles and

The professional groomer acts as a veterinarian's assistant by checking the dog for potential health problems.

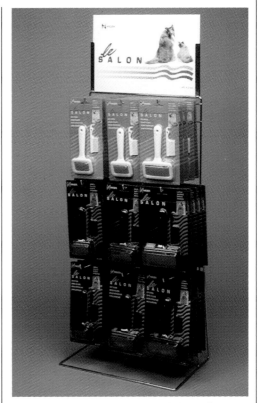

Selecting the right grooming tools is the first step to a healthy, well-groomed dog. Your local pet shop or veterinarian offers a variety of high-quality brushes, combs and rakes. Photograph courtesy of Hagen.

mats.

The slicker brush is the best bet for most dogs. This brush is used by parting the hair and brushing from the skin out in layers. The bent wire bristles grasps and removes the undercoat before your client finds it on carpeting and furniture. The slicker brush comes in a variety of sizes, shapes and stiffness of bristles and helps prevent matting when used regularly. The smaller, gentle variety can be used safely on sensitive-skinned pets. The curved, firm variety is used on larger double-coated breeds to loosen and remove

Brushes come in a variety of styles and sizes to fit any job. From left to right: Bristle brush, pin brush, small and medium gentle slicker, small and medium universal slicker.

undercoat. It is important to loosen mats with a slicker before using a dematting tool. Doing so prevents more damage to the coat than is necessary.

Combing

A comb is used to test what you have brushed. It is very important that the comb be placed in the coat parallel to the skin. Allowing comb tips to rake the skin is uncomfortable for the dog.

When choosing a multi-purpose comb, the diameter of the individual comb's teeth is an important consideration. The teeth should be as narrow as possible with at least an ⅛" spacing. Instead of pushing the coat flat, the comb will penetrate

the hair making best use of your time and efforts. Many professional groomers prefer the Belgian stainless steel greyhound combs.

A longer, 2" tooth comb with ¼" spacing, sometimes called a poodle comb, works well for fuller coated dogs. A large wide-tooth comb (Resco #80) is one of the best tools for removing undercoat in large double-coated breeds. Placed behind the thick undercoat of the neck or rump,

Brush from the skin out in layers when using a slicker brush.

parallel to the skin, it makes removing undercoat less time consuming and uncomfortable. I have never liked working with "rake type" tools as I feel the tips of the tool can create a great deal of discomfort for the dog. The removal of undercoat, especially in neglected dogs, is not always a pleasant experience for them or us. No sense making it worse!

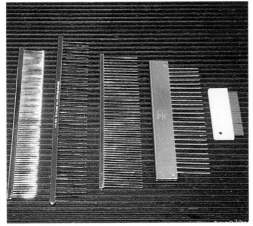

An assortment of combs for use on different coats. From left to right: A Belgium greyhound stainless steel comb, Aaronco coarse comb, Resco poodle comb, Resco #80 comb and flea comb.

Dematting

Dematting is a necessary evil we groomers must learn to do quickly and effectively. Trying to humanely handle each dog, save coat and please the customer (and not have our arms fall off while we are doing all of the above) is a big challenge. There is a limit to the miracles that a professional groomer can create. Experience in dealing with different coat types can help you to be more realistic in what you can and can not do. And it never ceases to amaze me in what the client expects of us.

If I felt a dog's coat could be saved with minimum discomfort to the pet, then I would attempt to demat the dog, usually with a compromise of style. But of course this is done after the client and professional groomer discuss all possibilities and repercussions.

There are lots of detangling and dematting agents, sprays and powders on the market. But nothing replaces elbow grease. There are no magic tricks when it comes to getting mats out of a coat. Basically, detangling or dematting products are worked into the mat to help the hair become "slippery". Then your fingers can be used to pull the mats apart in the best-case scenario or when matting is worse, loosened with a slicker brush then worked out with a dematting comb.

Mat combs are extremely sharp and can cut skin as easily as hair. Work with the sharp side of the blades facing you. Secure the dog's skin by pulling it taut and place the mat comb behind the mat. With short, quick strokes, pull the mat comb through the mat. I equate this to taking off an adhesive bandage, it hurts much less if you do it quickly. Contrary to what I have read, I never encourage a sawing motion. Keep your wrist straight and work as quickly as possible. Be aware of individual sensitivities of the dog. Geriatric pets and puppies are far less tolerant of the dematting process and rightfully so. If a generally good-natured dog must be held down or muzzled for dematting, it is my opinion that the dog be trimmed

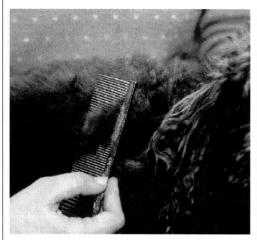

Insert comb into the coat parallel to the skin.

short. Or if the mats can be isolated and clipped out inconspicuously, then do so. We are not here to traumatize the dog. If at any time the dog's skin becomes red or irritated due to brushing or dematting, it is important to move to a different area of the dog and place a soothing lotion on irritated skin.

Also, matting can hide a variety of skin afflictions. Be sure to warn the owner of what clipping the mats might uncover. Many times professional groomers are wrongly blamed for exposing an existing problem. If the dog's coat is in firm clumps or

A mat comb saves time when dematting.

the hair is matted like a rug onto his skin (bullet proof as one groomer friend calls it), the dog must be clipped as short as needed to remove the mats. When a dog is in this kind of retched condition, the dog's aesthetics should be the last consideration. By this time the dog's health and comfort are definitely suffering.

Bathing

Once the pet has been thoroughly brushed, combed and dematted, it

Secure the dog in the tub.

is ready for a bath. All bathing supplies and tools should be gathered and placed in close proximity. *Never leave an animal unattended in the tub.* Secure the dog on a skid-free surface in the tub and put cotton in each ear to prevent water from penetrating the canal. Some groomers place a drop of mineral oil in each eye to protect from soap and dip. I find this messy and unattractive. Being careful can prevent problems.

Test the temperature of the water before wetting the dog. Holding the nozzle against the dog's skin will

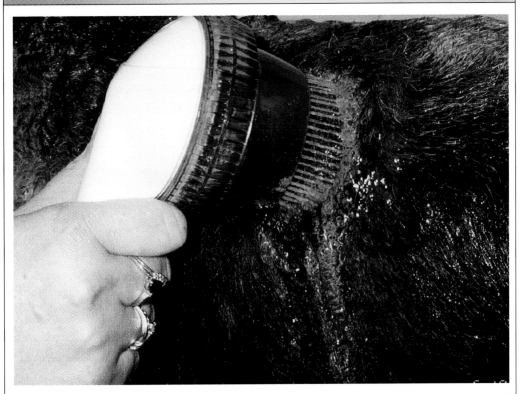

Hold nozzle against the dog's skin to avoid frightening him with spraying water.

avoid frightening him with spraying water. This also helps the water penetrate the coat quickly. Apply a good-quality shampoo formulated for the dog's coat and skin condition or color and lather well. Pay special attention to hard-to-reach areas like under legs, belly and extra soiled areas like facial hair, around ears and tail. If using a flea shampoo, be sure to leave it on the dog long enough to be effective. As the dog is waiting to be rinsed, use a flea comb to remove the fleas from the face and around the eyes. Hold the nozzle against the skin to lift the dead and fainted fleas out of the coat and down the drain. Rinse until you are reasonably sure the fleas are dead or off the dog.

Rinse and repeat the lathering process. If anal sacs (often incorrectly referred to as anal glands) are to be done, this is the time to do them. Be sure to wash the area well to remove all traces of gland excretion and odor. Your veterinarian can give you safe and correct instructions for expressing sacs.

Rinse until the water runs clear and hair feels "squeaky" clean. To prevent skin irritation remove all traces of soap. Gently run hands over dog to squeeze off excess water. Remember geriatric dogs need a very gentle touch. Remove cotton from ears.

The dog is now ready for conditioning. Long-haired breeds will benefit from the application of a cream

Lather well, paying close attention to face, ears and rump.

rinse which softens the coat and eliminates static. The finish will be less fly away and look silkier. For scissored breeds, a lighter rinse, mousse or spritz formulated to build body in the coat works well. Cream rinse on scissored breeds such as the Poodle, Bedlington or Bichon may weigh the coat, making scissoring more difficult. Hard-coated breeds will best benefit from a texturizing spritz. Be sure to read the product instructions and apply accordingly. Squeeze out excess water, and the dog is ready to be dipped or dried.

Use a squeezing motion when towel drying.

External Parasite Control

The professional groomer acts as a pet owner counselor. We have tremendous responsibility in educating our clients, and flea control is an important topic. Fleas and ticks can transmit disease and internal parasites to humans. Acute

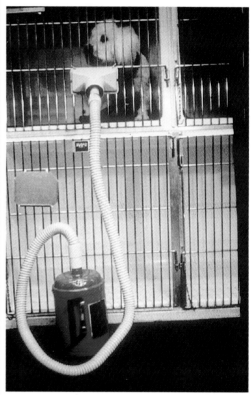

Cage drying saves time, but is best used on smooth-coated breeds.

anemia caused by flea infestation can cause death in young or geriatric pets.

It is our duty to not just go through the motions of "dipping the dog" but to remove every single flea or tick from the animal. After the bath squeeze as much water from the coat as possible. This prevents the dip from becoming too diluted to be effective. Apply the dip, mixed according to directions, by cup or sponge. Avoid the eyes and work the dip into the coat. Squeeze out excess dip and if possible wrap the dog in a towel to allow the dip to work. Be very sure you read product instructions carefully and follow them intently. Unless the product specifies that it is *safe* for use on cats, *never* use a product designed for dogs on cats. Organophosphates should be used in a ventilated area with gloves and impermeable clothing to prevent absorption into the groomer's skin. A busy groomer or bather may be dipping dozens of dogs a day, and preventative practice is the best solution to possible problems.

After the dog sits wrapped in a towel for 15 minutes, remove the wet towel and continue to dry with a fresh towel until the dog is just damp. On puppies, geriatric dogs or dogs in less than optimum condition, rinse the dip to prevent any additional absorption into the dog's system and condition the coat, making sure that all fleas were either picked or rinsed off.

It is not good practice to dry these dogs with a high-velocity dryer as the current sends tiny particles of the dip into the air. If the dog must be fluff dried for aesthetic purposes, it is in your best health to wear a surgical mask.

Drying

Towel drying is done to every dog bathed. Using a squeezing motion until the pet is just damp is a big

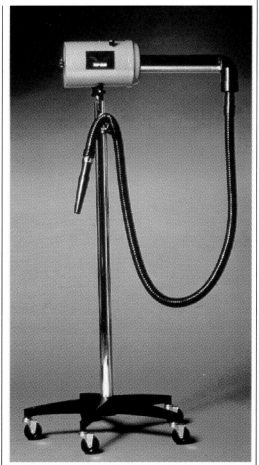

Some dryers offer both force and fluff drying features.

time saver, even when using a high-velocity dryer. Never rub, except healthy short-coated dogs, as this action can tangle a coat or irritate skin growths.

Cage drying in a busy shop can save manpower but is only practical for smooth- or short-coated breeds. Even a Poodle being clipped short will have a better finish when fluffed or force dried. If cage drying, be sure the dryer temperature is not too high and that there is sufficient ventilation. A grate will allow air

circulation beneath the dog and keep him clean if an "accident" should occur.

Fluff drying achieves the best finish and is typically done with a stand dryer and brush. Unfortunately fluff drying is time consuming as the groomer or bather brushes and dries a small area at a time. For best results a towel should be laid over the coat that is not being dried to prevent curling. For dogs that have flat coat on their backs, such as setters and spaniels, a t-shirt or towel pinned around their bodies can keep the coat lying flat while the furnishing are being fluffed. Be sure to dry from the skin out. High-velocity or force drying is quite popular and cuts a lot of time off this tedious but important aspect of grooming. However, the noise it creates can cause additional stress to employees and pets in the grooming shop. It is best to have a separate yet ventilated area for this service. Wearing ear plugs and a dust mask

Above: Hold the nozzle far enough from the skin to avoid swirling the hair.
Below: Ear cleaning is essential to good grooming. From left to right: Ear cleaner, cotton balls, ear powder, cotton swabs, hemostats and ear and nose scissors.

can eliminate most problems caused by high-decibel sound and airborne particles.

The rule of thumb for using the high-velocity dryer is that the shorter the coat the closer you can hold the nozzle to the dog. To prevent tan-

Poodles are high-maintenance companion dogs. Their ears are profusely feathered and need regular attention to keep clean; their coats, the most abundant of any dog, need professional care on a regular basis. Photograph by Isabelle Francais.

gling of longer-coated breeds, it is necessary to hold the nozzle 12 to 15 inches away from the skin. Experimentation helps the operator to become more comfortable with this technique. The angle and distance at which the nozzle is used will have great impact on the finish. Be sure to keep the nozzle away from the dog's eyes and ears.

Blind and deaf dogs may find this drying technique somewhat traumatic. Puppies and "first timers" should be worked into the force drying slowly, starting at the rear and at a low speed.

Ear Care

Dogs with naturally profuse facial hair grow hair in the ear canal. In most instances the removal of this hair is necessary to keep the ear canal dry and avoid ear infections. A depilatory powder is lightly dusted into the ears so that you can grasp the hair and gently pull it out. Hemostats can be used close to the skin to assist you in stubborn cases, but fingers are less likely to pinch. Blunt-tipped ear and nose scissors can be cautiously used on puppies when hair in their ears is not ready to let go or for dogs that object to the pluck-

Left unchecked, nails can grow painfully long.

ing. Remember to clean away traces of ear powder to prevent build up and possible problems. Swab ears with cotton ball and ear cleaner. Dogs with prick ears or with little hair growth in the ears will benefit from a swabbing and checking of the ears for mites, infection or other disorders.

Nail Care

Nails left to grow unchecked can become a very painful and disfigur-

Practice helps you to become faster and better at determining where the quick of the nail is.

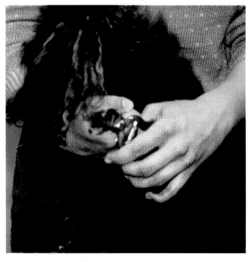

ing problem. Dew claws can grow completely around and back into the foot. Other nails can grow so long that the foot becomes splayed and twisted.

There are a couple different techniques used in shortening the nail. Some groomers prefer to clip them before the bath. Others prefer working on nails after the bath as nails may be softer and easier to cut, especially on large dogs.

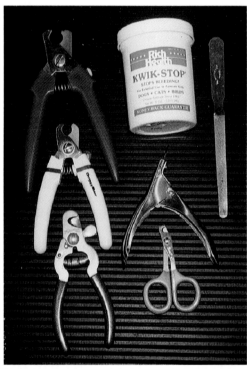

Nail trimmers for any job. From left to right: three types of plier trimmers, styptic powder, guillotine trimmers, cat claw scissors and stainless steel file for removing rough edges.

Nail scissors open completely and work well for toy breeds, cats and dew claws that have grown around. Plier-type nail trimmers were most comfortable for me for use on small to large dogs. Beginners may find the cutting guard of benefit, allowing you to trim a little at a time. Guillotine-type trimmers have replaceable blades and are probably the most widely used. Be sure to replace dull nail trimmers as they crush rather than cut the nail.

White nails are easier to trim than dark nails because the darkening of the quick is visible. Dark nails have a faint line and dull color where the quick begins. Only practice makes you faster and better at determining how much to take off. Always have styptic available for accidental cutting of the quick. Try to avoid, even at a customer's request, to cut the

nails so short that they bleed. It is possible for the nails to become infected through the open wounds. It is far better to have the client come in weekly to trim just a bit from the nail to force the quick to recede. I doubt the dog ever forgets the pain of a nail cut too short. Be sure to file the rough edges of the nail to prevent accidental scratching of the client as the dog jumps in happiness to see him!

MAINTENANCE GROOMING PROCEDURES

There are obvious differences between the breeds, so to simplify the description of maintenance grooming procedures, breeds can be categorized by coat similarities as follows.

The Beagle, a smooth-coated dog, has a short, close-lying coat and is among the most easycare of all dogs. Photograph by Isabelle Francais.

Smooth-coated Breeds

These dogs all possess a short, close-lying coat with little or no undercoat. This coat type is the easiest to properly care for because shedding is minimal and matting is not a consideration.

The breeds are: American Staffordshire Terrier, Basenji, Basset Hound, Beagle, Bloodhound, Boston Terrier, Boxer, Bull Terrier, Bulldog, Bullmastiff, Chihuahua, Coonhound, Dalmatian, Doberman Pinscher, Foxhound (American and English), French Bulldog, German Shorthaired Pointer, Great Dane, Greyhound, Harrier, Ibizan Hound, Italian Greyhound, Manchester Terrier (Standard and Toy), Mastiff, Miniature Pinscher, Pointer, Pug, Rhodesian Ridgeback, Shorthaired Saint Bernard, Smooth Dachshund, Smooth Fox Terrier, Staffordshire Bull Terrier, Vizsla, Weimaraner, Whippet, and short-, smooth-coated mixed breeds.

STEP-BY-STEP APPROACH

1. Using a bristle brush or hound glove, brush against then with the grain of the hair.

2. Clean ears and trim nails.

3. Following the general bathing

Smooth-coated breeds benefit from a good brushing and conditioning spray.

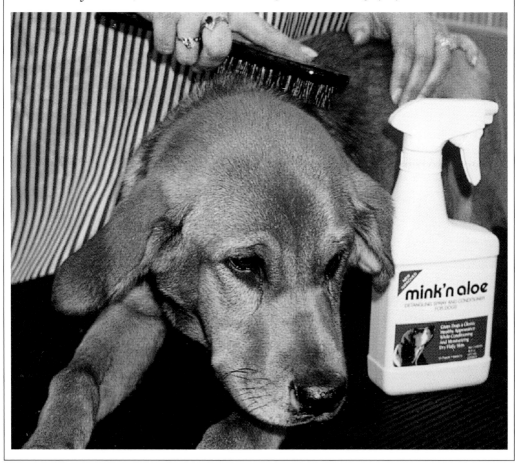

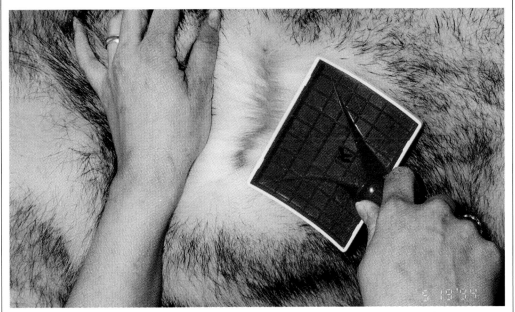

A slicker helps to remove undercoat from this Malamute.

instructions, apply the appropriate shampoo. Bathe thoroughly. Towel dry and apply a finishing spray such as Zema's Mink 'n Aloe Conditioner to enhance shine. Use a chamois or lint-free cloth to wipe the coat with the grain to remove dust, loose hairs and dander.

4. If the client desires or if the dog will be exhibited, trim the facial whiskers. Smooth the cowlicks at the rump and sides of neck with thinning shears and trim any stray hairs from around the ear opening to enhance the dog's profile.

Medium Double-coated Breeds

All these breeds have a double coat consisting of coarse, straight guard hairs that lie flat and soft undercoat in the rough of the neck, rump and tail. Though considered medium length coats, some breeds will have longer furnishings on the tail and legs. This coat type is fairly easy to maintain although excessive shedding occurs seasonally. Generally these breeds have water-repelling coats keeping them warm and insulated while working in water or cold climates.

The breeds are: Akita, Alaskan Malamute, Australian Cattle Dog, Belgian Malinois, Belgian Sheepdog, Chesapeake Bay Retriever, Flat-Coated Retriever, German Shepherd, Golden Retriever, Kuvasz, Labrador Retriever, Long-haired Saint Bernard, Norwegian Elkhound, Rottweiler, Schipperke, Siberian Husky, St. Bernard, Tibetan Spaniel, Welsh Corgis (Cardigan and Pembroke) and medium double-coated mixed breeds.

STEP-BY-STEP APPROACH

1. Using a slicker, brush against and then with the growth of coat. Be

sure to lift the coat, brushing from the skin out. Pay close attention to the rough of the neck and rump where undercoat is thickest.

2. Clean ears and trim nails.

3. Bathe the dog following general instructions using the appropriate shampoo. Be sure to hold nozzle against the skin to help penetrate the oily top coat. Rinse thoroughly.

4. Towel dry. Using a high-velocity dryer held close to the dog's skin blow the coat until damp. The dog can then be cage dried until completely dry.

5. Brush dog again using a slicker brush with the growth of the coat. Use a finer comb to remove any small clumps of undercoat. Use a finishing spray and wipe with a chamois or lint-free cloth to remove

Above: The Australian Cattle Dog, a medium double-coated breed, is a rugged outdoors dog that requires little more than a weekly once-over to keep his coat healthy and clean. Photograph by Karen Taylor.

Below: A high-velocity dryer helps to loosen and remove undercoat.

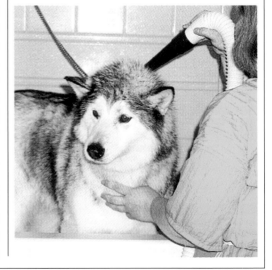

dust, loose hair or dander.

6. Trim facial whiskers and tidy up feet if desired. These dogs should be exhibited naturally with little or no additional trimming.

Long-haired Double-coated Breeds

Due to the size and amount of coat presented on most of these breeds, the grooming process can be back breaking work. A regular grooming schedule is important to keep these dogs in peak condition. Their coarse, straight outer coat is long and somewhat water-resistant with soft undercoat all over the body,

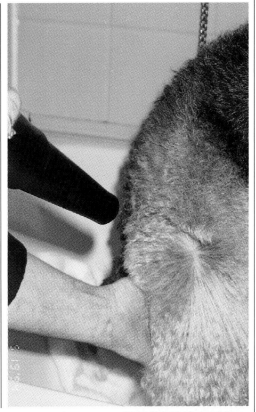

Right: Dry hard-coated breeds with the growth of hair.
Below: The Golden Retriever has a medium, double coat and requires regular brushing to keep looking its best. The coat should not be overly abundant else it hinder the dog when hunting in thick brush or when swimming in lakes or rivers. Photograph by Isabelle Francais.

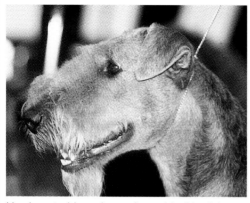

Hard-coated breeds, such as this Airedale require shaping to capture the expression and breed profile.

but most profuse on the neck, rump and tail.

The breeds are: Belgian Tervuren, Bernese Mountain Dog, Border Collie, Chow Chow, Collie, Great Pyrenees, Keeshond, Komondor, Kuvasz, Newfoundland, Pekingese, Pomeranian, Samoyed, Shetland Sheepdog and long-haired double-coated breeds.

STEP-BY-STEP APPROACH

1. Brush dog thoroughly with a slicker brush, be sure to part the coat and brush from the skin out. To remove the profuse undercoat, insert a large wide-tooth comb beneath the undercoat and parallel to the skin. The more coarse end of a small stainless steel comb can be used for the smaller breeds. Use a mat comb if severe matting around the neck, rump or tail is present.

2. Clean ears and trim nails.

3. Bath thoroughly with the appropriate shampoo. A high-velocity dryer can aid in the removal of undercoat. Dry using technique of your choice.

4. Repeat brushing. Use comb to finish removing any loose undercoat.

The coat on this Soft Coated Wheaten Terrier is obviously well cared for and groomed to perfection. (Grooming by Jaci Bowman of Hartland, Wisconsin).

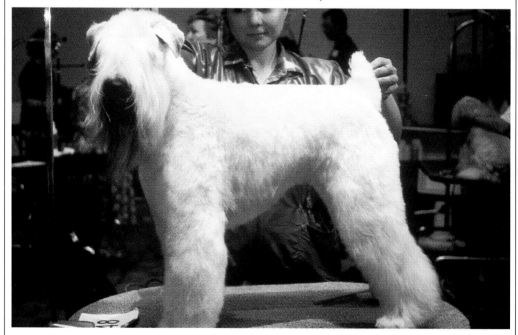

This Wheaten will require a great deal of elbow grease! What a mess!

5. Hair around feet may be trimmed to reveal a tight natural look. Trim facial whiskers if desired.

6. On occasion these breeds either out of necessity or client request will need to be trimmed short. Be sure the owner understands that once the outercoat has been cut it may not grow back with the same texture. A compromise might be to scissor the outline of the dog, so that hard-to-care-for areas (neck, rump and tail) are shortened to a reasonable length, giving a "puppy" appearance.

Hard-coated Breeds

Special treatment is required to keep the desired hard, flat coat on these breeds. The technique of hand stripping is used to remove the soft undercoat, keeping the crisp top coat. For a dog being exhibited, it is absolutely necessary that the coat be maintained properly. Work with a reputable breeder or handler to get specific instructions on maintaining this coat type.

For most pet owners, the thought of hand-stripping may seem unnecessary and, for a busy groomer, a time-consuming undertaking. It is possible to capture the proper breed profile using a combination of clipping and scissoring techniques, but this will usually soften the coat. Consideration to coat texture is important before choosing the shaping technique. Hard-coated breeds rarely become so matted that they would need to be cut down. Unfortunately, coat texture will vary from soft to hard due to breeding, grooming technique and upkeep. Some dogs may have a harsh jacket and silky furnishings, of coarse these dogs are much more vulnerable to matting.

The breeds are: Airedale Terrier, Affenpinscher, Australian Terrier, Border Terrier, Brussels Griffon, Cairn Terrier, Dandie Dinmont, German Wirehaired Pointer, Giant Schnauzer, Irish Terrier, Irish Wolfhound, Lakeland Terrier, Miniature Schnauzer, Norfolk Terrier, Norwich

A modified Wheaten style was done due to the severity of matting.

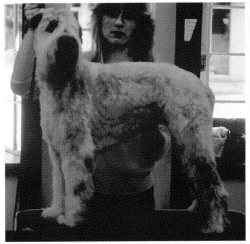

Terrier, Otterhound, Scottish Deerhound, Scottish Terrier, Sealyham Terrier, Standard Schnauzer, Welsh Terrier, West Highland White Terrier, Wire Fox Terrier, Wirehaired Dachshund, Wirehaired Pointing Griffon and hard-coated mixed breeds.

STEP-BY-STEP APPROACH

1. Brush the dog thoroughly using a slicker brush in layers from the skin out. Test what you have brushed with a metal comb.

2. Clean ears and trim nails.

3. Bathe according to instructions using a texturizing or protein shampoo. If the dog is to be hand-stripped and is not soiled, the bathing step may be eliminated.

4. Dry the coat. If force or fluff drying, be sure to blow the coat with the growth of hair.

5. Brush again and style the coat according to breed profile or client request using the technique of choice.

Long Straight-haired Breeds

With the exception of the Bouvier and Wheaten whose coats must be shaped to breed profile and the Afghan's saddle which may need to be stripped out or clipped, these breeds are are exhibited in a fairly natural state. Exhibitors generally use a pin brush on these dogs to leave as much coat as possible. As beautiful as these breeds are with a thick,

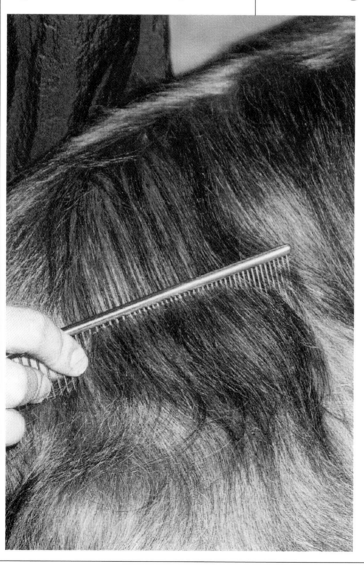

Test what you have brushed with a comb.

flowing coat, it simply is not practical for most pet owners. I recommend a slicker brush for both the pet owner and professional groomer when working on these breeds.

Coat texture varies from silky to coarse on the following breeds, but all the dogs have naturally long outer coats, most possessing a shorter, soft undercoat held against the skin. Their long, profuse coat can easily become matted necessitating a lengthy grooming session.

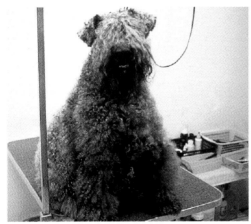

Without proper routine brushing, this Kerry Blue Terrier is a groomer's nightmare.

It is the professional groomers responsibility to make a humane decision in regards to what can and can not be brushed out. A mat comb can help, but sometimes the coat can not be saved. If this is the case, it is best to clip the matted hair off the dog before bathing. Another alternative would be to shorten the coat to a more manageable length to help the owner better care for the dog. Remember, the dog's comfort, health and safety should be your main concerns.

The breeds are: Afghan Hound,

A modified clip, such as done on this American Cocker, makes caring for the coat easier.

Bearded Collie, Bouvier des Flandres, Briard, Old English Sheepdog, Lhasa Apso, Maltese, Puli, Shih Tzu, Silky Terrier, Skye Terrier, Soft Coated Wheaten Terrier, Yorkshire Terrier, Tibetan Terrier and long-haired mixed breeds.

STEP-BY-STEP APPROACH

1. Brush out systematically, in layers from the skin out. Test with a comb. Use your fingers to pull apart any tangles or a mat comb for mats. A silicone spray, cream rinse water mixture, corn starch or dematting spray can be worked into mats to help facilitate their removal. But

After hours of dematting, a handsome dog was found! Another grooming miracle.

Grooming is definitely an art.

remember, there is no magic cure. Elbow grease is the only thing that really works on mats.

2. Remove hair from ear canal and clean ears. Trim nails.

3. Bathe and use a conditioner or cream rinse. Squeeze out excess

Most pet owners want their dog to resemble the dogs they see in books.

water and towel dry using a squeezing motion to prevent additional tangling of hair. Dry with the preferred technique. Remembering to keep the high-velocity dryer nozzle far enough away from the skin to prevent the hair from swirling. It is best to avoid cage drying to prevent the coat from looking stringy.

4. Repeat brushing. Part the hair down the dog's back and use a lanolin or finishing spray. Use a comb or pin brush for the final going over to help hair hang smoothly.

5. Hair in the feet can be trimmed out to prevent the collection of for-

Grooming competitions are a great place to sharpen your skills.

eign objects in the pads. Tidy up around the feet. On most breeds the headpiece may be trimmed or tied up to owner's specifications.

Flat-coated Breeds

The following breeds all possess a straight, flat coat with longer silky furnishings. The body coat is generally easy to care for since it is rather coarse and lies flat and has, in most cases, little undercoat. The longer furnishings which adorns the dogs legs, undercarriage and ears and in

Above: The Silky Terrier is a toy breed with a long, straight coat that never touches the floor. Photograph by Isabelle Francais.
Below: The Bichon Frise requires daily brushing and monthly shaping to stay as beautifully groomed as this prize. Grooming by Loretta Marchese.

a few breeds, the tail, can easy become matted as any groomer who has ever worked on an American Cocker in full coat can attest!

The breeds are: Borzoi, Brittany, English Setter, English Toy Spaniel, Irish Setter, Gordon Setter, American Cocker Spaniel, English Cocker Spaniel, Japanese Chin, Long-haired Dachshund, Papillon, Saluki, Sussex Spaniel, Welsh Springer Spaniel and flat-coated mixed breeds.

The American Cocker Spaniel, a flat-coated breed, has an abundant coat that requires much grooming. Photograph by Isabelle Francais.

STEP-BY-STEP APPROACH

1. Brush with a slicker brush, paying close attention to the long furnishings. Test with a comb and use a mat comb on problem areas. Sometimes a mat can be isolated and snipped inconspicuously out of the longer hair.

2. Clean ears and trim nails.

3. Bathe, paying close attention to ear leathers and use a cream rinse. Dry the dog being careful not to swirl the coat.

4. Repeat brushing and trim facial whiskers and feet if owner requests. A few of these breeds have a specific grooming style and will re-

quire clipping, scissoring or thinning to achieve the breed profile. A finishing spritz can be used to bring out the shine and wiped with a chamois to remove dust, loose hair or dander.

Curly-coated Breeds

The outercoat should be crisp and curly with a woolly undercoat. Together the coat is dense yet soft to the touch. These coats must be shaped, either by scissors or clipper to achieve the proper profile. Curly coats must be prepared correctly for shaping by drying the hair straight from the skin out. This procedure allows the coat to stand up off the body and retain its shape for a longer time. A properly dense coat will hold the loose undercoat, except when the dog is shedding excessively. That is why many believe the Poodle and other dense, curly-coated breeds to be good pets for someone with allergies.

The breeds are: American Water Spaniel, Bedlington Terrier, Bichon Frise, Irish Water Spaniel, Kerry Blue Terrier, Miniature Poodle, Portuguese Water Dog, Standard Poodle, Toy Poodle and curly-coated mixed breeds.

Step-by-Step Approach

1. Brush the dog thoroughly, paying close attention to friction points behind the ears, armpits and hocks where matting tends to be worse. Test with a comb and use a mat comb if necessary.

2. Remove hair from ears and clean well. Trim nails.

3. Bathe according to directions,

The Kerry Blue Terrier has a naturally curly coat that requires a professional touch. Photograph by Isabelle Francais.

rinse well and apply a body-building conditioner. Towel dry, then fluff or force dry from the skin out. Be sure curly coats are dried thoroughly for the best finish.

4. Brush again and dog is ready to be styled to breed profile or client request.

The right tools can save time stripping off matted coats. The wider cutting blade allows the professional groomer to remove more coat with less effort. Photo courtesy of Oster Professional Products.

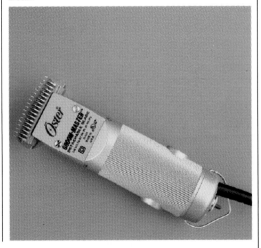

THE ART OF GROOMING

The professional groomer must have "a good eye" as well as adequate eye/ hand coordination and proficiency with shears, clippers and thinning shears to properly clip, scissor and sculpt the coat into a balanced, proportioned and eye-appealing example of the breed. For the mixed breed, imagination and appropriateness of the style to suit the coat and build of the dog leave endless possibilities. The clipping and scissoring styles will vary depending on the breed and coat texture. The professional groomer must also possess a knowledge of dog behavior and basic handling skills to enhance his or her ability to better work with the idiosyncrasies of the individual dog.

The art of grooming is much like sculpture, except that hair is the medium and the subject is not always cooperative. There is much satisfaction that can be gained by caring for and about dogs. But for the artist in each of us, creating that proverbial "silk purse out of a sow's ear" can be the greatest personal reward. Having a client gasp, "Is that my dog? She's beautiful" does wonders for your psyche. Even a novice pet owner will appreciate your eye and skill for creating a balanced, proportioned and properly angulated masterpiece.

Years ago, the general consensus was that any clip you put on any dog was acceptable because it was a "pet clip". Rest assured those days are gone. Pet owners are becoming much more sophisticated in the care of their pets. With few exceptions,

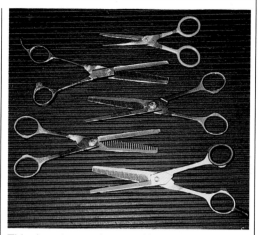

Thinning shears shorten, thin or blend.

they want their dog to look like the breed that it is. As professionals we owe this service to our clients.

Long gone are the terriers with long flowing "hula skirts" and Cockers wearing "pontune boats". Not only is this incorrect but downright unattractive and impractical. Knowing the correct look standardized by the American Kennel Club or other national body and educating your clients can do wonders in building

An assortment of clippers, blades and snap-on combs are the basic tools of the trade.

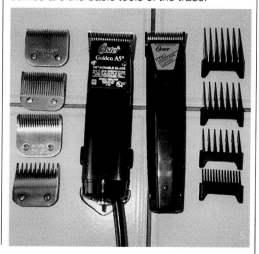

loyal clientele. A well-groomed dog and a happy customer are the best form of advertising.

The best way to develop your eye and learn about the breed profiles are to attend grooming contests, trade shows, breed shows and receive groomer publications. Viewing grooming guides in conjunction with a quality all-breed dog book, such as the latest edition of *The Westminster Kennel Club Winners* (TFH), is very helpful in applying directions in black and white to a three-dimensional full-color dog.

A number of tools will be needed to correctly trim a dog.

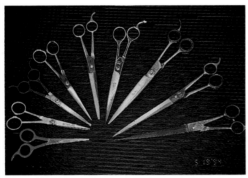

Shears are the professional groomer's prized possessions!

1. Clippers with an assortment of blades will be needed for the close trimming of a Poodle's feet, face, tail and setting patterns into the coat. Coarser blades can be used for short trims or removing mats in severe cases.

2. Snap-on combs are a great time saver in setting lengths on coats that will be scissored or leaving a nice length on long-coated dogs. Snap on combs also work nicely for leaving a more natural finish on hard-coated dogs and helps

to keep crispness in the coat.

3. Thinning shears blend, thin and shorten, depending on the technique and application.

4. Scissors, or shears are the most prized possession of the professional groomer. From moderately cheap to very expensive, there is a shear for every budget and every job. Short blunt-tipped scissors can be used safely around the dog's face. Curved shears can help the groomer more easily create a topknot or pompon. Straight shears in a variety of lengths and weights can help the groomer create a glass-smooth finish with minimal hand and finger stress.

Professional groomers must possess myriad talents and skills to best serve their client. From our role as veterinary assistant, dog trainer and psychologist to sculptor—balance is key. Perhaps the best professional groomer is one that marries well the art and science of grooming.

A handy clipper allows the professional to work on small areas more efficiently. Feet, face and tail, as well as pattern placement on Toy and Miniature Poodles, can be a breeze. Photo courtesy of Oster Professional Products.

COAT CHARACTERISTICS OF MAJOR DOG BREEDS

Legend: SC=Short-coated breeds; MDC=Medium double-coated breeds; LHDC=Long-haired double-coated breeds; HC=Hard-coated breeds; LSH=Long straight-haired breeds; FC=Flat-coated breeds; CC=Curly-coated breeds.

Breed	SC	MDC	LHDC	HC	LSH	FC	CC
Airedale Terrier				•			
Affenpinscher				•			
Afghan Hound					•		
Akita		•					
Alaskan Malamute		•					
American Eskimo			•				
American Staffordshire Terrier	•						
American Water Spaniel							•
Australian Cattle Dog		•					
Australian Terrier				•			
Basenji	•						
Basset Hound	•						
Beagle	•						
Bearded Collie					•		
Bedlington Terrier							•
Belgian Malinois		•					
Belgian Sheepdog		•					
Belgian Tervuren			•				
Bernese Mountain Dog			•				
Bichon Frise							•
Bloodhound	•						
Border Collie	•		•				
Border Terrier				•			
Borzoi						•	
Boston Terrier	•						
Bouvier des Flandres					•		
Boxer	•						
Briard					•		
Brittany						•	
Brussels Griffon	•			•			
Bull Terrier	•						
Bulldog	•						
Bullmastiff	•						
Cairn Terrier				•			
Chesapeake Bay Retriever		•					
Chihuahua	•		•				
Chinese Shar-Pei		•					
Chow Chow		•	•				
Cocker Spaniel, American						•	
Cocker Spaniel, English						•	

Breed	SC	MDC	LHDC	HC	LSH	FC	CC
Collie		•	•				
Coonhound	•						
Dachshund, Smooth-haired	•						
Dachshund, Long-haired						•	
Dachshund, Wire-haired				•			
Dalmatian	•						
Dandie Dinmont Terrier				•			
Doberman Pinscher	•						
English Setter						•	
English Toy Spaniel						•	
Flat-Coated Retriever		•					
Foxhound (Am & Eng)	•						
French Bulldog	•						
German Shepherd		•					
German Shorthaired Pointer	•						
German Wirehaired Pointer				•			
Giant Schnauzer				•			
Golden Retriever		•					
Gordon Setter							•
Great Dane	•						
Great Pyrenees			•				
Greyhound	•						
Harrier	•						
Ibizan Hound	•			•			
Irish Setter						•	
Irish Terrier				•			
Irish Water Spaniel							•
Irish Wolfhound				•			
Italian Greyhound	•						
Jack Russell Terrier	•			•			
Japanese Chin						•	
Keeshond			•				
Kerry Blue Terrier							•
Komondor			•				
Kuvasz		•	•				
Labrador Retriever		•					
Lakeland Terrier				•			
Lhasa Apso					•		
Maltese					•		
Manchester Terrier (Std & Toy)	•						
Mastiff	•						
Miniature Pinscher	•						
Newfoundland			•				
Norfolk Terrier				•			
Norwegian Elkhound		•					
Norwich Terrier				•			

Breed	SC	MDC	LHDC	HC	LSH	FC	CC
Old English Sheepdog					•		
Otterhound				•			
Papillon						•	
Pekingese			•				
Pointer	•						
Pomeranian			•				
Poodle, Miniature							•
Poodle, Standard							•
Poodle, Toy							•
Portuguese Water Dog							•
Pug	•						
Puli					•		
Rhodesian Ridgeback	•						
Rottweiler		•					
Saluki	•					•	
Samoyed			•				
St. Bernard, Long-haired		•					
St. Bernard, Short-haired	•						
Schipperke		•					
Schnauzer, Miniature				•			
Schnauzer, Standard				•			
Scottish Deerhound				•			
Scottish Terrier				•			
Sealyham Terrier				•			
Shetland Sheepdog			•				
Shiba Inu		•					
Shih Tzu					•		
Siberian Husky		•					
Silky Terrier					•		
Skye Terrier					•		
Smooth Fox Terrier	•						
Soft Coated Wheaten Terrier					•		
Staffordshire Bull Terrier	•						
Sussex Spaniel						•	
Tibetan Spaniel		•					
Tibetan Terrier					•		
Viszla	•			•			
Weimaraner	•		•				
Welsh Corgi (Pem & Card)		•					
Welsh Springer Spaniel						•	
Welsh Terrier				•			
West Highland White Terrier				•			
Whippet	•						
Wire Fox Terrier				•			
Wirehaired Pointing Griffon				•			
Yorkshire Terrier					•		

Karen Kuhl received her Doctor of Veterinary Medicine degree from the University of Illinois in 1987. She was a primary care veterinarian in the Detroit area for two years prior to completing a residency in comparative dermatology at the University of Pennsylvania. She passed the dermatology board examination in 1992 and is currently practicing veterinary dermatology in Downers Grove, Illinois.

Fleas and Ticks

By Karen Kuhl, DVM,
Diplomate, American College of
   Veterinary Dermatology
Animal Allergy and Dermatology
Arboretum View Specialty Services
2551 Warrenville Road
Downers Grove, IL 60515

INTRODUCTION

This chapter is designed to help owners maintain effective flea and tick control for their pets. It is essential to understand the life cycle of the flea to have appropriate flea control since many of the insecticides are effective against different developmental stages of the flea. The types of insecticides available will be discussed. Unless otherwise specified, the products discussed should be available from veterinarians or pet stores. It is very important to read and understand ingredients since new flea and tick products are developed often. Additionally, the forms in which the products can be applied will be discussed.

Ctenocephalides felis, the cat flea. Closer than you'd ever want to be.

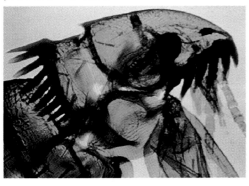

FLEA LIFE CYCLE

Although numerous species of fleas are known, the primary flea to infest dogs and cats is the cat flea, *Ctenocephalides felis*. Flea eggs are the size of a grain of sand. They are laid on the dog, but are not sticky and immediately fall onto the ground. Flea eggs hatch into larvae in one to ten days. All stages of the flea life cycle are very temperature and humidity dependent. Humidity 50% or less will desiccate (dry out) the eggs.

Flea larvae are yellow and approximately 2 mm long. They are free living and primarily feed on dry adult flea feces. As they ingest the adult feces, they become darker in color. Larvae dislike light so they try to bury themselves deep in carpet fibers or soil or under grass and branches outside. The larval stage lasts about five to 11 days. Temperatures below 65-70°F and humidity below 70% prolong their development. After this stage, the larvae spins a silk-like cocoon in which it pupates.

The cocoon is whitish and about ¼" long. This is sticky and often becomes coated with debris from the environment which makes it

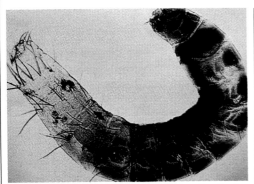

Flea larvae. These are the forms that live in the environment but can't yet bite.

difficult to visualize. The pupal stages usually lasts eight to nine days, but may last up to 174 days. This tends to be the stage that most resists flea control. The pupae are stimulated to emerge from the cocoon to become adult fleas by heat, vibrations and exhaled breath (carbon dioxide). Under average environmental conditions, the flea life cycle takes three to four weeks, but can take as long as six months.

Upon emergence from the cocoon, the adult fleas are attracted to a pet by the warmth of the animal's body, movement, changes in light intensity and exhaled carbon dioxide. The newly emerged fleas are found in the carpet and are at the stage that they most often bite humans prior to finding a suitable host. For many years, veterinarians were taught that adult fleas spend little time on the host and reside primarily in the environment. Recent research suggests that the cat flea resides on the host almost continuously since it requires a constant blood source. The cat flea can only survive ten to 14 days without a blood meal and can not mate until it has acquired its first blood meal. Then within 12 hours, it mates. Egg production begins within 48 hours of the first blood meal.

Female cat fleas may produce over 2000 eggs during their life. Only a fraction develop to adult fleas, but this method of reproduction does explain why fleas have existed for so long.

The higher the temperature and lower the humidity, the quicker fleas will die. Temperatures 68-72°F and humidity greater than 60% are the most ideal conditions for fleas. Fleas are unable to survive temperatures below 40°F for ten or more days. When people arrive in a home that is previously uninhabited for some time and are promptly bit by a number of fleas, it is usually due to the adult fleas emerging from the pupal stage or the attic, basement or crawl spaces are inhabited by raccoons, opossums or stray cats.

Squirrels, rabbits and birds are rarely infested with the cat flea.

TICK LIFE CYCLE

Ticks are very important due to the large number of diseases they are capable of transmitting to man and animals. They are capable of causing life-threatening anemia and paralysis. Two main families of ticks exist–soft shell and hard shell. This discussion will be limited primarily to the hard shell variety.

The most common ticks seen in small animals are *Rhipicephalus sanguineus*, *Dermacentor* species, *Ixodes*, and some species of *Amblyomma*. Their entire life cycle can take two to three years. They

may survive for long periods of time without food. The adults lay one large batch of eggs which hatch in one to four weeks and enter a resting period prior to molting to the nymph stage. The nymph feeds, rests and then molts into an adult.

Above: *Rhipacephalus sanguineus* tick. Photo courtesy of Allerderm/Virbac.
Below: *Dermacentor variabilis* tick. Photo courtesy of Allerderm/Virbac.

CLINICAL SIGNS OF FLEA-BITE HYPERSENSITIVITY

Flea-bite hypersensitivity is due to an allergic reaction to substances contained in flea saliva. Flea saliva is deposited in a dog's skin when a flea bites. An allergic dog may react minutes to several days after a bite occurs.

Dogs with flea-bite hypersensitivity tend to be extremely itchy. They "corncob nibble" at the base of

Egg-laying *Dermacentor* tick. Photo courtesy of Allerderm/Virbac.

their tails, their flanks/thighs, groin and anterior forelegs. They may also scratch around their necks, ears and sides. The scratching and nibbling may become generalized. When the scratching and chewing are moderate to severe, the dog may develop seborrhea (scaling), alopecia (hair loss), hyperpigmentation (dark discoloration of the skin) or lichenification (thickened and wrinkled skin) on their backs, tailbase, groins and inner thighs. Very often the dogs have a secondary bacterial infection. Occasionally, these dogs may have recurrent ear infections. Tapeworms, spread by fleas, are another sign that fleas are present.

These dogs tend to have fewer fleas than flea-infested dogs. This may be due to the constant chewing and mechanical removal of the fleas or the dogs' allergic reaction may decrease the number of fleas. Consequently, the fleas are often very difficult to find and the diagnosis may be based on clinical signs and response to appropriate flea control therapy.

Flea infestation differs from flea-bite hypersensitivity since there is no difficulty finding fleas on these dogs. Both they and their environment contain large numbers of fleas in various developmental stages. These dogs may or may not exhibit the clinical signs discussed above.

CLINICAL SIGNS OF TICK INFESTATION

Ticks congregate especially in the ears, between the toes and around the head and neck. If ticks are found, the tick should be soaked in isopro-

Ixodes scapularis, one of the ticks that cause Lyme disease. Photo courtesy of Allerderm/Virbac.

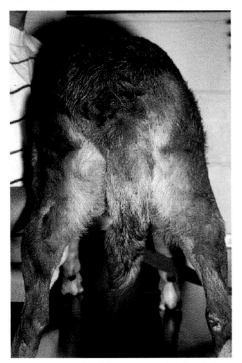

Typical area of hair loss seen with flea infestation and flea bite hypersensitivity.

pyl alcohol (not kerosene or lighter fluid). This will loosen its hold on the animal. Then the tick should be grasped with a forceps or gloved hand close to the point of attachment and removed with gradual pressure. Be careful to remove all mouthparts. If some mouthparts remain, the dog may develop a secondary bacterial infection. Unless paralyzed or otherwise debilitated, the animal should then be sprayed or dipped completely to kill any remaining ticks that may have been overlooked.

FLEA AND TICK CONTROL

Flea and tick control and prevention is important. Flea control and prevention consists of a "multipronged" attack. The flea-allergic animal not only must have the adult fleas on him/her killed but also should have a repellent applied to prevent any fleas from biting. Additionally, environmental control *must* be performed. It is essential that house treatment be done in cases of flea and tick infestation. Yard treatment is also important in most areas of the country.

Commonly Used Parasiticides

Pyrethrin is an extract of the chrysanthemum and has very low mammalian toxicity. It kills fleas quickly but needs to be used with a synergist to achieve maximum effect. Pyrethrins are also rapidly degraded by sunlight. Prolongation of activity can be accomplished by microencapsulation. No evidence of resistance to this substance has been noted.

Permethrin, a synthetic form of pyrethrin, has relatively low toxicity if used according to label directions. It is light-stable and does not need to be used with synergists such as piperonyl butoxide. It may adsorb to nylon carpet fibers and its effec-

Part the fur to see evidence of fleas and flea feces.

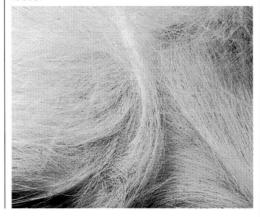

tiveness may be decreased for indoor environmental control.

Chlorpyrifos, an organophosphate, is extensively used in commercial products and by professional exterminators and has good efficacy against fleas. It is also available in microencapsulated form for good residual effect. Chlorpyrifos has also been used as a pour-on/dip for dogs. It should not be used with other organophosphate dips or yard treatments without further discussion with your veterinarian. Certain breeds, such as Greyhounds, do not handle organophosphates well. When using organophosphates, be sure to follow label directions on any product you use. These chemicals may have cumulative toxic effects resulting in neurologic signs. Immediate side effects in-

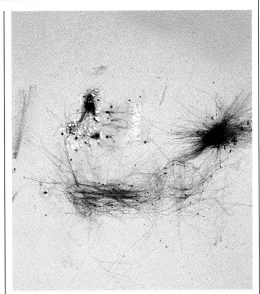

After flea combing, the material can be searched for evidence of fleas or their feces.

clude constricted pupils, tearing, vomiting, diarrhea, drooling, frequent urination, difficulty breathing, slow heart rate and low blood pressure.

Organophosphates should have very limited use on cats, older sick animals or very young animals. If used properly and under veterinary supervision, these products are very effective for good flea control.

Malathion is another commonly used environmental organophosphate. This is very effective against fleas and has relatively low toxicity. It should not be used with other organophosphates.

Diazinon, another environmental organophosphate, has a long residual effect, and insects do not easily become resistant. This is also available in a microencapsulated form. Again, do not use this with other organophosphates.

Carbaryl may also be applied to

Although no single method will eliminate fleas completely, specially designed flea combs can assist in the fight against parasites. Photograph courtesy of Interplex.

the yard. This is a carbamate that is often used as a pesticide for crops. The literature suggests this may not work as well in the southeastern United States. Toxicity is low, but fleas and ticks often become resistant to this insecticide. Carbaryl, diazinon and malathion can be obtained from yard-care stores.

Methoprene and fenoxycarb mimic insect growth regulators. Insect growth regulators are high in the larval stage of development but must decrease for the flea to enter the pupal stage. If methoprene and fenoxycarb levels are high in the environment, the larva can not pupate and will die. Both substances also kill eggs. Beneficial effects of this type of insecticide will not be seen for one to four weeks indoors. These two substances are usually used in conjunction with synergized pyrethrins (immediate kill) and an organophosphate (chlorpyrifos for extended activity) in the environment. Unfortunately, methoprene is broken down by sunlight and loses its effectiveness and therefore is not useful outdoors. Fenoxycarb can be used outdoors since it is light-stable. The insect growth regulators are an important part of good flea control.

Sodium polyborate is an inert substance that is ground into the carpets in certain areas of the country. This is an effective and safe means of flea control. The fleas are literally desiccated by this substance. This is available through a local distributor whose number can be obtained from a veterinarian.

Synergists are compounds that help other chemical work better. Insecticidal synergists help the insecticides they are paired with to be more effective. There are two types of synergists–piperonyl butoxide and N-octyl bicycloheptene dicarboximide. Synergists are safe and allow a higher level of killing by pyrethrins.

Repellents are chemicals that cause insects to move away. MGK326 (di-N-propyl isocinchomeronate), butoxypolypropylene glycol and DEET are examples. Pyrethrins and permethrins both have repellent activity.

Flea and Tick Control Indoors

A vacuum with a beater bar can remove between 15-20% of the larvae and 32-59% of eggs in the carpet. Therefore, vacuuming should be done prior to application of any insecticides. This will also allow more effective usage of any parasiticide products since the carpet fibers will be raised. The vacuum bag should immediately be taped and removed from the premises so any immature stages of the fleas do not further develop in your home. The pet's bedding should be washed at least weekly and dried on a high heat setting.

There are several types of insecticides available for application in the house. They primarily consist of permethrin, chlorpyrifos, microencapsulated chlorpyrifos, insect growth regulators (methoprene and fenoxycarb), synergized pyrethrins and sodium polyborate. Examples are Duratrol™ (microencapsulated chlorpyrifos), Sectrol™ (microencapsulated synergized pyrethrins), Ectoguard™ (synergized pyrethrin and fenoxycarb) and Ultraban™ (chlorpyrifos and fenoxycarb).

Flea control in the house differs somewhat in different areas of the country. In general, extermination by a professional exterminator tends to be somewhat more expensive but much less labor intensive. The professional exterminator does have access to some chemicals that are unavailable to veterinarians or consumers if an especially severe flea infestation is present. Application of the insecticides by the owner can be accomplished through the use of total-release aerosols or foggers. Aerosols are most easily applied with compressed air sprayers. These need to be applied after vacuuming to the surface of all rugs, carpets, baseboards and upholstered furniture. They should always be tested on an inconspicuous area to determine color fastness of fabric. In the author's opinion, application with a compressed air sprayer is much more effective than foggers. The foggers do not penetrate along baseboards or under furniture nearly as well. If foggers are used, a fogger should be used for each of the rooms. Follow the label directions for area. One fogger will not treat the entire home. Follow-up should be done with a sprayer in inaccessible areas.

Usually the commercially available products are applied two times two weeks apart after vacuuming and then monthly. The second application after two weeks is recommended due to the continued emergence of adult fleas from the cocoons which are resistant to most environmental treatments. Again, recommendations differ according to the area of the country. It is very important to seek the opinion of your primary-care veterinarian or veterinary dermatologist on application frequency for your particular area of the country.

Flea and Tick Control Outdoors

First, remember fleas will thrive in areas protected from the direct sunlight and where the soil is moist. Therefore, removing any organic debris and brush under bushes and mowing and raking the yard will help. Keep the doghouse, garage and areas under porches as clean as possible. Entrances to crawl spaces, attics and garages should be sealed. Finally, when applying flea treatments, do the shaded and sheltered areas primarily. Fleas and their offspring tend to inhabit the well-lit areas less frequently.

The most commonly used chemicals outdoors are chlorpyrifos (microencapsulated chlorpyrifos (e.g., Dursban™), growth inhibitors, malathion, diazinon and carbaryl. Be sure young children do not ingest or contact the organophosphate granules after application.

For best results outside, only light-stable products should be used. The yard and kennel preparations should not be applied to the animals. The liquids can be applied with a compressed air sprayer.

Finally, some new flea control products (BioFlea Halt™-Vetrinary Product Laboratories; and BioSafe™ -Ortho) which sound very promising are now available. The active ingredient is a beneficial nematode (worm) called Steinernema carpocapsae. This nematode is naturally occurring in nature. This product's key features are no odor or staining, environmentally safe to pets, children and wildlife, no contamination of water supplies and high efficacy and long-term effect. This flea product inhibits the pupal and larval stages and does not interact with any topicals or systemic preparations such as the organophosphates.

On-Pet Flea and Tick Control

On-animal flea control is the final prong. This begins using a flea comb (32 teeth/inch) daily in short-haired animals or puppies. The material collected can be examined for fleas and flea feces. Flea shampoos give the owner a false sense of security. It must be remembered that there is *no* long-term effect with a flea shampoo as it is all rinsed off. Therefore, a dip or flea spray will still have to be applied. Shampoos (pyrethrin-based) are best used on puppies (Be sure they are label-approved for puppies!) and in flea infestations. Alone, they are not effective for flea-bite hypersensitivities.

Sprays are highly effective if applied correctly. The entire haircoat should be dampened. Concentrate

Quality flea, fly and mosquito repellents are available at pet shops. The best of these promises to repel insects for up to 14 days. Photograph courtesy of Four Paws.

on the base of the tail along the back, under the chin and in the groin. The head and neck should be treated first before spray is applied to the rest of the body. Do *not* spray directly into the dog's eyes. Fenoxycarb-permethrin or methoprene-pyrethrin sprays are good since they provide adulticidal and ovicidal properties. Pyrethrin-synergist and repellent sprays are also good because they provide the quick kill and prevent fleas from biting. Examples of products containing permethrin and pyrethrin for use on animals include Duocide

LA™ (Virbac), Synerkyl™ (DVM), Mycodex 14 Day Spray™ and Two Way Pet Spray™ (3-M Animal Care Products). A straight permethrin spray (Preventic™-Virbac) recently developed has shown great efficacy. This product is to be used in dogs only. It tends to have a long residual and good repellent activity.

Flea collars also provide owners with a false sense of security and are not the most effective means of flea control. Therefore, they are not recommended. A new tick collar containing amitraz has shown promise. This is approved for use only in dogs and is available through veterinarians.

Dips or sponge-ons are highly effective for killing adult fleas and provide prolonged residual activity especially in long-haired dogs. Always follow label directions to be sure appropriate dilutions are maintained and wear gloves when applying the dips.

Any organophosphate dips such as phosmet (Paramite™ Zoecon/ VetKem) or chlorpyrifos (Duratrol™-3-M Animal Care Products) are primarily available through veterinarians and should be used with caution when other house or yard organophosphates are being used. When dips are applied, they should *not* be rinsed off.

Spot-ons are a small amount of fluid applied either above the tail or between the shoulder blades. Two popular compounds are permethrin (Ex-Spot™-Pittman-Moore) and fenthion (Pro-Spot™-Haver). Fenthion is another organophosphate. This drug has been responsible for a number of unintentional intoxications and should be used with extreme caution by both owners and their dogs. Since the fenthion is absorbed into the dog's system, the fleas are not killed until they have taken a blood meal. Therefore, this is very ineffective in flea-allergic dogs. The permethrin acts as a contact insecticide and repellent. Both are available from veterinarians.

Powders are a matter of preference. Many people do not like the dust on their animals. This is also evidence that powders are not as effective as sprays because they don't get to the skin surface where most of the fleas and ticks are actually found.

Systemic flea control products effectively kill fleas. Again, the flea must first bite the animal to get its dose of flea control. This is not effective in flea-allergic animals since the bite is the cause of the allergy. Systemic products are available from veterinarians. The currently licensed systemic in dogs is cythioate (Proban™-HAver), an organophosphate, which is given in pill form. Before the dog begins this medication, it is important to be aware of other organophosphates being used and any pre-existing liver or heartworm disease. This is easy but also gives a false sense of security. Another oral medication, lufenuron (Program: Ciba), promises to be effective. This seems to have low toxicity according to recent studies, but will need to be used with other topicals in flea-allergic animals.

According to research, ultrasonic flea collars, Brewer's yeast, B-complex vitamins and elemental sulfur products are ineffective in repelling or killing fleas.

SUMMARY

Flea control must be tailored for each situation. Most importantly, you must treat both the environment and the pet. Treating just one or the other will leave everyone frustrated. Finally, any questions or concerns regarding specific products should be addressed with your veterinarian or the product's manufacturer.

ADDITIONAL READING

Ackerman, L: *Guide to Skin and Haircoat Problems in Dogs.* Alpine Publications, Loveland, Co., 1994, 182 pp.

Garris, GI: Control of ticks. Veterinary Clinics of North America, *Small Animal Practice*, 1991; 21(1): 173-183.

MacDonald, JM: Flea allergy dermatitis and flea control. *Current Veterinary Dermatology*, Griffin, CE; Kwochka, KW; MacDonald, JM (Eds.). Mosby Year Book, St. Louis, MO, 1993, pp 57-71.

Muller, GH; Kirk, RW; Scott, DW: *Small Animal Dermatology*, 4th Ed., W.B. Saunders Company, Philadelphia, 1989, 1007 pp.

Sosna, CG; Medleau, L: The clinical signs and diagnosis of external parasite infestation. *Veterinary Medicine*, 1992; 87: 549-564.

Amitraz-containing tick collar licensed for use in dogs only. Photo courtesy of Virbac.

Facing page: Dog shows can be glamorous, but they can be dangerous too! Outdoor shows pose the hazard of external parasites—fleas and ticks—in addition to the possibility of contagious canine diseases. Photograph by Isabelle Francais.

Dr. Thomas P. Lewis II received his veterinary degree from Colorado State University in 1986. After a two year practice internship he entered an approved residency in dermatology in 1988. In 1991, he successfully completed the certification boards of the American College of Veterinary Dermatology. Dr. Lewis now operates animal dermatology referral practices in Arizona, New Mexico, and Utah.

Managing Mange

By Thomas P. Lewis II, DVM,
Diplomate, American College of
   Veterinary Dermatology
Mesa Veterinary Hospital, Ltd.
858 N. Country Club Drive
Mesa, AZ 85201

INTRODUCTION

Mites are microscopic parasites related to ticks that, in general, live permanently on or in the skin of their host. They usually prefer or require to live on one specific species. For example, the scabies mite of dogs can bite humans and cats but can't complete its life cycle on animals other than dogs. Mange refers to any skin problem that is due to mites; some are contagious and some aren't. As they feed, live, and die on the animal they cause damage to the skin. In addition, they may secrete irritating substances or produce allergic reactions. Sometimes severe secondary bacterial infections of the skin are seen due to mite infestation.

DEMODICOSIS (RED MANGE, FOLLICULAR MANGE)

Demodex canis is a cigar-shaped mite which is a normal inhabitant of canine skin. The mite lives in hair follicles and occasionally in the sebaceous (oil-producing) glands of the skin. The mite is only found on the surface of the skin when it travels between hair follicles. The life cycle begins with a spindle-shaped egg which develops into the first-stage larvae, followed by nymphs, and finally the adult mite. The entire life cycles takes 20-35 days to complete. The larvae have three pairs of legs, while the nymphs and adults have four pairs of legs. The mite is generally thought to feed on debris found within the hair follicle and material from the sebaceous glands. *Demodex canis* is not found on newborn puppies. They are passed by direct contact from the mother to the nursing puppy during the first few days of life. Mites have been found on the muzzle of the puppy during the first 16 hours of life. *Demodex canis* is therefore considered a normal part of the skin population in all dogs. *Demodex* mites are not contagious from one dog to another. Direct contact with dogs suffering from overwhelming infections have failed to result in the transmission or spread of mites to normal dogs. Experimental attempts to transmit the mite and cause disease have been unsuccessful. This has included direct contact as well as injection of the mite into the skin, abdominal cavity, and trachea.

A correct diagnosis is made by deep skin scrapings of the affected skin. Because the mites live deep in the hair follicle, the veterinarian needs to scrape deeply. The skin should be scraped in the direction of the hair until a slight oozing of blood is seen. It is often necessary to clip some of the hair so that an adequate sample can be obtained. The presence of a single mite will occasionally be seen but can be considered a normal finding if just one is found. In true cases of demodicosis there will be several mites seen, and many times all four stages are found. Occasionally skin biopsies are required to find the mites, particularly in the Chinese Shar-Pei breed, or in areas where there has been long-term inflammation and scar tissue formation, such as in the feet.

Demodicosis can appear as a localized region of hair loss and crusting.

There are two clinical types of demodicosis generally recognized, although in practice this difference is not always clear. In both forms the beginning of disease is usually in pups less than one year of age. A case is considered to be "localized" when there is one to several single or isolated areas of patchy hair loss. These patches are often accompanied by redness, scaling (dandruff) or an increased amount of dark pigmentation. The increased pigmentation is a result of the inflammation as well as plugged follicles (blackheads) which give the skin a dark appearance. Blackheads are formed by obstruction of the hair follicle pore by Demodex mites. Although the lesions can occur at any site of the body, the front legs, feet, and head are the most common areas affected. Occasionally the areas affected are limited to the feet or ears.

The other form, which is known as "generalized" demodicosis, is much more extensive and severe. This classification is reserved for those cases which initially involve large areas of the body, or those cases in which the number of single lesions has increased. This classification is important because treatment and prognosis are different between the two types. Generalized demodicosis is more common in purebred dogs, and a hereditary cause is strongly suspected. A less common form of demodicosis is adult-onset demodicosis. This is usually seen in middle-aged to older dogs who have no previous history of the disease. It may occur as either the localized or generalized form.

There are several theories as to why mites which are considered normal inhabitants of the skin sometimes cause problems in individual dogs. Studies of the immune system in these patients have been performed but the actual defect has not yet been identified. It has been shown that both the mites and bacteria are able to suppress the immune system even more, which leads to a vicious cycle of a suppressed immune system allowing more mites, leading to further suppression of the immune system.

Treatment of localized demodicosis in a dog less than 18 months of age should be conservative. Effective and safe topical therapy includes benzoyl peroxide shampoos

The Chinese Shar-Pei has one of the most unique coats in dogdom. A well-bred Shar-Pei may have few to no coat and skin problems; other dogs may exhibit a great many. Photograph by Paulette Braun.

and/or gels. Benzoyl peroxide has a follicular flushing action which helps remove the mite from the follicle, where it will quickly die. Topical rotenone is another safe treatment which can be used. Underlying infections with heartworm or intestinal parasites have been responsible for some treatment failures and worsening of the disease. It is important to realize and remember that 90% of the dogs with a localized form of disease will improve without *any* treatment. Amitraz (Mitiban™) dip is not needed in cases of localized demodicosis and should not be used. Use of amitraz in cases of

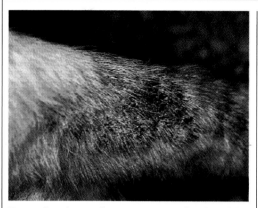

Demodicosis can be more generalized and involved large areas of body surface.

localized demodicosis may potentially lead to resistant strains of *Demodex canis.*

A diagnosis of generalized demodicosis can have serious implications because the tendency to develop the generalized form has been shown to be inherited. The American Academy of Veterinary Dermatology has recommended that all dogs with generalized demodicosis be spayed or neutered. Prior to beginning treatment of a patient with generalized demodicosis, the owner should be aware of the seriousness of the disease, including the potential length and cost of treatment and the likelihood of a complete or permanent clinical "cure." Secondary bacterial infections of the skin are very common in dogs with generalized demodicosis and can be so severe that blood-borne infection and death can potentially occur. Treatment of the secondary bacterial infection is always indicated with appropriate antibiotics for at least three weeks' time and often much longer. Whirlpool baths

or soaks can be very helpful when open draining wounds are present, or when the patient is "itchy."

Weekly baths with benzoyl peroxide can be helpful just as they are with the localized cases. The shampoo should be allowed to have contact with the skin for a ten-minute period. One of the more commonly used treatments includes weekly or biweekly dipping with amitraz. When this therapy is used, the dog should be bathed first, dried off (to prevent dilution of the dip) and then the dip is applied. For the best effect, the dog should be standing in a tub with the drain plugged and the dip is sponged onto the skin. The entire body should be treated, not just the areas with visible lesions. The feet are allowed to soak in the dip during this process which should take at least ten minutes' time. The dip is allowed to "drip dry" and should not be washed, rinsed or dried off. It is important that the patient be kept dry between dips. Walking on wet lawns, swimming or wading will make

Demodicosis can result in sores, attesting to its knickname of "red mange".

therapy less effective. Treatment *always* includes total body clipping of the hair in medium and long-coated dogs to allow proper contact of the dip with the skin.

After clipping the coat, all crusts (scabs) should be removed and the animal should be bathed with a shampoo containing benzoyl peroxide. The dog should be dry at the

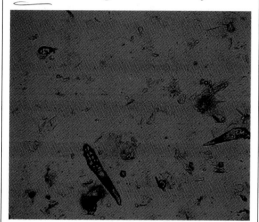

Microscopic view of a *Demodex* mite and egg. The mite (on the left) is cigar-shaped with short legs. The egg (to the right) is spindle-shaped and clear.

time of dipping, so the owner has the option of either toweling the dog dry, or applying the dip the following day. The dip should be sponged onto the entire body. The dog should be standing in a tub where the dip can collect and soak the feet. The dog should be allowed to drip dry or be blown dry. It's very important that the animal not get wet between dips. Amitraz is approved for dipping only every two weeks, but weekly dips have resulted in more successful case management. Treatment should continue until two successive skin scrapings are negative for live mites. Some dogs may require dipping on a maintenance basis every one to four weeks for the life of the dog.

Two additional therapies which have shown promise in the treatment of this condition are milbemycin oxime and ivermectin. There are several different treatment protocols used with these drugs but they have the advantage of oral administration. Clipping of the hair is not required as with dipping, although oral treatment may be used in addition to dips. Ivermectin should not be used in Collies or their crosses, and increased risk in Australian Shepherds and Shetland Sheepdogs (Shelties) is suspected. Because dogs with generalized demodicosis already have a suppressed immune system, drugs such as cortisone should not be used even if the patient is itchy. When excessive scratching is present, it may indicate the presence of a secondary bacterial infection. Treatment with antibiotics and antihistamines would then be helpful.

The Shetland Sheepdog is one breed that is particularly prone to demodicosis.

Underlying diseases which cause suppression of the immune system should always be considered in a dog with generalized demodicosis, especially if the affected animal is over 18 months of age. This should warrant a fecal examination, heartworm screen, blood count, chemistry panel, and thyroid hormone analysis. Estrus (heat) and pregnancy have been known to make the condition worse, which is another reason why all dogs with the disease should be neutered or spayed once they are stable. Additional tests based on the results of the physical exam and initial screening may be needed. When older dogs are diagnosed with demodicosis (adult-onset), it generally is a sign of some other underlying disease. The most common underlying causes for adult-onset demodicosis are a low thyroid or excessive amounts of cortisone. The source of the cortisone may be either prescribed (injectable, oral or topical) or be produced in excessive levels by the body itself by a disease caused Cushing's syndrome. Patients on chemotherapy will occasionally develop the condition due to their suppressed immune system.

CHEYLETIELLOSIS

Cheyletiellosis is commonly known as "walking dandruff" and is caused by three species, *Cheyletiella yasguri, C. blackei,* and *C. parasitovorax,* which generally affect dogs, cats, and rabbits respectively. There is some crossover between species and dogs can be infested with all three. All species of

Cheyletiellosis can be very variable in its clinical presentation. However, the most common symptom is scaling (dandruff).

Cheyletiella have prominent hooked-shaped mouth parts, which gives them a distinct appearance. All four pairs of legs extend past the body margins. These mites live on the surface of the skin where they feed on tissue fluids and debris. The life cycle requires two to three weeks to complete and is spent entirely on the animal. The mites may be spread between animals by either direct or indirect contact, and the infestation is highly contagious, especially between young animals in unsanitary conditions. These mites are most highly contagious by direct contact but can potentially spread through kennel or hospital cages or grooming tools if they are not cleaned, dried, and sprayed with insecticides.

The diagnosis is usually made by finding either the mite or its eggs on a skin scraping. Careful inspection of the scaly skin surface with a magnifying hand lens will sometimes reveal the white mites moving around on the skin and hair. This is not a very reliable method, however, as the mites must be actively moving in order to be seen. Skin scrapings do not have to be as deep as for Demodex, but multiple skin scrapings are sometimes necessary to find even one mite as the actual number of mites may be low. Material and debris collected from the scraping is then viewed with a microscope.

The clinical signs in dogs with cheyletiellosis will be variable. The most common initial problem is scale (dandruff) along the top of the body. Pruritus (itching) is variable, with some patients being very itchy while

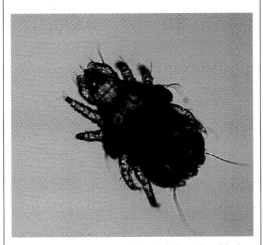

Microscopic view of a Cheyletiella mite. Notice the long legs and grasping mouthparts (palps).

others not being itchy at all. Dogs which have no symptoms have been found and are called "carriers." The animals with the most severe itching actually become allergic to the mite. Cheyletiella mites have the potential to infest humans and may result in a small red itchy rash (bumps and spots) on the arms, trunk, and buttocks. The mite cannot complete its life cycle on people

and will not reproduce; however, affected individuals should seek appropriate medical care.

Cheyletiella is unusual in that the female may survive off the animal for up to ten to 14 days. Therefore, successful therapy may require treatment of the environment as well as the animal. Cheyletiella is sensitive to most of the insecticides used for environmental flea control. Various therapies are effective for cheyletiellosis. Weekly lime sulfur dips (2-3%) have been the standard treatment and are still effective most of the time. Complete contact with the skin (not just the top layer of the coat) is necessary but difficult in long-coated patients. Other types of treatment in dogs include carbaryl and organophosphates, although these may have more side effects. Dips with amitraz with the same protocol as for demodicosis has also been used. Ivermectin has been found to be effective in both dogs and cats. This drug is not FDA-approved, and unexpected reactions in breeds such as Collies, Australian Shepherds and Old English Sheepdogs have been seen. The drug reaction seen in these breeds can be severe and can be fatal. All animals on the premises should be treated, as asymptomatic carriers do exist and could act as a source of reinfestation.

SCABIES (SARCOPTIC MANGE)

Scabies mites belong to the family Sarcoptidae, and the full name is *Sarcoptes scabiei* var. *canis*. The life cycle is spent entirely on the host and is complete in 17-21 days. These mites tunnel in the epidermis, which is the top layer of the skin. Female mites lay eggs behind them as they dig and crawl through the tunnel. The two pair of back legs are short and do not extend past the edge of the body. *Sarcoptes scabiei* var. *canis* will affect man and other mammals (cats, wild canids) for variable lengths of time. In approximately 30% of confirmed cases, humans in contact with the dogs will also have symptoms. These mites are highly contagious by direct contact but can potentially spread through kennel or hospital cages or grooming tools if they are not cleaned, dried, and sprayed with insecticides.

The most obvious symptom from the disease is intense itching, and often areas where the top layers of skin have been scratched away are seen. Because the mites prefer skin with little hair, the ears, elbows, abdomen, and hocks are areas that are affected more commonly. Clinically there is hair loss, yellow to red papules (small bumps), and crust. Patients which have been infested for longer periods of time develop very thickened skin with thick adherent scale and crust accumulations. The name "scabies" was derived from the word "scab." Many patients have lymph node enlargement. There is no age or sex of dog that gets the mite more commonly. In humans, itchy papules (bumps) on the trunk and arms are seen as soon as 24 hours after direct contact with the infested animal. The infestation in humans should be addressed by a human physician, because the human could poten-

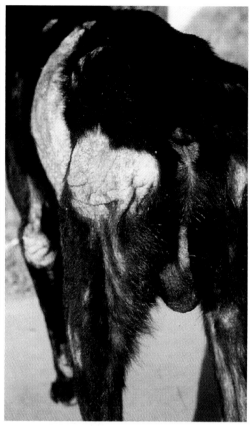

Sarcoptic mange is very itchy and can result in lots of scabs (crusts).

tially act as a reservoir for reinfestation of the animal.

The severe itching observed with scabies has several causes. Mechanical irritation to the skin from the burrowing female plays a role. There is also evidence that an allergic reaction to the mite (and some of its excretions) occurs. This further intensifies the itching and may account for the profound irritation and self-trauma created. Human volunteers experimentally infested with human scabies mites required a much shorter incubation time prior to developing symptoms the second time they were infested.

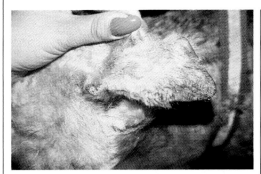

In the early stages of sarcoptic mange, the mites often prefer the ear margins.

The diagnosis is confirmed by finding even one mite or egg on skin scrapings. The elbows and ears are good places to scrape, and the scrapings should be extensive, with the accumulation of surface debris placed on the slide for examination. Even with multiple skin scrapings, canine scabies can be very difficult to recover. As an example, in some cases over 80 skin scrapings have been

Remember that sarcoptic mange is zoonotic and can spread to family members.

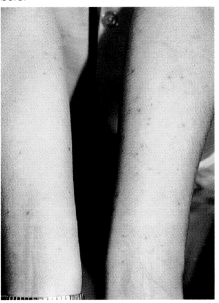

done before one single mite could be found. Therefore, if the history and physical exam evidence are suggestive of a diagnosis of scabies, the animal should be treated with appropriate medications.

There are various topical and systemic medications used to treat scabies, and some are better than others. When severe crust is present, shampoos designed to remove crust will be necessary in addition to the

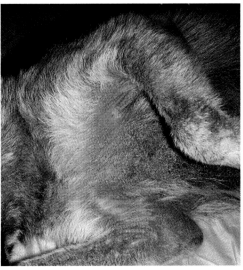

Sarcoptic mange is extremely itchy, and dogs can do a lot of damage by scratching.

mite treatment. Weekly lime sulfur dips of the entire body surface are a proven and safe treatment. Treatment for six to eight weeks, or two weeks past clinical remission is necessary. Organophosphates have also been used effectively; however, resistance to organophosphates is becoming more common and these insecticides can have side effects, and many have been removed from the market. Ivermectin has been shown to be very effective in killing these

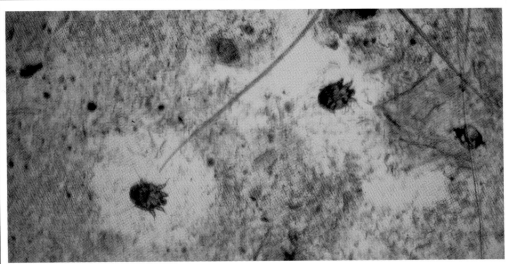

Microscopic view of two Sarcoptes mites. The mites are small and globose in shape.

mites. Although it is not approved for this use, it is generally considered safe except in Collies and related breeds. It can require several weeks for the itching to subside after treatment has been started.

EAR MITES (OTOACARIASIS)

Otodectic mange (ear mites) is caused by the mite *Otodectes cynotis*. The mite lives on the surface of the skin and does not burrow and has been shown to feed on lymph and blood. The life cycle is completed on the animal and requires three to four weeks. Transmission is by direct contact with infested animals; the mite dies quickly after it has been removed from the animal.

The outer ear canal is the favorite location for Otodectes, but the mite has been found in other locations such as the face, neck, feet, and tailhead. Clinical signs include variable degrees of itching and head shaking. Lesions include scratched skin around the ears and the accumulation of dark brown to black "coffee grounds-like" debris in the outer ear canal. Mites create irritation and damage to the ear and skin tissue because of their direct contact with the skin. In addition to irritation, the mites can also stimulate allergic-type reactions on the skin and ears, which intensifies the damage. Some dogs will carry the mite yet show no symptoms or signs. These patients have not yet developed an allergy to the mite.

Treatment includes cleaning or flushing the ear canal of all debris and then instilling miticidal (mite-killing) agents such as rotenone or thiabendazole topically into the ear. In addition, the rest of the animal should be lightly treated with a flea powder or spray to kill any mites outside of the ear canal. Many products which kill the adult mite will not kill the eggs. One single treatment will therefore not result in a cure. Treatment should either be continued for at least 30 days or be used daily for ten days, stopped for ten

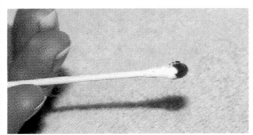

Ear swab showing debris collected from Sarcoptes mites.

days, then recommenced for ten more days. Ivermectin has been shown to be effective as well but is not licensed for this use.

DERMANYSSIASIS (MANGE CAUSED BY THE POULTRY OR RED MITE)

Dermanyssiasis is caused by the mite *Dermanyssus gallinae*. The mite generally feeds on fowl but has been known to infest dogs, cats, and man. The mite is gray to white but turns red from blood after feeding. The mite lives in cracks and crevices in the floor and walls during the day and feeds on the host at night. Clinical signs include an itchy, bumpy, crusty dermatitis of the head, back and limbs. Most affected animals have exposure to chicken houses. Almost all good insecticides safe for dogs which kill fleas will also kill these mites. Treatment should include the environment which is the source of the infestation.

TROMBICULIDIASIS (CHIGGER INFESTATION)

Trombiculidiasis is infestation with chigger mites. There are over 700 different species of chiggers. *Eutrombicula alfreddugesi* is the North American chigger. The adults do not live on or infest animals but instead live and feed on decaying vegetable debris. The larval stage is the only stage that affects mammals. Dogs get infested when they wander through wooded areas and acquire the larval forms. If the larvae attach to the skin they produce an itchy rash (papules, pimples and crust). The larvae are small (0.2-0.4 mm in length), bright orange in color and attach tightly to the skin. Because the larvae only attach to the host for a few days, they may be gone by the time of examination. Most affected patients have a history of exposure to wooded areas. Most cases are seen in the central region of the United States during the summer and fall season. Treatment involves one to two parasiticidal dips with any good, safe insecticide approved for flea control.

ADDITIONAL READING

Ackerman, L: Guide to Skin and Haircoat Problems in Dogs. Alpine Publishing, Loveland, Colorado, 1994, 182pp.

Sosna, CB; Medleau, L: The clinical signs and diagnosis of external parasite infestation. *Veterinary Medicine*, 1992; 87: 573-586.

Microscopic view of the ear mite, *Otodectes cynotis*.

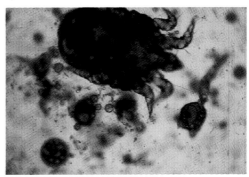

Dr. Jon D. Plant received his Doctor of Veterinary Medicine degree from Oregon State University in 1988. After a year in private practice, he completed a two-year residency in dermatology at the Animal Dermatology Clinic in Orange County, California. He is certified by the American College of Veterinary Dermatology. Dr. Plant and his associate see patients at the Animal Dermatology Specialty Clinic in three Los Angeles and Ventura County locations. He has lectured at numerous veterinary association meetings on veterinary dermatology subjects.

Ringworm (Dermatophytosis)

By Jon D. Plant, DVM,
Diplomate, American College of
   Veterinary Dermatology
Animal Dermatology Specialty
   Clinic
1304 Wilshire Blvd.
Santa Monica, CA 90403

INTRODUCTION

"Ringworm" is the common name given to fungal infections of the hair, skin, and nails caused by a group of organisms called dermatophytes. The medical name for these fungal infections is dermato-phytosis. Three groups of fungi which include many species are possible causes of ringworm, but in the dog only three are to blame for the vast majority of cases. These are *Microsporum canis, Microsporum gypseum*, and *Trichophyton mentagrophytes*. Most animal species, as well as humans, are susceptible to one or more types of ringworm organisms. Although each dermatophyte species is often found infecting a certain species of animal, this association is not rigid, allowing them to infect other species of animals as well when the opportunity arises. For instance, *Microsporum canis*, primarily infects dogs and cats but will also infect humans.

THE CLINICAL PICTURE

Dermatophytosis may take on several different appearances in dogs. The most common is an expanding, red, scaly, circular area in which the hair is lost. The center often become darker due to pigment production caused by the earlier inflammation. Although this may be suggestive of ringworm, it is not the only disease that can take on this appearance, so an accurate diagnosis is important. Some dogs will have only a solitary spot, while others will develop a more widespread infection with multiple circular areas blending together. In some cases, virtually the entire body is involved.

When a ringworm lesion becomes swollen and pustular, it is referred to as a kerion. Kerions are more inflamed than the more common, flat ringworm lesion. When dogs' nails are infected with dermatophytes (onychomycosis), the most common problem is crumbly, soft, deformed nails. The entire nail is

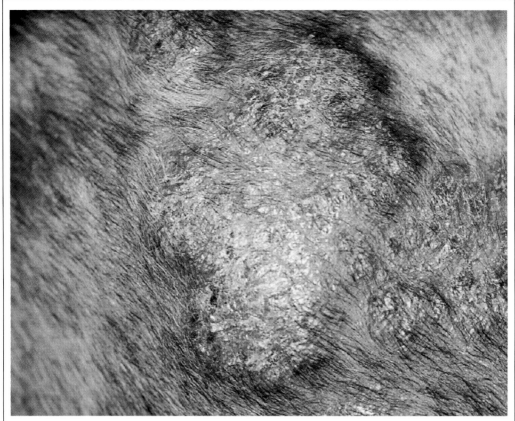

Ringworm on the hip of a Miniature Schnauzer caused by *Microsporum canis*. Note the rounded borders, redness, and scale.

sometimes shed. This type of infection can be very chronic and difficult to cure.

Another appearance that ringworm can take in dogs is that of widespread pimples and small bumps associated with erect-standing hairs and hair loss (a form of folliculitis, an infection of hair follicles). Because ringworm affects hairs as well as outer layers of the skin, hairs tend to be fragile and break off or pull out easily.

The areas of the body that are most commonly affected by ringworm in dogs are the muzzle, head, and extremities. The trunk may also be affected. When a solitary lesion is located on the top of the muzzle of a dog which digs and roots in the soil, *Microsporum gypseum*, a soil inhabitant, is often the cause.

Not all animals who come in contact with the fungi causing ringworm will develop the disease. What are the factors which make an animal more susceptible to ringworm infections? Any condition which suppresses an animal's ability to mount an effective immune response against dermatophytes makes that animal more susceptible to ringworm. These include: having an immature or aged immune system (very young or old animals); taking medications which suppress the immune system (like chemotherapy or chronic corticosteroids); and having a severe systemic illness (like hyperadrenocorticism also known as Cushing's syndrome). Other factors which may favor the development of ringworm include abrasions in the skin (like those that might be caused on a dog's muzzle by rooting in the soil), high humidity, and exposure to especially infectious strains of dermatophytes.

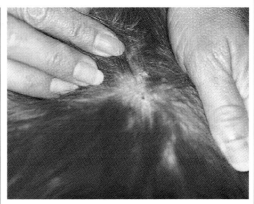

Scale and mild hair loss on a Golden Retriever with ringworm.

Ringworm is a zoonotic disease, which means people can catch it from animals. However, just because one is in contact with a pet that has ringworm does not mean he will necessarily catch it. Some of the same factors which govern whether or not a pet is susceptible apply to humans as well. People on immunosuppressive medications, children, and elderly people are more susceptible. The risk can be minimized by washing one's hands after each handling of an infected animal and cleaning up the pet's surroundings well. A person who is known to be at increased risk of contracting ringworm should consider avoiding all contact with the pet until it is judged by their veterinarian to no longer be contagious. If one suspects he has ringworm, he should see his physician.

DIAGNOSIS

The diagnosis of ringworm is made by the veterinarian based upon appearance and laboratory tests. A quick screening test involves illuminating the skin and hair with a Wood's light (a specific wavelength of ultraviolet light). Infections with some species of dermatophytes (principally *Microsporum canis* in dogs) will sometimes cause the hair to fluoresce under a Wood's light. However, this test is not very specific; some hairs that glow are not infected with ringworm and hairs that don't glow are not necessarily free of infection. Also, previous treatment with some medications may cause a non-ringworm spot to fluoresce while treatment with

The hair loss and redness on the leg of this dog was caused by *Microsporum canis*.

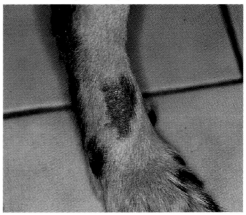

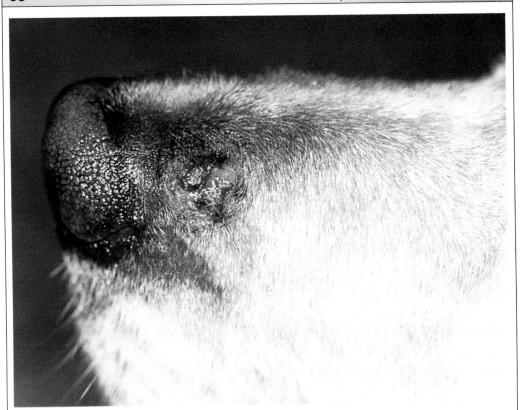

This type of lesion on the nose is often associated with the soil contaminant *Microsporum gypseum*, as in this kerion type of ringworm lesion.

another may obliterate the fluorescence of a previously fluorescent ringworm area. Due to these inaccuracies, a Wood's light should only be used as a screening test, and a fungal culture or direct microscopic examination of the skin and hair should be taken from suspicious regions.

A fungal culture is performed by placing samples of hair, scale, or nails on a culture material designed to support the growth of dermatophytes, allowing for identification. The most common material, dermatophyte test media (DTM) also contains a color indicator which aids in the early detection of dermatophyte growth. Positive cultures are best confirmed by the veterinarian examining the growth microscopically for characteristic structures. In this way, the species of ringworm can be identified. This may have important implications in identifying the source of the ringworm and how easy the infection will be to treat. It may take ten to 14 days for the DTM to become positive, although it often does so within seven days.

The veterinarian's direct microscopic examination of the hair or skin scraping can be aided by adding chemicals that dissolve keratin, leaving any dermatophytes present easier to see. This test can provide conclusive results of ringworm more quickly than a fungal culture but is more difficult to interpret.

TREATMENT

Treatment of infected dogs after a diagnosis of ringworm has been made by a veterinarian may involve topical as well as oral therapy. Recent studies have suggested that many topical treatments used alone may not speed the resolution of ringworm infections in cats. Similar studies have not yet been done in dogs. Only oral antifungal therapy helped significantly in this set of studies. Nonetheless, using antifungal shampoos, dips, and creams may help decrease the spread of ringworm to other pets, humans and the pet's environment.

Most veterinarians recommend clipping the hair in and around affected areas so that those hairs containing dermatophyte spores are removed and discarded. While whole body clipping was once recommended, recent studies suggest that this is not helpful, and may actually spread the disease to uninvolved areas.

Topical creams often used on individual ringworm areas include those containing miconazole, ketoconazole, and clotrimazole. Some studies have compared the effectiveness of topical therapy ingredients against various species of dermatophytes; however, the results have differed depending on the study, and there is no clear cut winner. Creams are usually pre-

scribed for use every 12 to 24 hours.

Antifungal shampoo ingredients that are commonly used to treat dogs with ringworm include chlorhexidene and miconazole. Active ingredients of antifungal dips include enilconazole, lime sulfur, dilute bleach, and chlorhexidene. Shampoos and dips are generally used every three to seven days.

Dogs with extensive ringworm are often treated with oral antifungal medications. Griseofulvin is the standard treatment for dogs. Side effects are uncommon. Several human antifungal drugs (e.g., ketoconazole, itraconazole) have also been used successfully in dogs. The veterinarian may choose to prescribe an oral medication based on the severity of the case, any underlying diseases present, and other factors.

Dogs with ringworm should receive treatment until their condition is completely cured and, ideally, until a negative culture is obtained. This takes from three to ten weeks in average hair and skin cases (and many months in nail

The widespread hair loss and red pimples on this Staffordshire Terrier were caused by *Trichophyton mentagrophytes*.

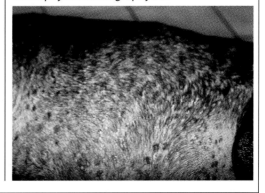

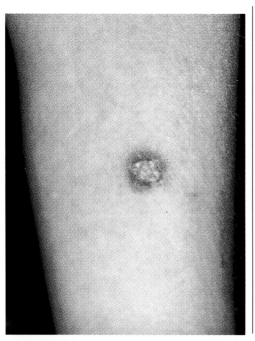

infections). Infections caused by *Trichophyton mentagrophytes* may also take longer to cure. When an underlying condition is identified that is suppressing the immune system, it must be corrected, or the ringworm is likely to be chronic, recurrent, and hard to cure.

A vaccine has recently been marketed for the prevention and treatment of ringworm in cats. It is of questionable value and, as of the time of this writing, not widely

Left: A circular lesion on the arm of a person who caught ringworm from an infected pet.
Below: Fluorescence under Wood's light of hairs on a dog's foot caused by infection with *Microsporum canis*.

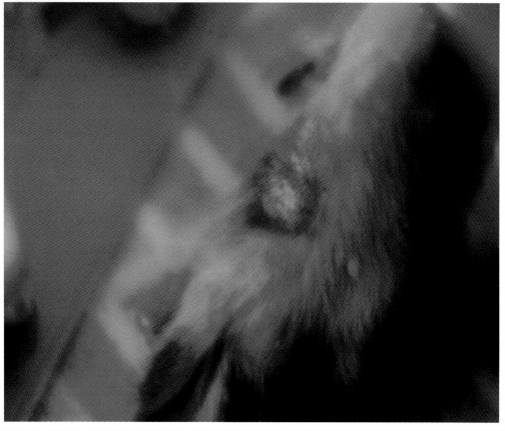

recommended by veterinary dermatologists. The main criticism is that even though cats may look better after treatment with the vaccine, they are potentially still infected with dermatophytes and can continue to spread the infection. Further studies may still prove the vaccine to be worthwhile for cats, but at this time it is not licensed for dogs.

Cleaning and disinfecting the environment are important part of effectively dealing with ringworm. All hard surfaces (floors and cages) should be cleaned with bleach, if possible. Bedding should be replaced or washed in hot water. Grooming supplies should be replaced or disinfected with bleach. Carpets should be thoroughly vacuumed daily. While steam cleaning may aid in removing infected hairs, it probably does not produce temperatures high enough to kill dermatophyte spores in the carpet. Environmental con-tamination and the subsequent repeat infection of a dog can be a serious obstacle in a household or kennel where multiple animals are infected.

SUMMARY

Ringworm is a fungal infection of dogs which may take on a number of appearances. People may catch it from their pets. The veterinarian may use a combination of tests to diagnose ringworm. Treatment usually involves topical therapy, environmental clean up, and sometimes oral medication.

ADDITIONAL READING

Muller GH, Kirk RW, Scott DW. *Small Animal Dermatology*, 4th Ed., WB Saunders, Philadelphia, 1989, pp 299-315.

Antifungal shampoos are useful in treating causes of ringworm. Photo courtesy of Virbac.

Dr. Bruce L. Hansen is a Diplomate of the American College of Veterinary Dermatology and is a practicing veterinary dermatologist in Springfield, Virginia. He received his Doctorate in Veterinary Medicine from the Veterinary School at the University of Missouri in 1980 and went on to do a dermatology residency program at the University of Pennsylvania. Dr. Hansen served one year as a clinical instructor in Veterinary Dermatology at the University of Pennsylvania prior to opening Dermatology and Allergy Services for Animals in Springfield, Virginia. He is currently serving as an adjunct clinical professor for the Virginia-Maryland Regional Veterinary School.

Problems with Hair Loss

By Bruce L. Hansen, DVM,
Diplomate, American College of
   Veterinary Dermatology
Dermatology and Allergy Services
   for Animals
6651-F Backlick Rd.
Springfield, VA 22150

INTRODUCTION

Hair loss that results in baldness is defined as alopecia. Alopecia may occur in small patches or be generalized and involve large areas of the body. Hair loss is a very common problem in pets and can be caused by a variety of diseases. Because animals are covered in a thick luxuriant hair coat, diseases that cause hair loss in the dog are very noticeable and distressing to the pet owner.

What causes hair to fall out? With modern medicine you might think that you should be able to call the local veterinarian to get a pill or shot to cure the alopecia. Unfortunately, hair loss is only a symptom shared by many different diseases. The patterns of hair loss in many diseases are identical, so that even the trained eye of a veterinarian can not identify the cause of alopecia in the pet; numerous laboratory tests are often required. Some cases are so complex that a veterinary dermatologist is needed to correctly diagnose the cause of the alopecia and prescribe appropriate treatment.

CAUSES

Diseases causing damage or death to the hair or hair follicle (which is the pore in which the hair grows) and diseases causing excessive traction or pulling on the hair can result in hair loss. Dogs with hormonal problems, from either too much or too little of certain hormones, often have fur that stops growing and falls out. The resultant hair loss is termed an endocrine alopecia (endocrine implying a hormonal nature). The hormonal alopecia that people have heard the most about is hypothyroidism, which is caused by an underactive thyroid gland. Other causes of hormonal hair loss include hyperadrenocorticism (Cushing's syndrome) caused by the effects of too much cortisol (a natural form of cortisone) in the body, adult onset growth hormone-responsive alopecia caused by too little growth hormone in the body, and a variety of sex hormone imbalances.

To the naked eye, all forms of hormonal hair loss are identical. The only way to identify the correct hormonal abnormality is to perform

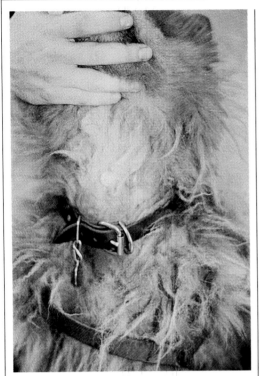

Hair loss on the neck of a Chow Chow with adult-onset growth hormone-responsive alopecia.

amples would include loss of hair after a very high fever or the sudden loss of hair in a mother dog (bitch) after delivering and nursing a litter of puppies. Some medications or toxins (poisons) can cause hair death and subsequent hair loss. In people hair loss of this type would include hair loss associated with chemotherapy. In animals the rodent poison thallium causes rapid complete hair loss (and later death) if ingested in sufficient quantities.

Diseases that affect the hair and hair follicle can cause patchy to widespread hair loss. Hair follicle infections loosen hair and eventu-

Complete hair loss along the chest and abdomen of a Boston Terrier with hyperadrenocorticism (Cushing's syndrome). Photo courtesy of Dr. Richard Hawe.

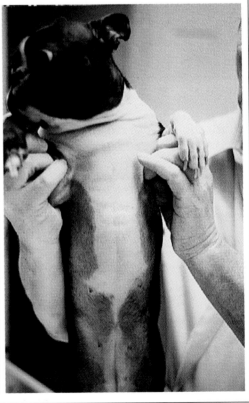

specific blood tests and to construct a careful history of other clinical symptoms such as excessive thirst and urination, recent weight gain, and decreased activity level. Because hypothyroidism is such a well-known cause of hair loss, many cases of hair loss, particularly hormonal alopecias, are incorrectly assumed to be from an underactive thyroid gland. However, each case must be evaluated individually. Some dogs with endocrine alopecia do have hypothyroidism, but it is important not to forget about the other important causes.

Conditions or events that are very stressful to pets can result in a sudden generalized hair loss called telogen or anagen dysfluxion. Ex-ally dislodge it to result in hair loss. In the dog follicular infections are usually a bacterial folliculitis caused by the bacterium *Staphylococcus intermedius*. In dogs with hair coats characterized by short stubbly hair (like the Doberman Pinscher), the resulting hair loss often resembles a moth-eaten blanket, what veterinarians term a "motheaten" alopecia. Long-haired dogs (such as the Shetland Sheepdog) usually develop large bald patches of reddened scaling skin in association with bacterial folliculitis. However, not all "motheaten" alopecias or circular, reddened scaly patches represent a bacterial folliculitis.

Young dogs and older debilitated dogs sometimes develop alopecia from a parasitic folliculitis, demodicosis, caused by the mite *Demodex canis*. This disease can manifest itself as one or two small bald spots or whole-body hair loss with severe crusting of the body. Actually, the mite is present in all animals, but, in animals with a depressed immune system, the mites multiply in large numbers to result in the disease. Therefore, the presence of demodectic mange in a puppy represents either an immature immune system, or potentially a defective immune system. Therefore, it is recommended that animals with generalized demodicosis not be used for breeding for fear that this genetic trait will be passed on to succeeding generations. Older animals that develop demodicosis have suffered a severe insult or debilitation to their immune system, and these animals should be exam-

Same Boston Terrier six months after starting therapy for hyperadrenocorticism. Photo courtesy of Dr. Richard Hawe.

Generalized hair loss in an adult male Poodle due to a castration-responsive dermatosis (sex hormone imbalance).

Generalized redness of the skin with hair loss in an Irish Setter with cutaneous lymphosarcoma.

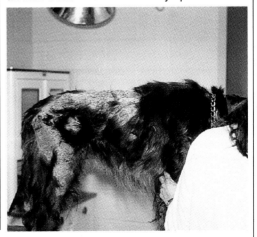

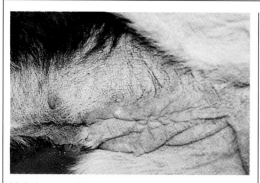

Hair loss and increased skin pigmentation on abdomen of dog with cutaneous *Malassezia dermatitis*.

ined very carefully for the presence of a severe internal disease.

Fungal infections, such as ringworm (dermatophytosis), cause hair loss from both disease of the hair shaft and fungal infection of the hair follicle. The resulting hair loss is clinically indistinguishable from demodicosis or bacterial folliculitis. Ringworm is occasionally seen in young puppies and is only a rare cause of alopecia in the adult dog. However, because ringworm is contagious to people, all cases of hair loss should be considered a potential fungal infection until proven otherwise.

Bacterial folliculitis resulting in a "motheaten" alopecia in a Doberman Pinscher.

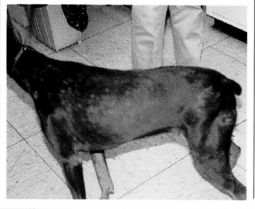

Hair follicle dysplasia is a genetic disease characterized by defective, brittle hairs that break and split easily resulting in patchy to complete hair loss. This disease is recognized in certain breeds of dogs such as the "blue" or "fawn" colored Doberman Pinscher in which the hair is normal as a puppy, but slowly as the animal matures the hair coat becomes more scaly and thin, until substantial hair loss is detected. Hair follicle dysplasia closely resembles bacterial folliculitis,

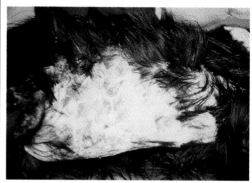

Bacterial folliculitis with hair loss on the chest of a long-haired dog.

demodicosis, and ringworm. Further complicating the picture is that animals with hair follicle dysplasia often have a secondary bacterial folliculitis.

Skin diseases not associated with hair follicles can cause hair loss by causing inflammation that secondarily affects hair and hair follicles. Sebaceous adenitis is a disease that attacks sebaceous glands, which are oil glands that empty into the hair follicle. The resulting inflammation affects the hair shaft and hair follicle, yielding a brittle, damaged hair that breaks off resulting in hair loss. Cutaneous lympho-sarcoma and other skin cancers can spread rapidly and cause severe inflammation, destroying and pushing hair follicles aside leaving bald nodules or growths on the skin surface. Unfortunately, treatment for most of these skin cancers is usually unrewarding.

Autoimmune skin diseases are diseases in which the body attacks its own skin. The result is destruction of skin and hair follicles with consequent hair loss and scaling. Pemphigus foliaceus and cutaneous lupus erythematosus are the most common autoimmune skin

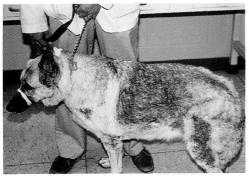
Hair loss associated with deep bacterial infection in a German Shepherd Dog.

diseases seen in the dog, but systemic lupus erythematosus, pemphigus vulgaris, pemphigus vegetans, pemphigus erythematosus, and bullous pemphigoid are encountered occasionally. Finally, diseases like toxic epidermal necrolysis and erythema multiforme are conditions in which the immune system attacks the skin (which is an innocent bystander), sometimes destroying the entire epidermis (or top layer of skin), completely oblit-

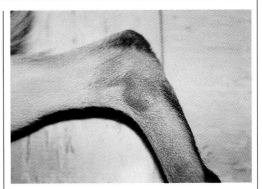
Focal patch of hair loss associated with a ringworm (dermatophytosis) in a dog.

erating all hair follicles in its path. The result is not only areas of hair loss but complete ulceration of the skin. The most common cause for toxic epidermal necrolysis and erythema multiforme is a drug allergy. From a clinical standpoint, these diseases can closely resemble demodicosis, ringworm, and bacterial folliculitis. Because treatment of autoimmune skin disease requires decreasing the body's immune response (to decrease the body's ability to attack itself), extreme care needs to be taken to ensure the correct diagnosis is made. Otherwise, if a bacterial folliculitis, ring-

Allergic inhalant dermatitis in a Yorkshire Terrier. Photo courtesy of Dr. Barbara Kummel.

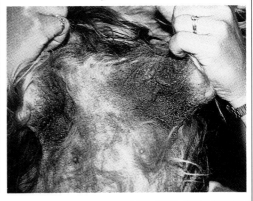

worm or demodicosis was present, the treatment for autoimmune skin disease would tremendously worsen the disease.

Diseases characterized by itching (pruritus) and manifested by licking, biting, chewing, and scratching of the hair constitute the most common causes of hair loss in the dog. Continued itching causes breaking of the hair and pulling of the hair right out of its hair follicle. However, not all cases of hair loss caused by continuous pulling or traction are caused by itching. In rare cases, hair barrettes applied too tightly for too long a period of time cause a permanent hair loss called *traction alopecia*.

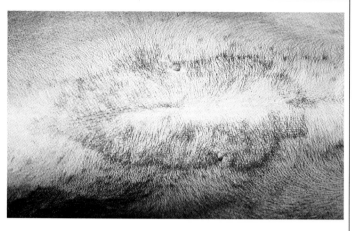

Allergic contact dermatitis with secondary bacterial folliculitis in a dog.

Allergic inhalant dermatitis with secondary bacterial folliculitis resulting in severe hair loss in a West Highland White Terrier. Photo courtesy of Dr. Barbara Kummel.

Flea bite dermatitis or flea allergy resulting in hair loss is the most common disease encountered in veterinary medicine during the summer time in much of the United States. Flea bite dermatitis causes severe itch over the entire animal with most cases being most severe over the lower back and rump region of the body. In many cases large numbers of fleas are necessary to cause sufficient itching to result in hair loss, but in some cases only slight exposure to fleas is needed. Treatment involves strict flea control on the animal and especially in the environment where the dog lives.

Fleas are not the only parasite in the dog capable of causing

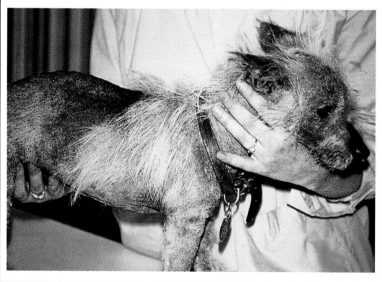

enough itching to cause hair loss. *Sarcoptes scabiei* mites (sarcoptic mange) are an occasional cause of an intensely itchy disease that results in extensive hair loss and crusting primarily on the ears, face, legs and belly of affected dogs. This mite is contagious and can transiently affect people.

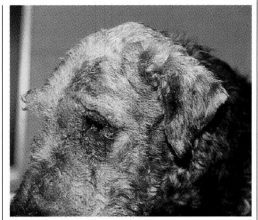

Airedale with sarcoptic mange resulting in significant hair loss due to excessive itching.

Doberman Pinscher with hair loss due to both sarcoptic mange and hair follicle dysplasia.

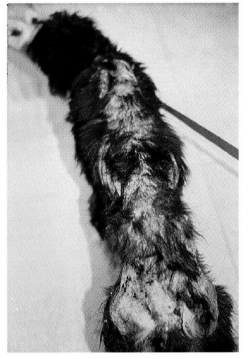

Generalized demodicosis and severe secondary bacterial folliculitis causing extensive alopecia in an Afghan Hound.

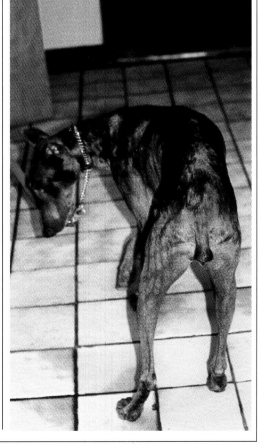

Cheyletiella mites (cheyletiellosis), *Otodectes cynotis* (ear mites), lice (pediculosis), and even chiggers (trombiculidiasis) can also result in severe alopecia from excessive scratching. Some of these parasites can also transiently affect people, so prompt veterinary care is recommended for all itchy dogs.

Allergic dermatitis in the dog usually manifests as itching and is a common cause of hair loss. Dogs can be allergic to pollens, grasses, trees, molds, and dust mites that are inhaled (and to a lesser extent absorbed from the skin surface). This type of allergy is called allergic inhalant dermatitis and is the second most common allergy (behind flea allergy) in the dog. Food allergy is also seen occasionally in the dog. Allergic contact dermatitis (an allergic reaction to materials contacting the dog's skin) does occur but only rarely since the dog's long hair coat acts as protection against prolonged contact with potentially allergenic substances. Finally, an intensely itchy disease caused by excessive colonization of the skin by a yeast, *Malassezia pachydermatis*, is increasingly being recognized as a cause of severe itching and hair loss in many parts of North America. This disease is often found to be secondary to allergic dermatitis or previous use of antibiotics.

SUMMARY

Numerous diseases are capable of causing excessive hair loss in the dog. Many are identical in the pattern and appearance of the hair loss. Furthermore, animals can suffer from several diseases that cause hair loss at the same time (for example, animals with flea allergy can develop bacterial folliculitis; hypothyroid dogs can catch sarcoptic mange, etc.), making evaluation extremely difficult. Therefore, a thorough medical examination is mandatory in all causes of hair loss in the dog.

ADDITIONAL READING

Ackerman, L: *Guide to Skin and Haircoat Problems in Dogs.* Alpine Publications, Loveland, Colorado, 1994, 182pp.

Campbell, KL; Small, E: Identifying and managing the cutaneous manifestations of various endocrine diseases. *Veterinary Medicine*, 1991; 86: 118-135.

Left: Fatty acid supplements are often used in dogs with inflamed skin, especially those with allergies or keratinization disorders. Photo courtesy of Virbac.

Facing page: Dog with hair loss over the lower back due to flea allergy dermatitis.

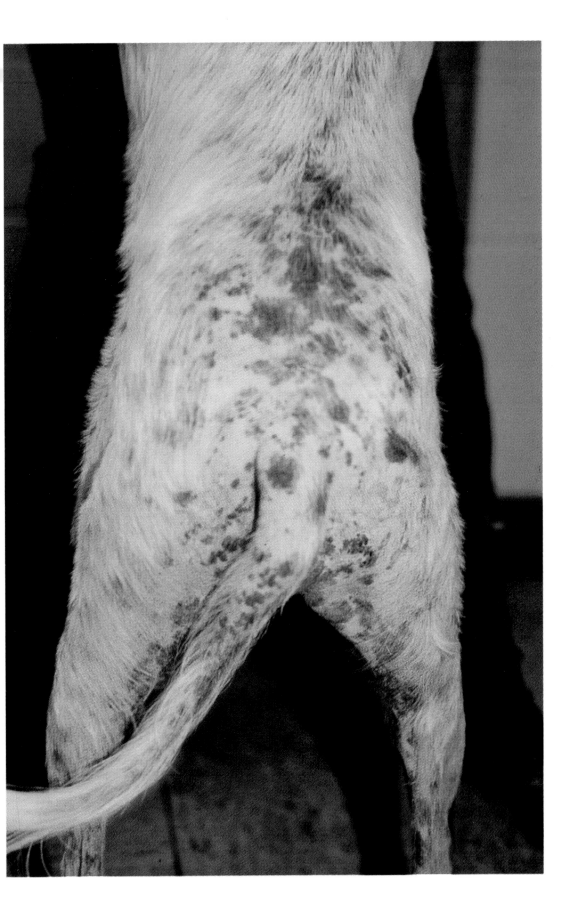

Dr. Bonnie Werner graduated from the University of California, Davis, School of Veterinary Medicine, followed by an internship at the Coast Pet Clinic in Hermosa Beach, California. She completed a residency in small-animal internal medicine at the Louisiana State University, School of Veterinary Medicine. Both Drs. Werner live in Southern California, where they practice together in a referral specialty clinic.

Dr. Alexander Werner graduated from the University of Pennsylvania, School of Veterinary Medicine, followed by an internship at the California Animal Hospital in Los Angeles, California. He completed a residency in veterinary dermatology at the University of California, Davis, School of Veterinary Medicine, where he met his wife Bonnie. Dr. Alexander Werner is a Diplomate of the American College of Veterinary Dermatology.

Ear Care and Ear Problems

By Alexander H. Werner, VMD,
Diplomate, American College of
   Veterinary Dermatology
and
Bonnie E. Werner, DVM
Animal Dermatology Centers
Valley Veterinary Specialty
   Services
13125 Ventura Boulevard
Studio City, CA 91604

INTRODUCTION

The canine external ear canal is a marvel of genetic manipulation. From the long, drooping, short-haired pinnae (ear flaps) of the Basset Hound, to the small, erect, long-haired pinnae of the Papillon, modern dog's ears are very unlike the more natural ones of the "original" dog (comparatively similar to the Dingo dog of Australia). With these changes has come a multitude of medical ear problems for the modern dog.

The anatomy of the canine ear canal conformation varies greatly between breeds, but the basic structures are present in all dogs. The pinna functions to direct sound into the external ear canal. The canal is divided into two components, a vertical, slightly tapering section and a horizontal section leading to the tympanum (ear drum). Both sections of the external canal are surrounded by cartilage, which supports the canal and keeps it open.

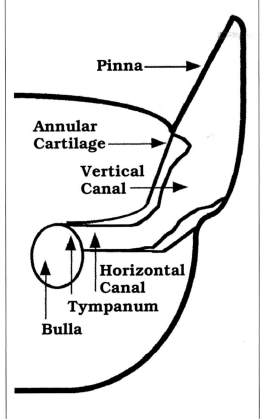

Schematic drawing of the canine ear canal.

Pinna

Annular Cartilage

Vertical Canal

Horizontal Canal

Tympanum

Bulla

The tympanum separates the external and middle sections of the ear and protects the middle ear from the debris and organisms found in the external canal. The middle ear consists of the bones of the ear and a large, hollow, spherical bone, called the bulla. The eustachian tube, which assists in equalizing pressures behind and in front of the tympanum, opens into the bulla from the throat. The inner ear resides entirely within the skull and contains the organs of hearing.

The ear canal is lined with skin, therefore any skin disease in general can have a direct effect on the ear canal. Special glands within the canal, called cerumen glands, produce the wax that coats and protects the ear. Depending on the breed, the external ear canal may be lined at its opening with hairs that guard against foreign objects entering the ear canal.

A normal dog should not have problems with its ear canals. Routine head shaking will remove excessive wax, and the occasional scratching will help to break up debris. A dog with ear disease, however, may continuously shake its head and scratch at either the base of the ear or the ear flap, damaging the skin. Ear infections are not normal and, if recurrent, the ears and the rest of the skin should be thoroughly examined.

CLINICAL SIGNS OF EAR DISEASE

Ear disease commonly presents as intense head shaking and itchiness around the ears. An exudate or discharge may also be present and the ears may have an unpleasant odor. While most ear infections may seem to appear suddenly, with the exception of plant awns or other foreign objects entering the ear, the majority of infections actually smolder quietly, with only occasional discomfort, until the disease becomes overwhelming and the ear seems "suddenly" painful. Answers to the following questions are useful clues for determining the cause of ear disease:

- Are both ear canals affected?
- Did ear disease occur suddenly?
- How long has ear disease been noticed?
- Has ear disease occurred in the past?
- Did itching or did a discharge occur first?
- Is just the canal diseased or is the pinna also affected?
- Are any other skin lesions present?
- Does the dog otherwise feel and act well?
- Does the dog swim?

Severe swelling of a pinna may indicate that the head shaking has caused blood vessels to break, resulting in a blood-filled pocket. This pocket is called a hematoma and requires surgical drainage and correction to avoid scarring. In addition, the underlying cause of the head shaking (e.g., ear disease) must be investigated.

Head tilting, disorientation, flicking of the eyes, vomiting, circling, and falling can be evidence that the ear infection has spread from the external canal to the middle and inner ear. These infections are more dangerous to the animal, and systemic antibiotics should be used. Statistically, more than half of all cases of chronic ear disease result in a ruptured ear drum and lead to middle ear infection. Luckily, the tympanum can regrow once the ear disease is eliminated.

FACTORS PRODUCING EAR DISEASE

The ear canal is a sensitive structure with a carefully balanced environment. Many diseases can produce inflammation and infection of the ear. The term, "otitis externa" literally means "inflammation of the external ear canal." It is a description, not a diagnosis, therefore the underlying cause of this inflamma-

tion must be discovered and resolved. Ear canal diseases can be separated into three categories:

1. predisposing factors;
2. primary factors;
3. perpetuating factors.

Each category will be discussed separately, however, all three categories combine to produce and to worsen ear disease.

1. Predisposing Factors:

A normal ear requires good aeration to reduce moisture accumulation and minimal wax production to prevent blockage of the external canal. The funnel shape of the ear effectively traps debris and wax. Many breed conformation specifications require a large, flaccid pinna that occludes the ear canal, preventing good air circulation. In addition, a large amount of hair on the

Cocker Spaniel with severe ear infection due to excessive folds and wax accumulation within the ear.

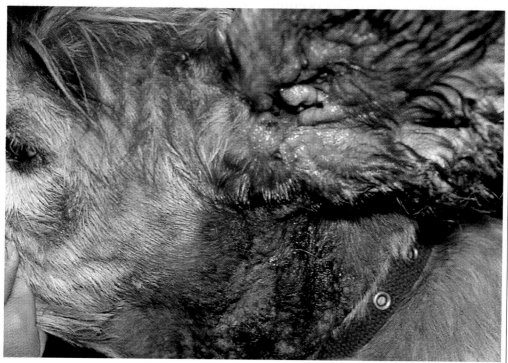

pinna and in the canal can further decrease air flow. Some breeds, such as the Chinese Shar-Pei, have very tortuous, deep, narrow canals; others, such as the Cocker Spaniel, have many folds inside their ear canals. Cocker Spaniels may also produce excessive amounts of ear wax. These changes result in decreased air flow in the canal, leading to increased moisture, wax accumulation, and ultimately, infection.

Several other factors can produce decreased aeration and increased moisture within the ear canal. Dogs that swim may frequently develop infections (known in humans as "swimmer's ear") due to water accumulation. Excessive or inappropri-

ate ear treatments can traumatize or irritate the lining of the ear. Build-up of medication can obstruct the canal and produce a moist environment. Tumors or polyps within the ear canal will also obstruct air flow. Lastly, any disease that affects the animal's health in general, and its skin in particular, can affect the ear canals.

2. Primary Causes:

Primary causes of ear disease are factors that will directly cause inflammation and infection within the ear canal in the absence of any confounding factors. Satisfactory resolution requires treatment of any secondary infection and elimination of the underlying cause.

Ear mites are implicated too frequently as the cause of ear infections. The most common ear mite,

Dalmatian with food allergy. Note severe redness of the ear flap and canal.

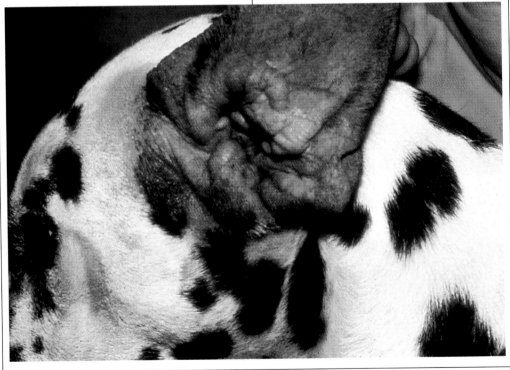

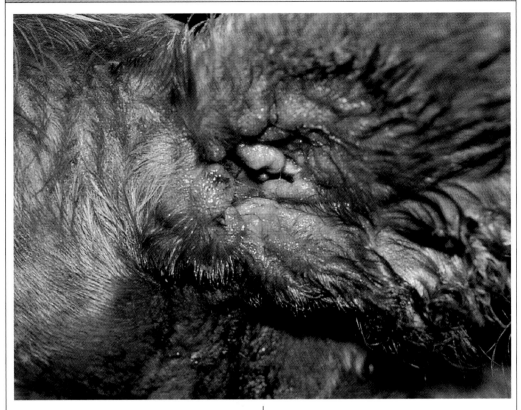

Otodectes cynotis, usually affects very young or ill animals. Mites are a rare cause of ear itchiness and infection in a healthy adult dog. Other parasites can produce ear disease and these possibilities should be explored by your veterinarian.

Hypersensitivities (allergies) are perhaps the most frequent cause of recurrent ear infections. Increased itchiness, either generalized over the body or confined to the ear canal itself, is a hallmark of allergy. Hypersensitivities include diseases such as atopy (inhalant allergy), food allergy, and contact allergy. In fact, some dogs can become allergic to medications commonly used to treat ear infections. Each of these hypersensitivity states must be di-

Above: Closer view of Cocker Spaniel's infected ear. Note the severe amount of wax accumulating within the ear canal, on the ear flap, and on the face. This ear was painful, inflamed, and odiferous.

Below: Labrador Retriever with contact allergy. Multiple regions of scabbing and hair loss are present on the ear flap.

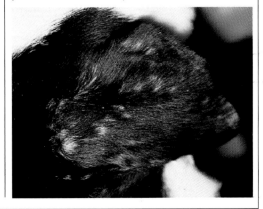

agnosed and controlled in order to prevent the ear disease.

Abnormalities in wax production result in an unhealthy ear. The most common cause of increased wax production is any type of inflammation in the ear. The cerumen glands of the ear canal respond to inflammation by producing more wax. In disease states, this increased wax production results in a vicious cycle of inflammation, wax production, infection, more inflammation, and even more wax production. The goal in these cases is to break the cycle and return the ear to its normal state. Examples of primary causes of excessive wax production include hormonal disease, idiopathic

seborrhea (dandruff), and the increased wax production seen in such breeds as Cocker Spaniels.

3. Perpetuating Factors:

Once otitis externa has developed, secondary events will complicate the problem. Severe bacterial infection with such pathogens as *Pseudomonas* and *Proteus*, or yeast infections with *Malassezia pachydermatis* (or both bacterial and yeast infections together) are common. These infections perpetuate the ear disease by producing even greater inflammation, pain, and wax production. With long-standing or recurrent ear infection, the lining of the ear canal will form thick scar tissue, closing down the canal further and preventing effective treatment. The cartilage surrounding the canal (annular cartilage) will also thicken and then accumulate cal-

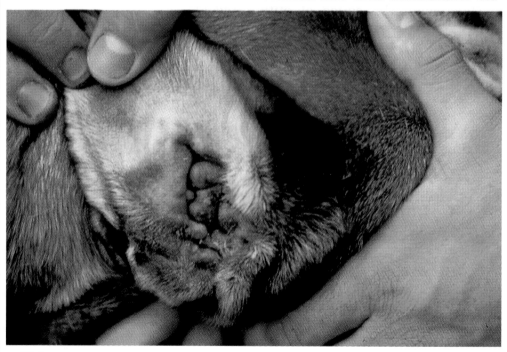

Complete obstruction of the external ear canal caused by chronic ear disease in a mixed-breed dog.

cium, becoming bone-hard. The lack of pliability and the narrowing of the canal may ultimately lead to complete obstruction. At this point, the ear canal disease is considered end-stage, and medical treatment cannot reverse these changes. In these cases, surgical removal of the ear canal (ear ablation) by a qualified veterinary surgeon may be the only option to make the dog comfortable. It is interesting to note that some dogs that have their ears ablated seem to have better hearing after the surgery than before. It is possible that all of the inflammation, infection, and thick accumulations of tissue and debris prevent the inner ear from receiving vibrations and, once they are removed, residual hearing through the skull bones returns.

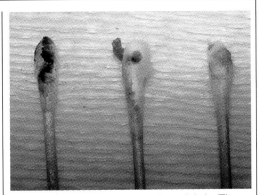

Examples of different types of ear debris. These samples were collected from normal-appearing ear canals.

DIAGNOSIS

Diagnosing the cause of otitis externa necessitates identifying the perpetuating causes as well as any primary or conformational problems. Specific diagnostic tests include direct examination of the ear canal (otoscopy), microscopic examination of canal debris, bacterial culture of canal debris, allergy testing, and general, comprehensive blood tests.

The otoscopic examination is important in order to answer several key questions:

- Are one or both canals affected?
- Is the ear canal inflamed?
- Is the ear canal thickened or stenotic (narrowed)?
- Is the ear canal obstructed by a mass or by debris?
- Is there a foreign body (plant awn) in the canal?
- Is the tympanum intact?

The conscious dog with painful ear disease may not allow complete examination of the ear canal without sedation. Your veterinarian will decide whether it is better to attempt cleaning of the ear first, before examination of the canal, or if sedation to allow a full examination and cleaning is best. Therapy for the ear will be based on both the direct examination of the ear canal and the microscopic examination of canal debris.

Examination of canal debris helps to determine if an infection or infestation is present. Simple visual inspection of the debris can direct the veterinarian toward a particular diagnosis. However, it is not possible (without microscopic examination) to determine the exact type of debris that is present in the ear. For example, it is sometimes believed that a dark brown, crumbly, coffee-ground appearing ear exudate is diagnostic of ear mite infestation. This is incorrect. While this type of debris is commonly found with ear

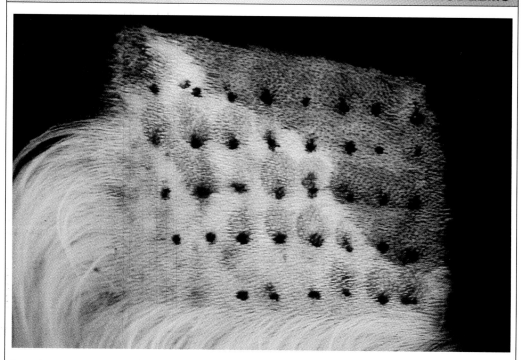

Intradermal allergy test. Positive reactions are recognized as reddened welts above the black pen-marks.

mite infestation, many other non-infested ears may have this type of debris. Microscopic examination of ear exudate is a mandatory part of the diagnosis and treatment of ear disease.

Microscopically, ear debris may contain only wax, or wax and various organisms. The presence or absence of white blood cells within the debris can indicate the degree of infection within the ear. Wax without white blood cells indicates inflammation with minimal infection. The presence of many white blood cells indicates severe infection. Finding red blood cells in the debris indicates that the skin lining the ear canal has been damaged and is bleeding.

Bacterial or fungal cultures of ear debris is commonly performed so that appropriate antibiotic therapy can be prescribed. In general, when infection occurs, the bacteria present are merely opportunistic invaders. These bacteria do not grow in a normal ear. Only when inflammation, debris blockage, or other damage is present does the environment in the ear become favorable for bacterial growth. Therefore, establishing a normal ear environment is paramount to resolving infection. Culturing ear debris should be reserved for resistant cases or for individual animals that have received many medications without successful resolution. Bacterial cultures yield sensitivity results for antibiotics based on the level of these antibiotics in the bloodstream. The ear canal interior is far removed from the bloodstream, therefore these results are not always applicable. Since systemic (oral or injectable) antibiotics rarely penetrate into the ear canal, they cannot replace appropriate topical therapies.

If the cause of recurrent ear disease is suspected to be of allergic origin, referral to a veterinary dermatologist is recommended. The work up for allergic skin disease may require specialized diagnostics such as intradermal skin tests or serum testing that may not be available to the general practitioner. Remember, an itchy or infected ear is a common manifestation of allergy. Without correct diagnosis and treatment, recurrent disease and severe sequelae may be expected.

As part of a general work up for disease, routine laboratory blood work is recommended in chronic cases of ear infection. In particular, hormonal diseases such as hypothyroidism and hyperadrenocorticism can produce changes in the ear canal environment and decrease the immune system's ability to fight infection. Before beginning intensive therapy, and certainly before anesthesia for ear cleaning, documentation of good general health is important.

TREATMENT

Treatment of otitis externa relies on resolving underlying causes and returning the ear canal environment to normal. This is only possible if permanent damage to the canal has not already occurred. If the ear canal has become severely constricted and secondary changes in the cartilage surrounding the canal have occurred, surgical re-

Owners should check their dogs' ears regularly. Since infections can be very serious, always contact your vet with any persistent problem. Veterinarians offer a variety of high-quality ear care products. Photos courtesy of Virbac.

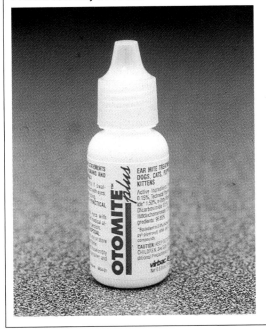
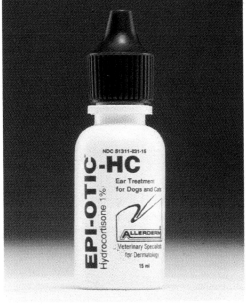

moval of the diseased canal may be the only effective therapy. Systemic antibiotic therapy is necessary if infection of the middle or inner ear is suspected. Medical treatment of the external ear canal involves using products that clean, dry, reduce inflammation, and resolve infection. Severely affected ears usually require thorough cleaning under general anesthesia, possibly more than once, followed by at-home treatment.

Most otic (ear) treatment preparations contain a mixture of antibiotics, antifungals, parasiticides, and anti-inflammatory agents. Therefore, whatever the current cause of

Severe erythema (redness) of the inner aspect of the ear flap secondary to drug administration.

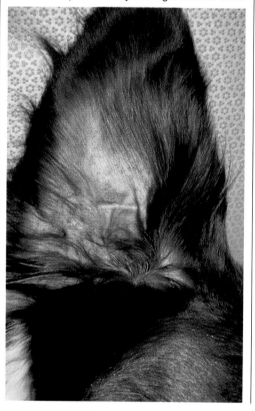

infection may be, these mixtures usually resolve it. However, it is better to determine which type of organism is producing the infection and to use an appropriate, specific medication. Anti-inflammatory agents (corticosteroids) are recommended to decrease wax production, reduce canal swelling, and provide comfort to the dog. Excessive use can cause systemic corticosteroid side effects, if enough is absorbed. Additionally, if an allergy work up is planned, corticosteroids may interfere with diagnostic testing.

Regardless of the topical medication used, the ear should become more comfortable, with less debris formation, within one week. If the ear appears to worsen with therapy, stop administering the medication and contact your veterinarian. Allergic or irritant reactions can occur with topical therapy and will worsen any pre-existing disease.

In addition to specific medications for ear infection, routine cleansing is required for healing. Medications cannot penetrate ear wax and debris and therefore cannot reach the lining of the ear. This debris must be removed for medical treatment to be effective. This can be accomplished by either veterinary sedation and ear flushing, or by frequent home use of ear cleansers. Ear cleansers are solutions that dissolve wax, kill organisms, and chemically dry the ear. Cleansers should be used throughout therapy to keep the ear canals clean and free of debris so that the medications can work effectively.

Holding the ear flap firmly up, fill the ear canal completely with a prescribed ear cleanser.

Frequent examinations of the ear canal are important to monitor the response to therapy. Once infection has been eliminated, debris has been removed from the canals, and inflammation has been reduced, the ears should remain disease-free if any underlying causes have been resolved. Some animals require occasional ear cleaning to keep them comfortable. Regular maintenance of the ear canals is strongly recommended to reduce the incidence of recurrent infections. This is particularly important in ears that have suffered permanent changes from chronic disease and in breeds with abnormally narrow or waxy canals.

ROUTINE EAR CARE

Every dog, regardless of the presence or absence of ear disease, should have its ears cleaned regularly. The most convenient time to do this is when the animal is bathed. Ears should be cleaned at least every other week with a routine ear cleanser. Dogs that swim may require more frequent cleanings to reduce the amount of moisture and the number of organisms in the ear canal. Dogs with a history of ear disease, or those breeds predisposed to ear disease, should have their ears cleaned more (often enough to prevent wax accumulation within the canals).

To clean the ear, hold up the ear flap (pinna) in one hand and introduce the tip of an ear-cleaning solution bottle just into the opening of the canal. Never stick anything down the canal. Fill the canal with the solution. Prevent the animal from shaking its head by keeping a firm grasp on the ear flap. Massage the canal by firmly grasping the pinna between your thumb and forefinger and move in an up and down mo-

Gently massage the canal from the base upwards. A characteristic "squishing" sound indicates correct technique.

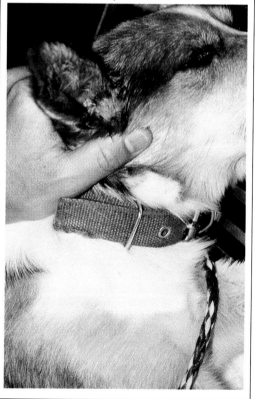

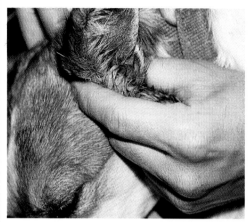

Massage the upper aspect of the canal. Reduce the pressure applied if pain is noted.

tion. If you are manipulating the ear correctly, you will hear a squishing sound. Allow the animal to shake out the solution and dislodged debris. Do not attempt to clean the canal with cotton swabs, but you may dry the inside of the pinnae with towels or cotton balls. Most animals enjoy this therapy because of the relief it provides. If the dog objects to treatment, make sure you are not being overly aggressive with your massage technique, especially if the canal is inflamed. For several

Allow the dog to shake out the solution from its ears. Do not introduce swabs or other objects into the canal unless specifically directed to do so by your veterinarian.

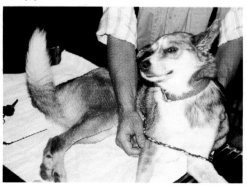

days you may need to gently fill the canal and allow the animal to shake out the debris without massaging, until the ear is less inflamed. Following cleaning, use the prescribed topical medication. This medication must also be massaged into the canal to provide complete coverage of diseased tissue. If you are unsure how to clean and medicate the ear correctly, always contact your veterinarian for a demonstration.

SUMMARY

Ear disease can be a chronic and frustrating problem for you and a painful, sometimes dangerous, condition for your dog. Routine ear cleansing can reduce the incidence of disease. When ear disease does occur, diagnosis of the underlying cause should be attempted or recurrence can be expected. When properly performed, ear cleaning should be enjoyable to your dog. Do not hesitate to ask for a demonstration from your veterinarian if you are uncertain whether you are cleaning your dog's ears correctly.

ADDITIONAL READING

Griffin CE, Kwochka KW, MacDonald JM. Current Veterinary Dermatology: The Science and Art of Therapy. Mosby Year Book, 1993. Chapter 24.

Muller GH, Kirk RW, Scott DW. *Small Animal Dermatology.* Fourth edition. W.B. Saunders Company, 1989. Chapters 5, 6, 7 and 8.

Facing page: For a dog with as much as earage as the Basset Hound, good ear hygiene is an absolute must! Photograph by Isabelle Francais.

Dr. Alice Jeromin received a Bachelor of Science in pharmacy from the University of Toledo (Toledo, Ohio) and was a practicing hospital pharmacist for ten years before earning her Doctor of Veterinary Medicine degree from The Ohio State University in 1989. She completed a three-year residency in veterinary dermatology and currently is in private practice in Cleveland, Toledo, and Pittsburgh. She is actively involved in research in conjunction with Procter & Gamble in the area of canine skin lipids and sebaceous adenitis.

Nail Care and Nail Problems

By Alice Jeromin, DVM,
Diplomate, American College of
   Veterinary Dermatology
Veterinary Allergy & Dermatology,
   Inc.
8979 Brecksville Rd.
Brecksville, OH 44141

INTRODUCTION

Nails (more correctly termed claws) serve important functions in the dog and cat including protection, ability to walk properly, defense, and grasping abilities. Those who have witnessed a cat climbing a tree or defending itself against another animal (humans, included!) recognize the important function of nails. Although dogs do not use their claws for climbing trees, they are still important for grasping and locomotion. There is essentially little difference between the nails of animals and humans.

Nails are extensions of the epidermis, the nails consisting of more tightly compacted tissue (keratin). Whereas in nature animals keep their claws sharpened and short, domestic animals (man included) need to keep their nails trimmed in order to walk or run properly. The most common consequence of long, untrimmed nails is trauma due to the nail catching on a rug fiber, tree root, etc. The nail is either pulled out as a result or the entire toe (digit) can be dislocated or fractured.

Dew claws are "extra", vestigial claws that are located on the inside aspect of the front or back legs, approximately three to four inches up from the digits. Some dogs are born with both front and back dew claws while others have only those on the front legs present. Dew claws on the rear legs should be surgically removed when the dog is still a pup. These rear dew claws, particularly in a hunting dog, will pose problems later in the field as the dog runs

A dog with normal claws that are neither too long nor too short.

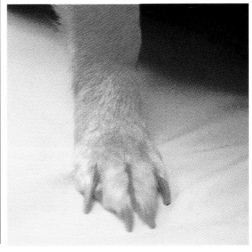

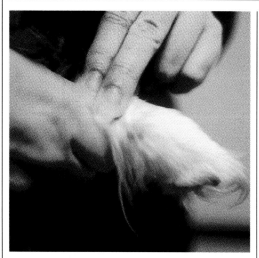

The dew claw is an extra digit found on the inside aspects of the legs.

through brush and weeds and may "rip" a dew claw. If removed when the dog is older, the blood supply to the area is greater and an actual bony joint develops which is more difficult to remove. Usually dew claws on the front legs are not a problem if kept properly trimmed. If allowed to grow too long, the nail associated with the dew claw will grow in a curved fashion into the foot pad.

ROUTINE MAINTENANCE

Keeping a dog's nails properly trimmed is not difficult for an owner to learn to do. Some adult animals do not like having their feet touched, let alone have their nails trimmed. When the dog is still a puppy is the best time to get him used to having his feet touched. At first, do not try to trim the nails but rather just touch or gently examine the foot, talking in a low, soothing manner. Make this a positive experience. After touching the feet and praising

the pet, present him or her with a treat. After the pet gets used to his/ her feet being handled, then try to trim one nail and gradually build to trimming all of them over the next month. When a dog is very young, their nails grow more rapidly, then reach a slower steady growth as they get older. Most dogs will require nail trims every four to six weeks.

Pets with white nails are much easier to trim than those with black nails because the blood supply (the

When the nail on the dew claw is not kept trimmed, it can grow around in an arc and into the foot pad.

"quick") to the nail is visible as a dark pink area. Just as when trimming human nails, only the white portion should be trimmed. Several types of clippers can be used. I prefer the "Rescoe" of "White" clippers for a small dog and "Rostfrei" clippers for larger dogs. If nails are trimmed back a little bit at frequent intervals, the quick will be kept short. However, if nails are let go, the quick will slowly grow down to the length of the nail and even if a

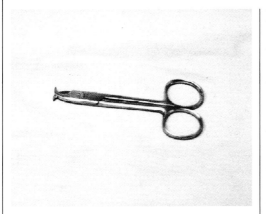

White clippers are also useful for small dogs.

small amount of nail is trimmed, bleeding may occur. If bleeding does occur, hold a piece of cotton with direct pressure on the bleeding portion of the nail for five minutes. If bleeding continues, styptic powder may need to be applied.

If your pet is ever under anesthesia for surgery, dental cleaning, etc., ask your veterinarian to trim the nails back (many veterinarians do this routinely). The pet will get the benefit of a short nail trim without suffering pain because he/she is under anesthesia. This is especially

For large dogs, these Rostfrei clippers make it easier to generate enough power to cut through thick nails.

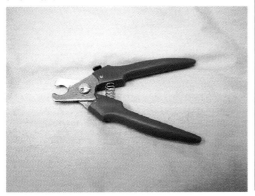

helpful in dogs with black nails. In dogs with black nails, the nail trimmer can really only guess where the quick will be located. It is helpful to use Rescoe nail trimmers and "shave" back gradually until the coating (cuticle) surrounding the blood vessel is located. Once this is seen, stop trimming the nail. If this is done repeatedly every few weeks, it is possible to work the quick farther back into the nail.

DISEASES OF THE NAIL AND NAIL BED

The Latin derivation of nail is "onycho" and various nail diseases may include this prefix. For ex-

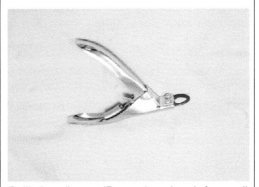

Guillotine clippers (Rescoe) are handy for small dogs.

ample, "onychomycosis" means fungal infection of the nails, "onychodystrophy" means abnormally shaped nails, and "paronychia" denotes infection around the nails. Many diseases can affect the nails, ranging from trauma affecting one nail to infections that involve all nails.

Bacterial infection of a single nail is a common consequence of trauma (i.e., ripping out a nail, cutting the

It is more difficult to trim black nails because the pink quick is not plainly visible underneath.

nail bed on glass or other foreign objects, etc.). Infections usually respond to soaks in an antiseptic solution and oral antibiotics. When bacterial or fungal infections of all the nails occur, an underlying internal disease should be suspected. Poor thyroid function, diabetes mellitus, or Cushing's syndrome are just some of the medical conditions that can cause secondary infections of the nails.

The nails will occasionally be malformed or easily split as well as inflamed, bloody, or swollen in the nail bed area. Other diseases such as immune-mediated conditions (such as lupus erythematosus or pemphigus) and nutritional imbalances can affect the appearance of all the nails. Cancer, depending upon the type, can affect one or all of the nails. Cancers that affect only a single nail include squamous-cell carcinoma (seen especially in dark-skinned dogs), melanoma, and mast-cell tumor. Lymphosarcoma, a cancer affecting the lymph tissue, can affect all the nails. Most of these cancers are more commonly seen in elderly pets.

A sore that does not heal on a digit or nail bed should be examined by your veterinarian. To properly diagnose a nail or nail bed problem, the veterinarian may need to remove the entire nail as well as submit a piece of the nail bed (in formaldehyde) to a pathology laboratory.

Sometimes no underlying reason can be detected to explain abnormal nails. The term idiopathic is used to describe these cases for which a cause can't be found. Rottweilers, Dachshunds, and Siberian Huskies have all been reported to have idiopathic nail abnormalities. These nails can be painful, and it is best to have your groomer or veterinarian keep the nails clipped short.

Finally, it must be emphasized that many early signs of potential nail disorders may be detected by examining the nail beds or skin surrounding the nails. Bacterial or fungal infection, nutritional deficiencies, seborrhea, or cancer in their early stages can present with nail bed changes before the nail is ever involved. It is important for the owner, groomer, and veterinarian to routinely check these areas on all four feet to detect early changes that are amenable to therapy.

SCRATCHING DOES DAMAGE

As any pet owner with a scratching pet knows, dogs can do a lot of damage to their skin by scratching. They can irritate the skin as well as cause abrasions, hot spots and excoriations. There is a new nail enhancement that can protect the skin from the damage caused by scratching. A vinyl nail cap can be applied to blunt the sharp tips of dogs' nails, reducing the likelihood of damage done to the skin. For dogs that inadvertently claw people or furniture, the nail caps help prevent damage there too. These nail caps are not a substitute for proper diagnosis and treatment but can be a temporary measure to help a dog over an itchy time when it could be doing a lot of damage to its skin.

SUMMARY

Nails require routine maintenance. This usually means that they need to be trimmed every four to six weeks. Suitable clippers are commercially available for all types of dogs, regardless of size. There are also many different diseases that can affect the nails and nail bed, and sometimes arriving at a correct diagnosis can be difficult. Whenever possible, a diagnosis should be reached so that therapy can be its most effective.

ADDITIONAL READING

Muller, GH; Kirk, RW; Scott, DW: *Small Animal Dermatology*, 4th Ed. W.B. Saunders Co, Philadelphia, 1989.

Griffin, CE; Kwochka, DW; MacDonald, JM: Current Veterinary Dermatology. Mosby Year Book, 1993.

Scott, DW; Miller, WH: Disorders of the claw and clawbed of dogs. *Compendium on Continuing Education for the Practicing Veterinarian*, 1992; 14(11): 1448-1456.

Nail caps remain securely in place for several weeks on most breeds. Photo courtesy of SmartPractice.

Dr. Phyllis Ciekot got her Bachelor of Arts from the College of Notre Dame of Maryland in 1985 and veterinary medical degree from Ohio State University in 1989. She completed an internship in small-animal medicine and surgery at North Carolina State University and went on to complete a residency program in Small Animal Oncology (and a Master's degree in Veterinary Clinical Sciences) at Colorado State University. Dr. Ciekot then became board-certified in the specialty field of veterinary medical oncology and is a cancer specialist for animals. Dr. Ciekot practices her specialty at her office in Scottsdale, Arizona.

Lumps and Bumps

By Phyllis Ciekot, DVM,
Diplomate, American College of
  Veterinary Internal Medicine
  (Oncology)
Sonora Veterinary Surgery &
  Oncology
6969 E. Shea Blvd., Suite 200
Scottsdale, AZ 85267

INTRODUCTION

Pet owners can easily recognize skin abnormalities in their companions, which explains why skin cancer is usually diagnosed earlier than tumors located in other organ systems. Tumors (synonyms are neoplasms, cancerous growths) are abnormal tissue masses that arise by proliferation of the body's own cells. Today's constantly expanding knowledge and skill in the practice of veterinary medicine, improved nutrition, and the use of vaccines have resulted in an increased life span for canine companions.

Many contributory causes of skin tumors have been recognized, including solar and ionizing radiation, viruses, chemicals, hormones, genetic and immunology factors. Skin neoplasms represent more than 30 percent of all tumors in dogs; dogs have approximately six times as many skin tumors as cats. Tumors can appear during all periods of an animal's life; however, the peak age of tumor incidence is six to 14 years of age in the dog. Canine breeds having a high prevalence of neoplasia are the Boxer, Boston Terrier, Scottish Terrier and Labrador Retriever. More recently reported data indicate that the five breeds with the highest overall tumor incidence are Basset Hound, Boxer, Bullmastiff, Scottish Terrier and Weimaraner.

Careful breeder selection and screening for hereditary cancers reduce the incidence of tumors in the Boxer and other purebred dogs. Photograph by Bob Pearcy.

CLASSIFICATION OF SKIN TUMORS

The first step in the clinical assessment of a skin mass by the veterinarian is to differentiate neoplastic tissue from non-neoplastic masses such as an abscess. If the diagnosis is a cancerous growth, the clinician will then attempt to distinguish whether the mass is benign or malignant in nature. In general, malignant neoplasms are characterized by sudden onset, rapid enlargement, ulceration, invasion into surrounding tissues and spread to distant sites (metastases). Another important consideration highly suggestive of malignancy is the tendency of the tumor to regrow at the original site after surgical removal. Neoplasms are classified as malignant based on certain microscopic criteria.

Tissue from a tumor can be sampled in a variety of ways depending on the location and the size of the neoplasm. Fine needle aspiration biopsy and excisional biopsy are the most frequently used methods.

The prognosis partially depends on the microscopic appearance of the cells taken from the tumor described under the microscope. Tumors are "graded" based on the structure and degree of maturation of the cells observed. In general, well-differentiated, mature-appearing tumors have a better outcome than undifferentiated immature-appearing tumors. Tumor size, location, involvement of lymph nodes and evidence of metastasis (spread) to other body organs define the "stage" of the neoplasm. Blood tests, radiographs (x-rays) and other diagnostic tests may be performed by the veterinarian to determine the extent of the process. If the tumor is confined to the original area of occurrence, the overall outlook is more favorable. Cancer which has been found to be spreading to distant

A tissue biopsy of a tumor is the definitive method to obtain a diagnosis.

areas of the body, such as the lymph nodes or lungs, has a more guarded prognosis.

GENERAL METHODS OF TREATMENT

The type of therapy recommended for a skin tumor will depend upon the tumor type, size, location, the local or distant spread (metastases) determined to be present and the overall health of the patient. For some tumors, no treatment may be the most appropriate decision, particularly when dealing with obviously benign tumors in geriatric patients. In such cases, the risks of treatment exceed the risk associated with the tumor if left untreated.

For most neoplasias, however, treatment is usually warranted. Therapeutic efforts include surgery, radiation therapy, chemotherapy (medical therapy) and cryosurgery (freezing). More recent innovative treatments include photodynamic therapy, immunotherapy and hyperthermia (heat therapy). The science of veterinary oncology is a constantly expanding field and new treatments are constantly evaluated for many tumor types.

COMMON SKIN TUMORS OF THE DOG

Cutaneous neoplasms are classified according to their tissue of origin: epithelial tumors, tumors of melanin-producing cells and mesenchymal (soft tissue) tumors. Epithelial tumors of the skin include basal-cell tumors, squamous-cell carcinoma, papilloma, sebaceous-gland tumors, sweat-gland tumors, tumors of the hair

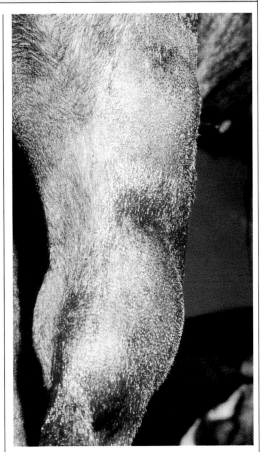

The swelling in this dog's hind leg is an enlarged lymph node located near the original tumor site. Some tumors have a higher tendency to spread (metastasize) to distant sites such as lymph nodes and the lungs.

follicles, and intracutaneous cornifying epithelioma. Tumors of the melanin-producing cells are divided into benign melanoma and malignant melanoma. Soft tissue tumors include those which occur in the region under the epidermal layer (dermis and subcutaneous region). Other tumor types in their own category include mast-cell tumors, transmissible venereal tumors, histiocytomas and lymphomas.

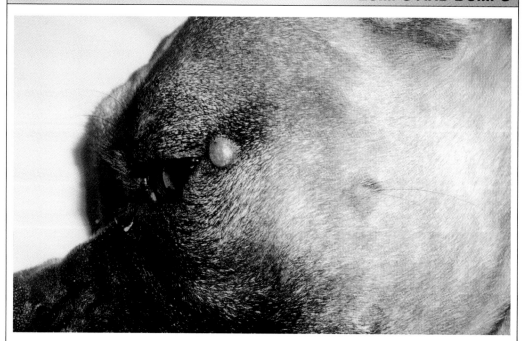

Above: This basal-cell tumor appeared near the left eye of this Boxer approximately two months prior to presentation to the veterinarian.

Below: Basal-cell tumors are raised, hairless benign tumors commonly located on the face of dogs.

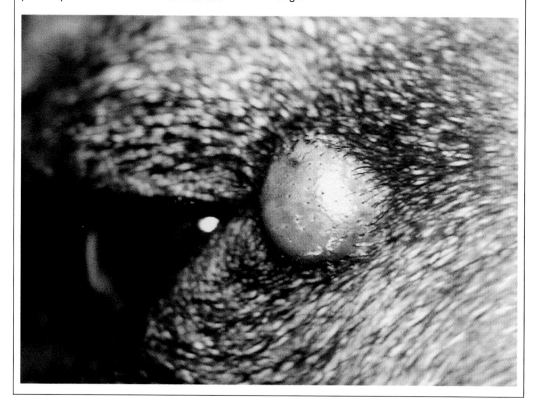

EPITHELIAL TUMORS

Basal-cell Tumor (basal-cell carcinoma, basal-cell epithelioma)

Basal-cell tumors are most often seen in dogs over six years of age and are usually benign. They grow slowly and usually occur around the head, neck and shoulder as a single, firm spherical structure. Although there is no sex predilection, Poodles, spaniels and mixed-breed dogs may have a higher incidence than other breeds. Occasionally, secondary pigmentation of this tumor can occur. Although approximately one of every thousand basal-cell tumors in human patients will metastasize, spread of basal-cell tumors to other sites in the dog is rare.

Basal-cell tumors are treated by surgical excision. Cryosurgical treatment (freezing) is an alternative approach. Prognosis is favorable and recurrence following adequate excision is rare. The topical application of fluorouracil cream for basal-cell carcinoma, although effective in humans, has *not* been demonstrated to be effective in the dog, and is actually hazardous.

Papilloma (wart, fibropapillomas, squamous-cell papilloma)

Papilloma is a benign growth of epithelial cells which can occur anywhere on the body as pedunculated or cauliflowerlike growths usually less than 0.5cm in diameter. In the dog, this tumor can also appear in the mouth or in the eye. Viral infection appears to be involved in some of the canine cases. Although cutaneous papillomas are usually benign, apparent transformation into squamous-cell carcinoma (a malignant skin tumor) has been recog-

Papillomas (warts) occur commonly in the mouth region. This dog has multiple papillomas on the lips, gums and nose.

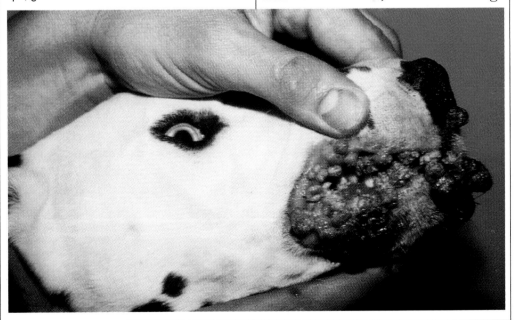

nized. These tumors appear to be more common in Cocker Spaniels and Kerry Blue Terriers. Male dogs may have an increased incidence. The prognosis following complete surgical excision or cryotherapy is excellent for complete cure.

Squamous-Cell Carcinoma

Squamous-cell carcinoma (SCC) in the dog most commonly affects the following areas: trunk, limbs, digits, scrotum, lips, and nose; this tumor can also occur inside the mouth. Squamous-cell carcinoma has been reported to occur more frequently in Scottish Terriers, Pekinese, Boxers, Poodles and Norwegian Elkhounds. These tumors can be proliferative (warty outgrowths) or erosive (ulcers and erosions) in appearance. The surface tends to be ulcerated and bleeds easily. The proliferative type of tumors may have wart-like growths of varying size with a cauliflower appearance. The erosive tumor types initially appear as shallow, crusted ulcers that can become deep and craterlike. This tumor is usually only locally invasive but metastasis (spread) can occur to the regional lymph nodes and lungs.

There is evidence indicating that solar irradiation is responsible for some canine squamous-cell carcinomas. The condition generally progresses from chronic inflammation (redness and swelling) secondary to sunlight exposure to superficial and invasive squamous-cell carcinomas. In general, surgical excision and cryotherapy are most helpful for this tumor. Radiation therapy has also been proven effective. Medical therapy with retinoic acid (vitamin A) may be beneficial in preventing the transformation of chronic inflammation to squamous-cell carcinoma and has been used extensively for this purpose in people.

Sebaceous-gland Tumors (sebaceous adenoma, sebaceous epithelioma)

Sebaceous-gland tumors are the most common benign skin tumors of the dog. The tumor tends to occur on the head and back and, frequently affects the eyelid; however, it can occur anywhere on the skin.

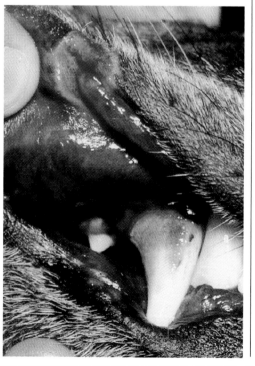

This squamous-cell carcinoma on the lip of this dog is an ulcerated lesion which bled easily when manipulated.

Cocker Spaniels, Kerry Blue Terriers, Boston Terriers, Poodles, Beagles, Dachshunds, Norwegian Elkhounds and Basset Hounds are commonly affected. Solitary or multiple tumors can occur and usually are superficial lobulated hairless growths that are yellow to tan in color. Many owners refer to them as "warts", which they are not. Untreated lesions will ulcerate and become inflamed and bleed. Surgical removal and cryosurgery are highly effective for treatment. A malignant form of this tumor, sebaceous-gland adenocarcinoma, can potentially spread to the lymph nodes and lungs. However, this is quite rare compared to the common benign growths.

Sweat-gland tumors (apocrine gland tumors)

These are much less common than the sebaceous-gland tumors in the dog. Male dogs are affected more frequently than females and Cocker Spaniels appear to be predisposed. These tumors are usually solitary and occur on the back and flanks. These tumors can be benign (adenomas) or malignant (adenocarcinomas). Malignant sweat-gland tumors can metastasize (spread) to lymph nodes and lungs. Surgical removal is the treatment of choice with radiation

Sebaceous adenomas are benign lobulated, hairless growths which commonly occur on or near the eyelid.

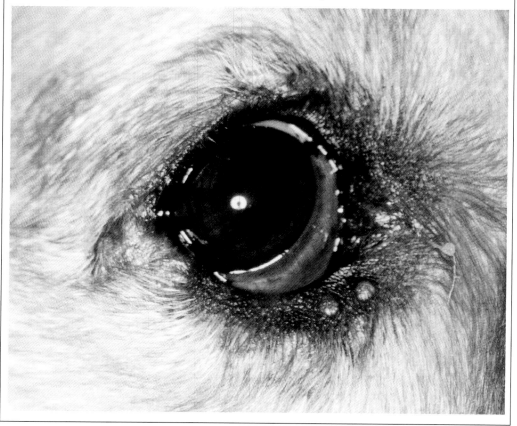

therapy administered if the tumor is incompletely removed. Chemotherapy is indicated if the tumor has spread beyond the lymph nodes.

Tumors of the Hair Follicles (trichoepithelioma, pilomatrixoma)

These are quite common skin tumors and are benign. Usually found in dogs over five years of age, these tumors are solitary, firm masses which can become quite large (10 cm) in size. Poodles, Cocker Spaniels and Kerry Blue Terriers are breeds commonly affected. The overlying skin surface is frequently hairless and ulcerated. Although these tumors are rarely invasive and are slow growing, surgical removal is indicated for therapy.

Intracutaneous Cornifying Epithelioma (keratoacanthoma)

This is a benign neoplasm which usually occurs in dogs five years of age or less. The Norwegian Elkhound, Keeshond, Old English Sheepdog, Collie and German Shepherd Dog are predisposed. These tumors are not invasive and can vary in size from 0.5 cm to 4.0 cm in diameter. A large pore opening to the skin surface with a plug of keratin (hard, cheese-like material) is characteristic. Surgical removal of the mass not only will improve the patient's appearance but may offer relief as well, since these tumors can cause pain and discomfort. It is important to note that despite removal of one or several masses, affected dogs tend to develop new tumors at other sites.

Perianal-gland Tumors (circumanal or hepatoid tumors)

These are common in the dog and also occur in sites other than perianal tissue, such as the tail, prepuce, vulva, trunk and hind limbs. Perianal adenomas are benign tumors which occur in males five times as frequently as in females; perianal adenocarcinomas occur with equal frequency in both older males and females. All breeds are affected by this cutaneous neoplasia. These tumors can be solitary or multiple, variable in size (1 cm to 10 cm), lobular and can ulcerate. Treatment consists of surgical removal primarily, with cryosurgery and radiation therapy also used. Because perianal adenomas are known to be testosterone dependent tumors, castration of male dogs is recommended to eliminate recurrence.

Melanocytic Tumors (melanoma)

These are relatively common skin tumors in the dog and can be benign or malignant. These neoplasms can also develop in the mucous membranes (particularly the mouth) and the eye. No evidence exists that prolonged sunlight exposure is associated with the incidence of melanomas in the dog, unlike in humans. Heavily pigmented, black-skinned dogs such as Scottish Terriers, Cocker Spaniels and Boston Terriers are at high risk. The tumor occurs mainly on the face, trunk, feet and scrotum and may vary in appearance from dark gray to gray in color. They may be flat plaquelike lesions or dome-shaped nodules.

Malignant melanomas are usually rapidly growing, larger than 2 cm in diameter and frequently ulcerated. Canine cutaneous melanomas located in the scrotum region or in the digits have a higher tendency to be malignant. Evidence of metastasis occurs in the lymph nodes and lungs. The treatment of choice is tiple and occur in older dogs, especially females. They can occur anywhere on the body, but usually occur over the chest, abdomen and limbs. The skin is freely moveable over the tumor and it is not typically attached to underlying tissue. Although benign, these fat masses can grow to be quite large and can

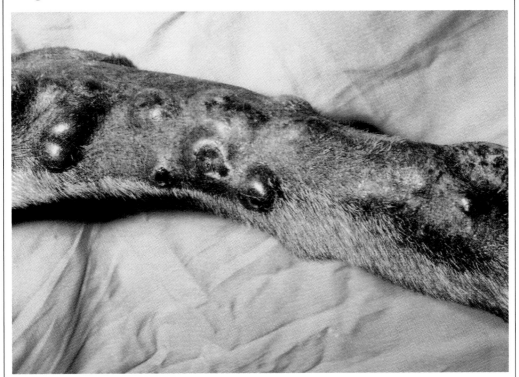

Cutaneous melanomas can occur anywhere on the body, but especially on darkly pigmented skin. Multiple melanomas are shown on the hind limb of this dog.

surgical removal. However, with evidence of distant spread, treatment options should also include medical therapy.

SKIN TUMORS ORIGINATING FROM CONNECTIVE TISSUE

Lipomas (fatty tumor)

Lipomas are the most common mesenchymal (connective tissue) tumors in the dog and are benign. These fat tumors are single or mul- interfere with walking or lying down. They can also become ulcerated and rarely can infiltrate into the underlying muscle and connective tissue. A rare malignant form of fatty tumor, liposarcoma, can spread to other areas of the body. Surgical removal is the treatment of choice;

however, "benign neglect", i.e., observing the tumor carefully for rapid growth or interference with movement, can be prescribed in selected cases.

Fibromas and Fibrosarcomas

These are firm, rubbery growths arising from fibrous connective tissue. Fibromas are benign tumors reported to occur more commonly in Boxers, Boston Terriers and Fox Terriers. Fibrosarcomas are the malignant form of fibrous tumor which can occur anywhere on the body, tend to be locally invasive, and can spread to regional lymph nodes and lungs. The cellular characteristics (degree of differentiation, maturation) have been shown to

correlate with the tendency of these tumors to regrow at the site of removal and with the tendency to spread to other areas. Surgical removal is the treatment of choice although radiation therapy, hyperthermia (use of high temperatures to kill tumor cells), and chemotherapy may also be beneficial for therapy.

Leiomyomas/Leiomyosarcomas

These are uncommon neoplasms which arise from smooth muscle cells. They are usually solitary, firm and rarely metastasize. More commonly these tumors occur internally in the gastrointestinal tract or in the vagina or vulva of the bitch.

Hemangiomas/Hemangiosarcomas

These arise from the cells surrounding blood vessels and can occur in any location. Hemangiomas

Mast-cell tumor after a biopsy has been performed. This tumor was a red, raised nodule which suddenly appeared on this dog's foot.

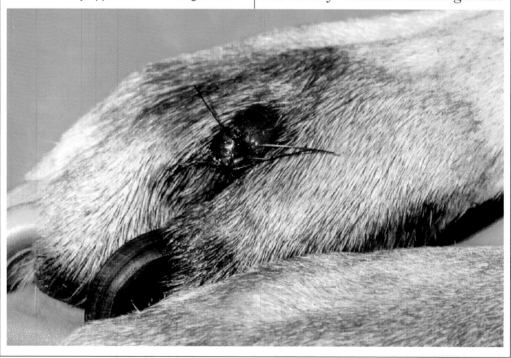

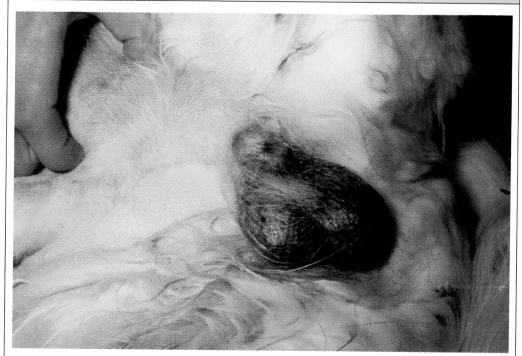

Mast-cell tumor located near the scrotum. These are particularly aggressive cancers which can metastasize (spread) early to nearby lymph nodes. Clinician is palpating an enlarged inguinal lymph node.

are usually solitary benign tumors occurring on the limbs and flank. They are bluish to reddish black in color. Hemangiosarcomas are malignant, rapidly growing, invasive tumors which tend to occur in multiple areas. They often ulcerate and bleed readily. Surgical excision is the treatment of choice and medical therapy has demonstrated significant benefit in improvement of survival time for dogs with hemangiosarcomas located in the skin.

OTHER TUMOR TYPES

Mast-cell Tumor (mastocytoma, mast-cell sarcoma)

Mast-cell tumors occur commonly in dogs and can be benign or malignant. Several breeds are predisposed, notably Boxers, English Bulldogs, Labrador Retrievers and Weimeraners. These tumors occur most frequently on the trunk, perineum and limbs and vary tremendously in appearance. Canine mast-cell tumors arising from the genital area and digits appear to have greater malignant potential. Dogs affected with mast-cell tumors can show symptoms of gastrointestinal ulcers and altered ability of their blood to clot. These tumors can spread to lymph nodes, liver, spleen and bone marrow. Surgical removal with a wide margin of normal tissue surrounding the tumor is the therapy of choice. Radiation therapy and medical therapy can also assist in the control of this cancer.

Transmissible Venereal Tumor

This is an uncommon neoplasm which can be transmitted between dogs through coitus. Additionally, dogs can contract the tumor by licking or biting affected areas in the genital region of infected dogs or bitches. These tumors present typically as ulcerated, nodular or cauliflowerlike areas in the skin of the genitalia or face. This tumor grows rapidly at first, then more slowly. Metastasis is uncommon, and the cancer can be effectively treated with medical therapy.

Lymphosarcoma on the lip of a German Shepherd Dog. Multiple ulcerated plaques were noted in this dog.

Histiocytoma (button tumor)

This is a benign, fast-growing tumor commonly found in young dogs. Boxers, Dachshunds, Cocker Spaniels, Great Danes and Schnauzers are predisposed. The tumors are typically solitary and occur commonly on the head, ears and limbs. Spontaneous regression can occur within one to three months after recognition. Surgical excision is the treatment of choice, and recurrence is unusual.

Cutaneous Lymphosarcoma (lymphoma, mycosis fungoides)

This is a rare malignant skin tumor in the dog. Boxers, Golden Retrievers, German Shepherds and

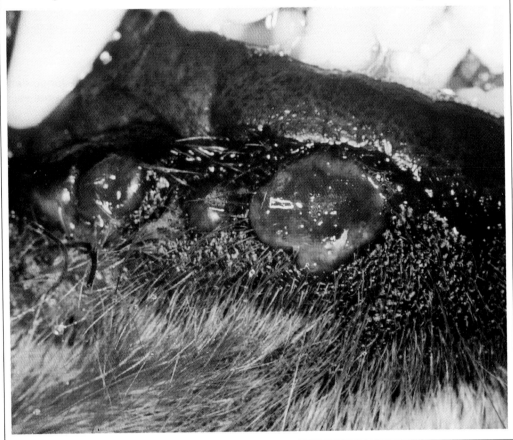

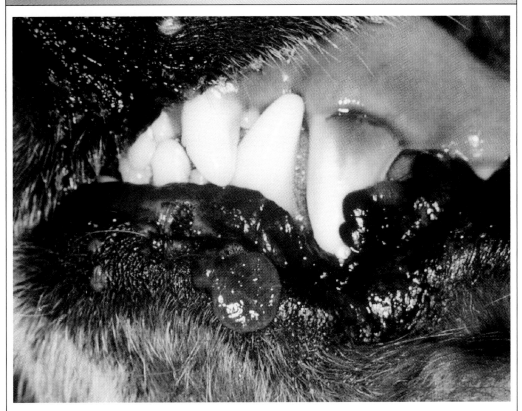

Scottish Terriers are more commonly affected. Cutaneous lymphosarcoma is usually generalized, with multiple nodules, plaques or ulcerative lesions occurring throughout the body. Systemic involvement of other organs can occur and other symptoms such as weight loss, inappetence, or changes in urination and bowel habits can be noted. Treatment is best achieved with medical therapy. Recently, treatment with vitamin-A-derived drugs has been shown to be beneficial.

Also known as mycosis fungoides, lymphosarcoma needs to be recognized early so that appropriate treatment is used. A tissue biopsy was obtained from this dog (note suture material to left of lesion).

cer. Each type of cancer has its own biological behavior and anticipated response to different therapies. Your veterinarian can provide you with additional information and, if necessary, a referral to a veterinary cancer specialist, an oncologist.

SUMMARY

Oncology is the medical specialty dealing with cancers. Now, more than ever, there are new methods of diagnosis and treatment that can help pets who are afflicted with can-

ADDITIONAL READING

Barton C.L.: Cytologic Diagnosis of Cutaneous Neoplasia, An Algorithmic Approach, *Compendium of Small Animal Education*, 1987; 9(1): 20-33.

Conroy, J.D.: Canine Skin Tumors, *Journal of the American Animal Hospital Association*, 1983; 19(1): 91-114.

Moriello, KA: Rosenthal R.C., Clinical Approach to Tumors of the Skin and Subcutaneous Tissues, *Veterinary Clinics of North America, Small Animal Practice*, 1990; 20(4): 1163-1190.

Strafuss, A.C.: Skin Tumors. *Veterinary Clinics of North America, Small Animal Practice*, 1985; 15(3): 473-488.

Susanek, S.J., Withrow, S.J.: Tumors of the Skin and Subcutaneous Tissues. *Clinical Veterinary Oncology*, Withrow and MacEwen, E.G., editors, J.B. Lippincott, Philadelphia 1989.

Theilen, G.H., Madewell, B.R.: Tumors of the Skin and Subcutaneous Tissues. *Veterinary Cancer Medicine*, Theilen and Madewell, editors, Lea and Febiger, Philadelphia, 1979, pp. 123-191.

White, S.D.: Rosychuk, R.A.: Use of Isotretinoin and Etretinate for the Treatment of Benign Cutaneous Neoplasia and Cutaneous Lymphoma in Dogs. *Journal of the American Veterinary Medical Association*, 1993; 202(3): 387-391.

Facing page: Modern-day research by veterinarians and responsible screening by breeders have helped to lessen the occurrence of cancer in many purebred dogs. Golden Retriever photographed by Karen Taylor.

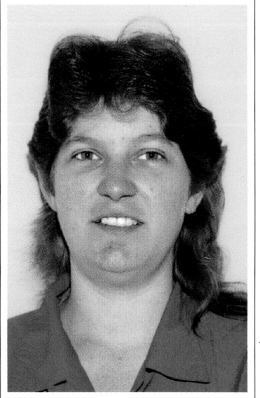

Dr. Julie M. Delger grew up in Gretna, Louisiana, a suburb of New Orleans. She obtained her Doctor of Veterinary Medicine degree from Louisiana State University in 1990. After a one-year Small Animal Rotating Internship at Auburn University in Alabama, she completed a two-year Dermatology Residency at North Carolina State University in Raleigh, NC. In August 1993 she successfully completed the American College of Veterinary Dermatology Board Certification Examination. In November 1993 she started full-time private practice at the SC Dermatology Referral Service in Columbia, SC. Her practice is limited to diseases of animal skin. All patients are referred by a family veterinarian.

Environmental Causes of Skin Problems

By Julie Delger, DVM,
Diplomate, American College of
    Veterinary Dermatology
South Carolina Dermatology
    Referral Service
Columbia, SC 29210

INTRODUCTION

The skin is an amazing organ. It is the largest organ of the body, and serves more functions than you might think. In addition to covering the body and protecting it from infection and contamination, the skin is also involved in regulating body temperature and keeping body and blood fluids inside where they belong. Other equally important but less apparent functions are touch sensation and the production of vitamin D.

Dogs are exposed every day, just as people are, to environmental factors and substances that may cause skin problems. Whether or not the damage is permanent depends on the factor and how long the dog has been exposed. Skin thickness is also important, and you might be surprised to learn that dog skin is much thinner than human skin.

Most skin problems having an environmental cause are not linked to age, breed or sex of the dog. As you might suspect, exposure is the primary clue. In general, areas of the body where the skin is the thinnest are most susceptible to environmental damage. These areas include the ear flaps (called the pinnae), the abdomen and inner thighs, and the skin between the toes. This is just a general guideline and there are many exceptions. In all cases, the goal must be to stop the exposure so the problem can be relieved. Prompt veterinary care is critical in treating and reversing the damage done to the skin, if reversal is indeed possible.

Specific diseases will not be discussed in-depth; rather, larger categories or classes of disease will be presented, with individual conditions mentioned when appropriate.

SOLAR DAMAGE

Sunburn

Sunburn is seen in virtually all domestic animals and man. As in humans, dogs with less skin pigmentation (white or pink skin) are more susceptible to damage from the sun. Breeds in which sunburn is most often seen include Bull Terriers, Staffordshire Terriers, English Bulldogs, Dalmatians, and Pointers. Most affected dogs have large

Redness, hair loss, and crusting of the nose, bridge of the nose, and eyelids caused by excessive sun exposure.

patches of white hair with an underlying pale pink skin coloration. Many may be entirely white. Dogs of any age may be affected, although older dogs are more likely to have problems. This is because the effects of solar damage, which are due to ultraviolet radiation, are cumulative. That means that it is repeated exposure over periods of time that are most likely to cause problems.

Ultraviolet light can cause permanent changes in the genetic makeup of the skin cells, as well as altering the structure of skin collagen and elastic fibers. These fi-

Sun exposure can damage both the haired and non-haired regions of the skin.

bers are responsible for normal skin elasticity and texture.

Clinical signs (symptoms) of sunburn include reddened, tender or painful skin in those areas which have been exposed to the sun. Parts of the body most likely to be sunburned are the pinnae (ear flaps), abdomen, inner thighs, and the rela-

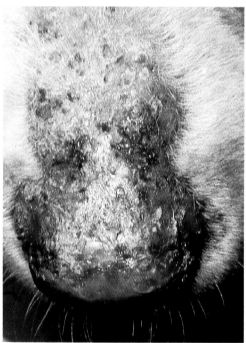

Notice that the inflammation and crusting extends right into the tissue of the nose.

tively hairless area between the eye and ear. If sun exposure is discontinued, these damaged areas may resolve and heal on their own with no major consequences. If, however, exposure is persistent and prolonged, the reddened areas may progress to blistered, ulcerated areas which may be quite painful or pruritic (itchy). Large yellowish or bloody crusts may be seen as the ulcers attempt to heal. The skin may become thickened in these areas, which also represents an attempt at healing.

It is best to seek veterinary attention before the lesions become ulcerated; however, once this has happened, prompt veterinary care is essential to prevent progression of the disease to an irreversible point. In any case, sun avoidance is re-

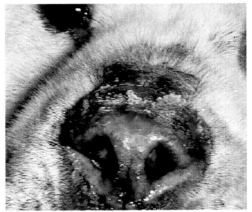

Dogs that lack full pigmentation on their noses are more susceptible to ultraviolet damage.

quired, and is a good preventive measure which should be taken with any dog which has a predominantly white coat or any dog excessively fond of sunbathing. If outdoor exposure is necessary during peak daylight hours, susceptible skin is best treated with sunscreens (SPF 15 or greater) before the dogs go outside.

Skin Cancers' Association with Sun Exposure

Most people are aware that sun exposure can cause skin cancers in people, and the same is true of dogs. In addition to changing the structure of the skin, ultraviolet light also causes a decrease in the numbers of skin cells responsible for detecting and eliminating abnormal or neoplastic (cancerous) cells. This is why prolonged sun exposure predisposes dogs (and people) to skin cancer.

Several types of cancer can be induced by ultraviolet light. The most common of these by far is called squamous-cell carcinoma, but other types exist. Most kinds of skin cancer are relatively slow-growing and can invade nearby areas although they are slow to spread to other parts of the body. Thus, with very early detection, a partial to complete cure may be possible.

Skin cancer most often arises at sites which have been subjected to chronic sun exposure, with or without previous sunburn. These body parts are the same ones most prone to sunburn: the pinnae (ear flaps), abdomen, and inner thighs. Dogs with light-colored noses may develop these types of cancers on their noses also. Once the skin has become ulcerated, continued ultraviolet irradiation can alter the genetic structure of the skin cells trying to heal the wound, which can lead to development of cancer. Skin cancers can also develop on non-sun-exposed skin if there is a problem with the immune system, such that abnormal cells are not recognized and removed.

The appearance of sun-induced skin cancers is variable. Some tumors are simply reddened, angry-looking raised lesions, while others are barely noticeable. These latter types may simply be reddened ar-

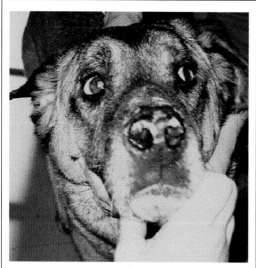

Persistent ulceration of the nose due to sun exposure in a dog with autoimmune disease. This particular dog had discoid lupus erythematosus that was complicated by exposure to ultraviolet light.

eas with blackish crusts, and they may or may not be painful or itchy. In most cases, there is some degree of hair loss in the affected area. Once the problem has progressed to this stage, your veterinarian will need to be consulted and biopsies (pieces of the affected area) taken to confirm his or her clinical suspicion of cancer. Again, if detected very early, there is a reasonable chance for at least prolonged remission of disease, if not a cure. Like other forms of cancer, skin cancer can be fatal if left untreated.

AUTOIMMUNE DISEASES

While solar exposure and ultraviolet radiation do not cause this type of disease, almost all forms of autoimmune disease are made worse by sun exposure. The most obvious examples are systemic lupus erythematosus and its more benign counterpart, discoid lupus erythematosus. Most autoimmune skin diseases target sensitive skin areas and the damage done makes the skin more susceptible to solar damage. Then, the sun can cause additional damage, as described above. This also makes the autoimmune disease more clinically resistant to proper therapy. Any dog which has been diagnosed as having an autoimmune disease should be kept out of the sun, especially between 10 a.m. and 4 p.m. Sunscreens are necessary for dogs that need to be outdoors during peak daylight hours. Once again, sun exposure doesn't cause autoimmune skin disease, but it may be a complicating factor.

MISCELLANEOUS CONDITIONS

Photosensitivity

In rare instances, dogs may have genetic defects which lead to the deposition of substances in the skin that react to sun exposure. The result is that exposure to sunlight causes severe damage to the skin. Fortunately, these types of genetic problems are rare in dogs, as they are in people.

A non-genetic but still troubling sensitivity to sunlight (photosensitivity) can be seen in some dogs receiving certain prescription drugs. Just as in people, some medications cause individuals to be sensitive to sunlight and to develop rashes with sun exposure. Even though this type of drug reaction is rare, owners should be aware and react promptly if the situation arises.

Frostbite

One of the functions of the skin is to maintain normal and consistent body temperature. This is achieved by sweating (evaporation of moisture from the skin) in warm weather and by limiting the amount of blood that circulates to the skin (constriction of the small blood vessels in the skin) during cold weather. Of course, dogs also regulate their body temperature by panting. When the temperature is very low for prolonged periods of time, the small blood vessels in the skin remain constricted. If those vessels constrict long enough, the skin dies from lack of circulation. We call this reaction "frostbite".

Dogs of any age, breed, or sex can get frostbite. There seems to be an extra danger for short and short-legged dogs in regions with moderate to heavy snowfall and standing snow for long periods. Undoubtedly this is because the underside gets dragged through the snow and may be subjected to very cold temperatures. Other parts of the body that can be affected are those that tend to have poor circulation. These include the pinnae (ear flaps), nose, tail tip, scrotum, and toes. The appearance of frostbite lesions varies with its duration. When warmed, the affected areas will often appear very red and may be quite painful. If the area is not warmed, then it will eventually appear purple-black and will usually be painless since the nerves in the skin have also died. Often the skin just adjacent to the blackened dead skin will be very red and painful.

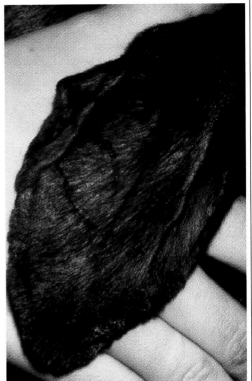

Frostbite in a Dachshund, affecting the ears and tip of the tail. Notice the darkness on the ear margin.

The damaged areas are quite evident on the underside of the ear flap in this Dachshund.

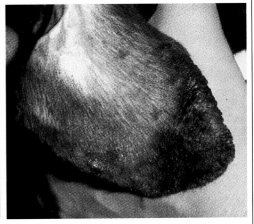

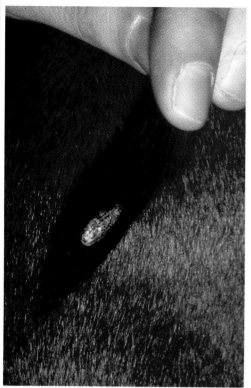

The Dachshund's tail has been affected by frostbite as well.

Your veterinarian should be consulted immediately when frostbite occurs. As with most health problems, the sooner this is done, the better the outcome is likely to be.

Burns

Burns may be caused by increased temperature, by caustic or corrosive chemicals, or by radiation. The appearance is similar for all of these causes, in most cases, and all ages, breeds and genders are susceptible. Thermal burns may be due to hot liquids contacting the skin, by direct contact with hot solids (such as space heaters, radiators, heating pads, etc.), or by prolonged exposure to heated air, as with hair dryers or heat lamps. Heat causes skin damage by altering the physical structure of the individual cells, actually cooking the skin. The hair may be singed, but this does not happen in all cases. Areas of the body most often affected are the abdomen, back, and sides.

At first, the skin is red and painful. As the lesions age, depending on the severity of the burn, blisters may form. Since dogs' skin is so thin, blisters are not always seen. Ulcers and weeping, or oozing of serum through the skin, follow the blister stage. The hair over these areas often becomes matted down to the skin. The skin, which is now dead, will slough off to leave large ulcers which ooze blood, serum and

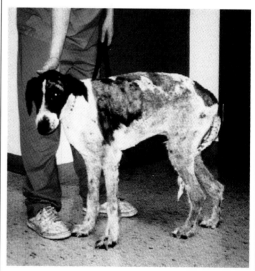

Burns can be severe and even fatal in dogs.

sometimes pus. When large areas are burned, the dog's ability to maintain a normal temperature is impaired. Massive amounts of fluid can be lost through the ulcerated areas, leading to dehydration. The raw areas are also prime colonization sites for bacteria, which can easily gain access to the bloodstream and cause severe illness or death.

Many chemicals are caustic and corrosive and will literally digest the skin upon contact. The appearance is usually identical to those of thermal burns. If exposure to any corrosive or caustic chemical occurs, the skin should be rinsed immediately

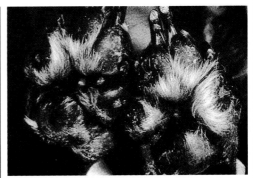

Ulceration and peeling of the footpads caused by contact with corrosive chemicals.

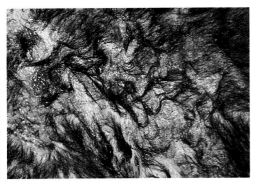

Closeup of a burn. In the early stages the areas are inflamed and ooze serum, blood, and sometimes pus.

with cool water and your veterinarian should be consulted.

Because of the potential devastating after-effects of burns, any burn must be treated promptly by your veterinarian. Quick care may save your pet's life and a lot of money in medical bills.

Contact Dermatitis

Contact irritation differs from chemical burns in that the offending substance, rather than killing the skin cells outright, causes inflammation of the skin. The list of substances capable of causing such a reaction is exhaustive and includes salt on roadways, cleaning

solvents, flea collars, shampoos, garden sprays, and plants. In many ways the reaction resembles an allergy, but there are some important differences. With contact irritation, exposure to the substances causes irritation in the skin and inflammation. Without prompt recognition and treatment, the skin can become darker in affected areas as the inflammation persists.

Parts of the body most affected by contact irritation depend upon the specific irritant compound. For instance, irritation of the chin, lips, and nose may be due to plastic resins in a food dish, while irritation caused by a carpet deodorizer will

Another example of contact irritation of the footpads.

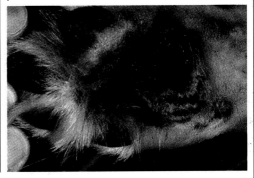

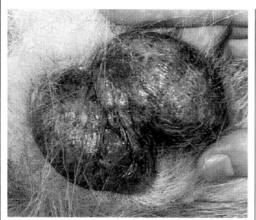

Ulceration of the scrotum caused by contact with caustic chemicals.

cause inflammation on the paws and abdomen.

Early cases of contact irritation may appear as red areas which the dog licks, chews, rubs, or scratches, although the problem may not be itchy at all. These areas may then become thickened, hairless, and may gain (hyperpigment) or lose (hypopigment) skin coloration. When contact irritation is suspected, your veterinarian will question you about possible irritants in the home. Try to prepare a short list before consultation with him or her. Think about shampoos, cleansers, carpet

Contact irritation causing loss of pigment of the gums.

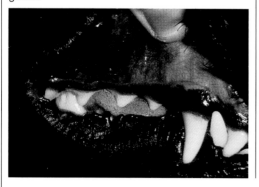

cleaners, disinfectants, insecticides, or plants to which your pet may have been exposed.

Bites and Stings

Bites and stings can be very variable in their appearance and diagnosis is not always easy. In some cases the bites just cause irritation, while in other cases there may also be an allergic component. Dogs most likely to be bitten or stung tend to be young, curious dogs and breed doesn't seem to be a factor. Body parts usually affected are the face, paws, and abdomen, although any

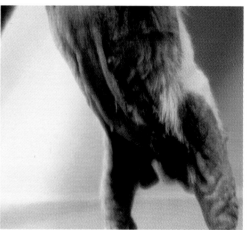

Contact irritation causing hair loss, hyperpigmentation, and thickening of the skin of the abdomen and legs of a dog.

site may be injured. In some dogs kept outdoors, the ear tips may be attacked by biting flies, causing crusting and hair loss. Usually, the most common problem seen with bites and stings is a red bump or pimple, or sometimes a small welt. These may or may not be itchy. Most will resolve without treatment in two to seven days if no more bites

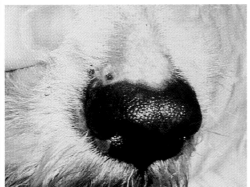

Red bumps and ulcers on the nose caused by insect bites.

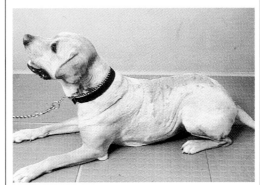

Hives over a dog's back. Seek veterinary attention immediately because the problem can become more severe and even life-threatening.

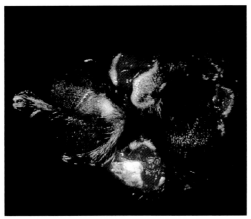

Ulcers of the footpads caused by spider bites.

Closeup of footpad injury caused by spider bites.

Ulcers on a dog's face, caused by an allergic reaction to a bee sting.

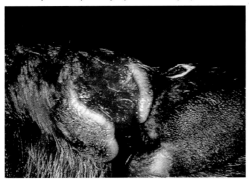

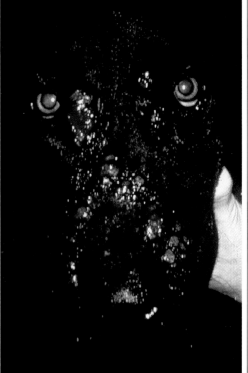

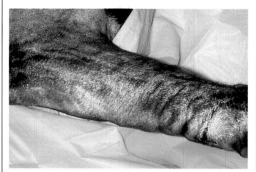

Severely swollen leg caused by snakebite.

occur. In the case of some types of spiders, these inflamed areas may progress to areas of dead, blackened skin with subsequent ulceration, or to areas of intense inflammation and swelling, which may then become ulcerated.

In those dogs that have allergic reactions to bites or stings, the reaction is a little more intense. Hives may be seen and are generally considered a mild form of allergic reaction, but they may also be the first sign of a much more serious condition called anaphylaxis, or anaphylactic shock. Anaphylaxis can be fatal; therefore, any animal showing hives should be taken immediately to a veterinarian for treatment.

Ulceration in swollen leg caused by snakebite.

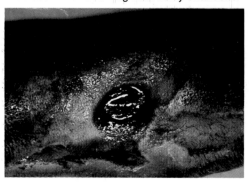

Another variant of allergic reaction to insect bites or stings is extreme itching with subsequent ulceration of the face and nose. Again, prompt treatment by your veterinarian may prevent more serious problems from occurring.

Snakebite

Any kind of snake may cause skin damage by biting a dog, even if it is not poisonous (venomous). Snakes' mouths are full of bacteria, which become implanted in and under the skin when a bite occurs. Again, as with insect and spider bites and stings, young, curious dogs as well as hunting dogs are most likely to be snakebitten. The face and legs are most commonly bitten. A variably painful, swollen lump may result, which may progress to an abscess or ulcer.

In cases of bites by venomous snakes, the affected area quickly becomes quite red and painful, and extremely swollen. When the face or head becomes swollen, one must be concerned about the dog's ability to breathe, as the swelling is often internal as well as external. The reason for the intense swelling is damage to blood vessels caused by the venom itself. If the swelling involves a leg, the blood supply to the entire limb may be compromised, resulting in a sort of gangrene. Some venoms contain a toxin which damages the nervous system and can be fatal.

Snakebite is one of the most pressing medical emergencies. Do not wait for serious problems to occur if you know your dog has been bitten—seek veterinary care immediately!

Hot Spots

Hot spots, also called acute moist dermatitis and pyotraumatic dermatitis, may be caused by any itchy skin problem. The most common cause is flea infestation or flea allergy, which can result in hot spots of the rump, thighs, or tailhead. Hot spots may occur anywhere on the body, but the rump, tail, cheek, and sides are most common. A dog of any breed, age, or sex can develop hot spots, although those breeds most predisposed to allergic skin diseases are more often affected. Hot spots under the ears and on the cheek are often due to ear inflammation or infection. Your veterinarian should be contacted for proper treatment before the hot spot becomes badly infected or ulcerated.

Fleas in the coat of a dog.

Skin Fold Dermatitis

In dogs with excessive folding of the skin upon itself, such as Chinese Shar-Pei, Bulldogs, Pugs, Basset Hounds, Boston Terriers, and obese dogs, the skin folds trap moisture and create a favorable environment for the growth of bacteria and yeasts. Any age dog of either sex may be affected. Body parts with excess

Fleas being removed using a flea comb.

folds include the face in flat-faced breeds, the tail in corkscrew-tailed breeds, around the vulva, and anywhere that the skin folds upon itself. The inner part of the fold is reddened and moist, and is usually hairless. Sometimes pus is present, and a foul odor is common. Occasionally, red bumps or crusts are seen.

Generally, keeping the folds clean and dry is all the care required for treatment and prevention. If bumps are seen, the problem should be treated by a veterinarian because the skin is likely infected. In severe cases, surgery may be needed. Again, consult your veterinarian for his or her advice regarding your personal pet.

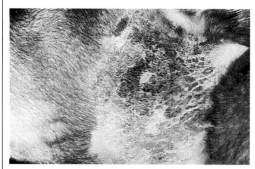

Hot spot under the ear of a dog.

Foreign Body Reactions

The major function of the immune system is to detect and eliminate invaders of the body. However, the process is often much more successful for bacteria and viruses than for large particles such as thorns, grass seeds (awns), burrs, pins, needles, or other foreign bodies. The skin of the paws and face is most commonly involved, but foreign bodies may also get lodged in the eyes, ears, mouth, nose, and body cavities. Any age, breed, or sex can be affected. Often, the foreign body goes undetected, especially if it is small, until the immune system has responded to its presence by mounting an inflammatory attack. Some signs which may be typical of foreign body reactions include swollen red bumps, with or without pus, hair loss from the dog's persistent licking, and sometimes lameness. Owners are often shocked to learn that a grass awn lodged in the paw can make its way under the skin surface for quite a distance, often tracking bacterial infection in its wake.

Foreign bodies often carry bacteria and hairs, which are also seen as foreign by the immune system, into the tissues, further complicating the situation. A deep-seated infection may ensue, the severity of which depends upon the type of bacteria involved. A veterinarian should be consulted at the earliest detection of a suspected foreign body, or as soon as exposure to potential foreign bodies (grass awns, broken glass, splinters, etc.) is verified.

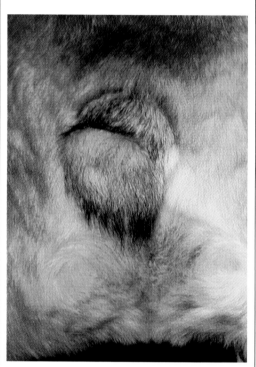

Hair loss and redness in the tail fold of an English Bulldog.

Pressure Sores and Calluses

When the skin is chronically irritated, it responds by getting thicker and turning darker in color. Calluses are seen as hairless, often reddened areas of thickened skin, usually over bony points, where there is not much muscle or fat between the skin and underlying bone. Generally, adult large-breed

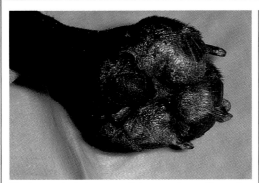

Redness, hair loss, nodules, and swelling of a paw caused by foreign bodies.

dogs more commonly develop calluses, usually on the elbows, hips, and hocks. There is often a history of the dog preferring to sleep on hard surfaces, although small dogs and those who sleep on well-cushioned beds can also be affected. Infection may occasionally occur in calluses, indicated by the presence of small bumps over the surface of the callus, or by pus.

In dogs which are forced to remain laying down for long periods, whether by injury or illness, the skin over the bony points may become ulcerated rather than thickened. This is due to pressure of the body weight on the skin and its

Deep infection of a callus on the elbow of a dog.

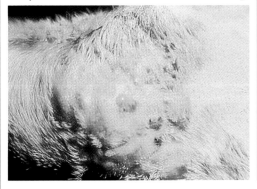

blood supply. Again, once the skin loses its blood supply, it dies and sloughs, leaving an ulcer. This type of ulcer is generally very slow to heal, because the blood supply is still poor and the healing process requires a greater than normal blood flow. A veterinarian should be consulted in cases of pressure sores or infected calluses.

Trauma

Trauma is very common and can afflict any age, breed, or sex of dog. Any part of the body may be injured, although the paws and legs are more

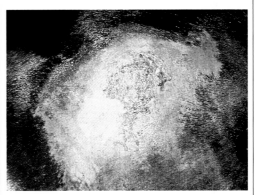

Pressure necrosis (pressure sore) over the shoulder. Note the hair loss, loss of pigment, ulceration, and oozing.

commonly hurt. A traumatic wound may be nothing more than a scratch, or it may be a deep laceration, abrasion, or complete tearing away of the skin from the underlying tissues (called a degloving injury). The latter are quite painful.

While simple first aid may be all that is required for most small scratches and abrasions, any wound that extends through the full thickness of the skin should be seen by a veterinarian as soon as possible.

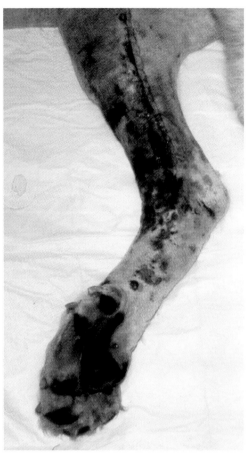

Deep laceration of the paws of a dog.

A wound prone to fly-strike. See your veterinarian immediately.

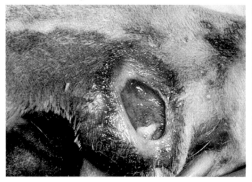

Myiasis (fly strike)

Undoubtedly one of the most abhorrent conditions seen by veterinarians, fly-strike is caused by some species of flies depositing eggs in and near open wounds. The result is the presence of fly larvae (maggots) in the wound. This condition can occur whenever there is injured skin and exposure to flies. Even very small wounds may become infested. A special kind of myiasis is caused by the burrowing of a type of fly larva (*Cuterebra*) into the skin of dogs, usually around the head and neck. The fly larvae are in the soil around the openings of rodent burrows, and the dog becomes infected when investigating the hole. The lesion caused by these larvae is usually seen as a small hole in the skin with some clear fluid draining from it. Occasionally, the "worm" can be seen moving inside of the hole.

If larvae are seen in any wound, the dog should be taken as soon as possible to a veterinarian for removal of the larvae and for wound cleaning and disinfection.

ADDITIONAL READING

Ackerman, L: Guide to Skin and Haircoat Problems in Dogs. Alpine Publications, Loveland, Colorado, 1994, 182 pp.

Muller, GH; Kirk, RW; Scott, DW: Small Animal Dermatology, 4th Edition, W.B. Saunders Company, Philadelphia, 1989, 1007 pp.

Incidence of hereditary diseases and other disorders is often attributed to the more populous breeds, which of course veterinarians see most frequently. Less common breeds, due to their lack of numbers and the more controlled breed base, are cited only rarely in veterinary papers. This handsome unusual dog is the Perro de Presa Canario or Canary Dog. Photograph by Isabelle Francais.

Dr. Lowell Ackerman is a board-certified veterinary dermatologist, a diplomate of the American College of Veterinary Dermatology. He is the author of nine books and over 130 articles and book chapters dealing with pet health care, including Guide to Skin and Haircoat Problems in Dogs. Dr. Ackerman has lectured internationally on the subject of canine dermatology. At present he acts as a consultant in the fields of pet dermatology and nutrition.

Miscellaneous Skin Conditions

By Lowell Ackerman, DVM,
Diplomate, American College of
    Veterinary Dermatology
Mesa Veterinary Hospital, Ltd.
858 N. Country Club Drive
Mesa, AZ 85201

INTRODUCTION

There are many conditions in veterinary dermatology that are newsworthy but may not warrant a complete chapter. We will examine some of the more interesting here, in a more abbreviated forum.

PYODERMA

Pyoderma refers to a bacterial infection of the skin. The most common bacterium involved is called *Staphylococcus intermedius*. This microbe is a frequent contaminant of dog skin and is involved in over 90% of skin infections. However, pyoderma is not as straightforward as you might think. If they were, antibiotics would be effective far more often than they are. What happens in most cases is that the infection is secondary to some underlying process. If that problem is not addressed, the pyoderma becomes chronic. Antibiotics may give relief initially, but eventually they lose their effectiveness.

The secret to treating pyoderma is thus to examine the situation closely and determine what the underlying cause is that is allowing bacteria to flourish on the skin surface. Sometimes the cause is an underlying allergy, sometimes an immune problem and other times a problem with thyroid function. There are so many different problems that can result in pyodermas that an in-depth search is often needed. In some cases, this requires referral to a dermatologist, a specialist in skin problems. And, in other cases, the detective work is much more straightforward.

Bacterial infection (folliculitis) in a dog.

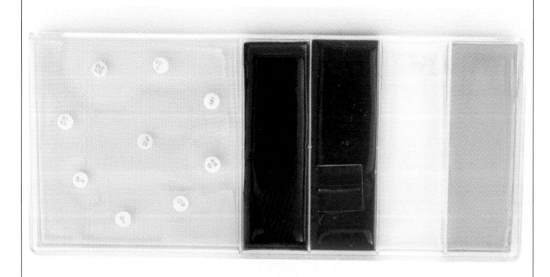

Pyo-Dermplate, a medium for growing bacteria. Courtesy of Bacti-lab, Mountain View California.

Superficial Pyoderma

Superficial pyodermas occur when there is a mild interference with the skin's defense mechanisms. The most common examples are fold pyodermas in dogs with wrinkled skin and infantile dermatitis or pimple belly seen in young pups. The fold pyodermas are caused because the wrinkles trap moisture and surface bacteria near the skin. The infantile dermatitis is harder to explain but might involve some mild urine scalding on the abdominal skin. In any case, treatment is straightforward in both cases, and antibiotics are rarely required. A mild antiseptic such as triclosan, chlorhexidine or cetrimide applied several times a day for seven to ten days should resolve most cases. Of course, if the underlying problem is not resolved, the problem will recur. The only permanent cure for fold pyodermas is to surgically remove the wrinkles. The most practical alternative is regular cleansing with a gentle antiseptic.

Intermediate Pyoderma

Intermediate pyodermas usually affect the hair follicles (pores) so that surface bacteria extend into the pores and inflame and infect the whole follicle. The body is designed to guard against such invasion, so the underlying cause in some way is affecting the body's peripheral defenses. These dogs usually have crops of pimples, often on the belly and over the back. Short-coated breeds may just look motheaten, as the hairs fall out from the compromised follicles. In all breeds, the skin may appear red, may have expanding rings that can be confused with ringworm, and often the final phase involves black spots where the infection used to be and associated hair loss. Common underlying problems that result in intermediate pyodermas include allergies, hypothyroidism (poorly functioning thyroid) and mild-to-moderate immune problems. Antibiotics must often be used for three to eight weeks to control the infection, but it is also important to identify the underlying cause during that time. If not, the infection is sure to recur. For those cases in which a cause cannot be determined, immune stimulants such as Staphage lysate® may be beneficial.

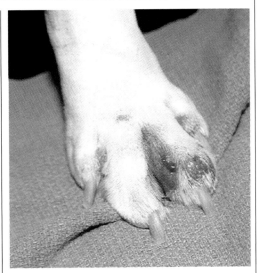

Interdigital pyoderma due to sterile pyogranuloma syndrome. Courtesy of Dr. Thomas Lewis, Dermatology Clinic for Animals, Albuquerque, New Mexico.

Deep bacterial infection (pyoderma) in a dog.

Deep Pyoderma

Deep pyoderma occurs when bacteria extend into the deeper tissues and almost always signals a major compromise of the immune system. These dogs have serious problems. They may have lumps and bumps associated with their infection, draining tracts, and infections of other body systems. Young animals with deep pyoderma usually have some congenital or inherited immune dysfunction such a T-cell immunodeficiency, IgA deficiency, or demodicosis. Older animals that suddenly develop deep pyoderma should be examined for evidence of underlying diseases such as cancer, diabetes, hypothyroidism or liver disease.

The treatment for deep pyoderma involves potent antibiotics and correcting the underlying problem. Preferred antibiotics include the cephalosporins and the potentiated penicillins. Treatment may be needed for many weeks or months, depending on the status of the underlying disease. For animals with problems that cannot be medically corrected, long-term antibiotics and immune stimulants offer the best course of action.

KERATINIZATION DISORDERS (SEBORRHEA)

The term seborrhea is widely used, but often incorrectly used. The term is so ingrained in the veterinary literature that it is difficult to re-

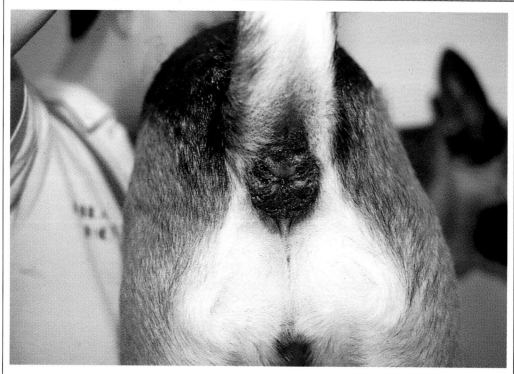

Perianal fistulae in a German Shepherd Dog.

move, but we should try. The fact is that so-called seborrhea in dogs has very little relationship to the human condition known as seborrhea. In dogs, the term is used to describe any condition that is dry, greasy or smelly. That can apply to almost any canine skin condition.

The term keratinization disorder is preferred and suggests that the dog has a problem with surface scale formation. It is thus a description, not a diagnosis. Most keratinization disorders in dogs have an underlying problem, such as allergies, hypothyroidism, nutritional problems, infections, autoimmune diseases and even some cancers.

On the other hand, there are some primary keratinization disorders in which the defect is in the skin and not due to an underlying problems. One of the primary causes is actual seborrhea (seen most commonly in Cocker Spaniels), but it is only one of many. There are also several nutritionally responsive skin disorders, including those that respond to zinc and vitamin A. Chronic blackheads in Schnauzers (schnauzer comedo syndrome) is yet another example of a keratinization disorder. The only thing most of these conditions have in common is that they cause scaly, greasy or smelly skin; their treatments are entirely different. Therefore, it can be very misleading to use the term seborrhea, because it implies you know the diagnosis, and hence the preferred treatment.

Keratinization disorders can be diagnosed in many different ways, but biopsies for histopathological analysis are usually the most direct route. A pathologist examines the samples and determines if the changes are secondary to some other process or whether there is actually a defect in the skin accounting for the change. Although it allows an exact diagnosis for most cases of primary problems, it can only be suggestive of what is accounting for secondary changes. Thus, a biopsy can be quite exact in diagnosing an inherited seborrhea, but if the changes are secondary, it can only suggest possible causes (e.g., allergies, hormonal problem, etc.).

The treatment for all keratinization disorders must be individualized based on the actual cause. Thus, a keratinization disorder secondary to inhalant allergies will only

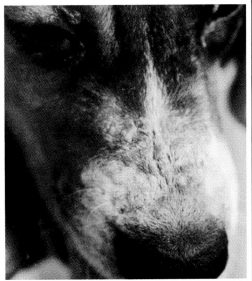

Skin problems, reminiscent of zinc imbalances, seen in dogs fed a generic dog food. Courtesy of Dr. Thomas L. Huber, Department of Physiology and Pharmacology, College of Veterinary Medicine, University of Georgia, Athens, Georgia.

Facial crusting associated with zinc-responsive dermatosis.

resolve when the allergy problem has been addressed and treated. A greasy dog with hypothyroidism will only respond once thyroid replacement therapy has been instituted. Zinc-responsive dermatosis will only improve with appropriate zinc supplementation. For those skin problems in which there is a defect in the turnover of the skin, derivatives of vitamin A (retinoids) are often used in treatment. They often have a normalizing effect on the skin turnover process. Unfortunately, these products are expensive and not without side effects. They should only be used once the diagnosis has been confirmed and it is one of those variants known to respond to retinoid therapy.

Medicated shampoos are an important adjunct to treating all kera-

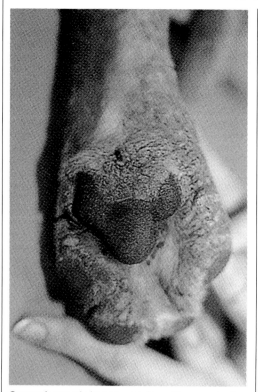

Crusty footpads in a young dog with generic dog food disease.

mal. The loss of dead skin cells in an accelerated fashion is a phenomenal nutritional drain on the body. Affected dogs should be fed a high-quality and easily digestible dog food; supplements are often helpful as well. Fats have often been added to the diets of these dogs, but now we know which fats are most effective. Products high in linoleic acid (e.g., safflower, sunflower seed oils), gamma-linolenic acid (borage or evening primrose oils) and eicosapentaenoic acid (cold-water fresh fish oil) have been shown to decrease inflammation and improve the condition of the skin. Moderate levels of zinc and vitamin A have also been advocated. Finally, some current research has suggested that plant-based enzyme supplements may be beneficial, purported because they increase blood levels of zinc, selenium and linoleic acid.

Marked follicular crusting of the ears in a Cocker Spaniel with vitamin A-responsive dermatosis.

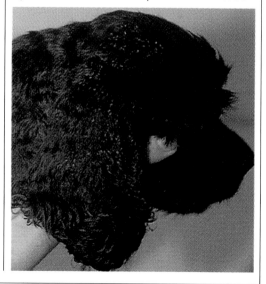

tinization disorders. Antiseborrheic ingredients include benzoyl peroxide, tar, sulfur and salicylic acid. Most of these need to have adequate contact time with the skin (usually five to 15 minutes) before being rinsed off. These products help strip away dead skin cells, which improves the situation, but they are not a cure. If the underlying problem has not been addressed, the shampooing will need to be used indefinitely to achieve results. Medicated shampoos only offer symptomatic relief; they do not address any underlying problem.

Nutritional fortification is also important for the seborrheic ani-

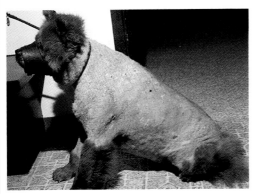

Hair loss associated with sebaceous adenitis, a form of keratinization disorder.

ALLERGIES

Allergies represent a heightened sensitivity to things in the environment. The most common allergens (substances causing allergies) are pollens, molds, housedust and dander. This is referred to as inhalant allergy, atopy, or hay fever. The second most common cause of allergy (not including flea-related reactions) is foods. We will briefly examine each of these entities.

Inhalant Allergy (atopy)

Inhalant allergies are extremely common, affecting perhaps 15% of the purebred dog population. Although not a predictable genetic trait, allergies clearly run in families. Some of the breeds most commonly affected include terriers (especially the West Highland White Terrier), Golden Retrievers, Chinese Shar-Pei and Dalmatians. However, any dog can be afflicted by allergies, depending upon the allergic history of its parents.

Whereas people with hay fever often sneeze, respiratory problems associated with allergies are not commonplace in dogs. Most affected dogs are itchy; they particularly lick at their paws and may have redness and inflammation on the flaps of their ears, on their bellies or around their eyes. The pattern can be quite individualized and not all dogs are affected the same way. However, the most common form of presentation is licking and chewing at the paws. Other areas are variably itchy.

Although dogs of any age can develop allergies, most are between six months and three years of age when they first start to show signs.

Scaling associated with a primary keratinization disorder in a Cocker Spaniel. Suture present marks the biopsy site used in diagnostic testing.

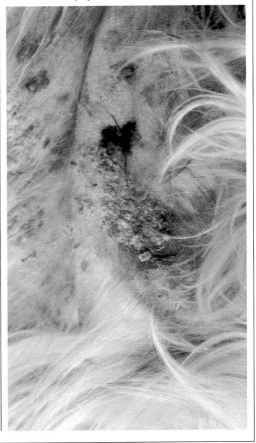

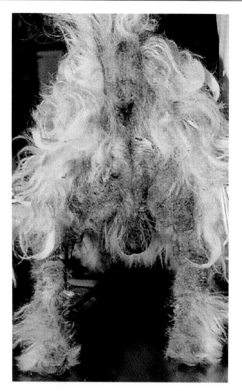

Then, with each passing season, they tend to get progressively worse. Some dogs may be itchy all year, while others may only be seasonally affected, such as when weeds pollinate in the fall, or grasses in the summer. Regardless, in time, about half of those dogs that were seasonally affected will begin to scratch year 'round.

The best diagnostic test for inhalant allergies is intradermal allergy testing, similar to skin testing in people. Small amounts of potentially allergy-causing ingredients are injected into the skin and the reac-

Left: Scaling associated with epidermal dysplasia in a West Highland White Terrier.
Below: Scaling associated with a secondary keratinization disorder.

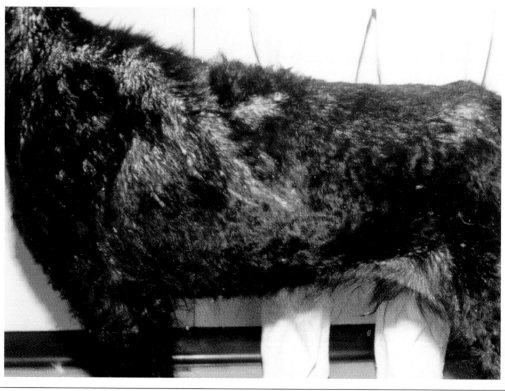

tion observed about 15 minutes later. From start to finish, the whole test only takes about an hour. Many veterinarians refer patients to specialists (dermatologists) to have the test done because there is some expertise required to read and interpret the results. Blood tests have also become available in the last ten years. Although these tests are convenient, skin tests are still the most reliable means of diagnosis and determining the most effective treatment.

There are many different ways that allergies can be effectively managed. One of the simplest is a cool, itch-relieving bath. Although the benefits are short-lived, it is a quick, effective and inexpensive way to give relief to the itchy pet.

Medicines can also be used to give relief from itchiness. Some are prescription items whereas others can be purchased over-the-counter. Antihistamines are effective in about one-third of cases; products with clemastine (Tavist), diphenhydramine (Benadryl) and chlorpheniramine (Chlor-Trimeton) are preferred. Special fatty acids known as omega-3 and omega-6 fatty acids can give relief to about 20% of allergic dogs. The effective ingredients include gamma-linolenic acid and eicosapentaenoic acid. These are found in seed oils (borage, evening primrose) and fish oils, respectively. Your veterinarian can recommend products with the most effective combinations. The old stand-by treatment for allergies is prednisone, a form of corticosteroids. The good news is that prednisone relieves

itching in the vast majority of cases. The bad news is that long-term use is fraught with side effects. Since inhalant allergies are invariably long-term, corticosteroid use should be considered either a temporary or a last-ditch effort. Corticosteroids can be used safely long-term, but this requires regular monitoring of blood parameters and carefully regulated dosing, preferably on an alternate-day basis.

Ceruminous (oily) otitis externa, a frequent complication of both primary and secondary keratinization disorders.

Immunotherapy represents the best long-term control method for inhalant allergies. Commonly referred to as allergy shots, immunotherapy consists of giving repeated injections of the things causing the allergies in the hope of creating resistance or tolerance. In some ways, this resembles vaccination. Immunotherapy is safe (no drugs are involved) and effective (about 75% of the time) but is a long process. In general it takes six to eight months before the benefits will be realized, in those animals capable

A housedust mite. Courtesy of Greer Laboratories, Inc., Lenoir, North Carolina.

of responding. Although 75% of allergic dogs benefit from the exercise, there are still 25% that go through the series of injections without benefit.

Adverse Food Reactions

Adverse food reactions can be due to either food allergies or food intolerance, although it is often difficult to distinguish between the two. The topic really isn't that confusing but owners are quick to jump to conclusions about diets and their prejudices greatly complicate the picture. Some owners will be adamant that their dog doesn't have food allergies because it's been eating the same diet for years, without problems. Others will claim that their dog doesn't have diarrhea after eating and therefore couldn't possibly have a food allergy.

Let's look at some facts. Food allergies almost never occur when a new diet is fed. Allergy or sensitivity to food items happens after repeatedly feeding the items over time: weeks, months or years. Food allergy can be caused by several different mechanisms, so the clinical presentation is quite variable. Some dogs do have diarrhea, but most do not. Some dogs have itching which is indistinguishable from inhalant allergy or flea bite hypersensitivity. Another dog may have a recurrent ear infection, limited to only one ear. Because of the variability, it is impossible to paint a picture of what the food-allergic dog should look like. Food-allergic dogs react to ingredients, not brand names. Therefore, the dog may have problems when eating beef, soy, or corn, and this is true regardless of the packaging. Most commercial dog foods have many of the same ingredients.

Food intolerance refers to an adverse food reaction which isn't caused by allergy. For instance, lactose intolerance is common in people and is prevalent in dogs and cats as well. It's not that people are allergic to dairy products, but they may lack an enzyme necessary to digest it properly. Some pet foods are high in histamine or saurine which can have adverse effects. Some dogs have difficulty digesting soy; some have medical problems so that they can't properly digest high-fat meals. And, of course, some of the pet food preservatives have also been implicated as problem-causers.

Diagnosing adverse food reactions is also not difficult to comprehend but there is so much misinformation around that many people get confused. Since dogs develop problems to ingredients, not brand names, simply switching brands is not helpful most of the time. One would have to be quite fortunate to switch to a brand that didn't have the ingredient that was causing problems. Remember, we haven't yet identified what the problem ingredient is! Therefore, that is our first order of business.

A hypoallergenic diet trial is performed by feeding a special home-cooked meal for a minimum of four weeks but preferably for as long as two to three months. Recent studies have shown that it may take up to three months on a hypoallergenic diet before improvement is noticed. The diet should be homemade so we have full control over ingredients and preservatives. It's risky to believe pet food labels. The hypoallergenic diet consists of a protein and carbohydrate source that the dog has not eaten before. For example, depending on the previous feeding history, lamb and rice might be sufficient. The diet would be prepared by feeding one part cooked lamb with two parts boiled rice in the same total amount the dog is used to eating. Add nothing to this diet except for fresh water (preferably distilled). This is only a test. The diet is not balanced for long-term feeding and should not be used in puppies, pregnant or nursing bitches, or on working animals. The diet should be fed only for four to 12 weeks (depending on your patience and how exacting you want to be) never longer. The purpose is only to determine if the problem is diet-related. If it is, further tests will be done to find out the problem ingredient(s). If it isn't, the diagnostic testing has just begun—the prob-

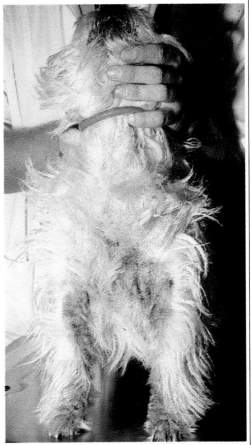

An allergic dog that might benefit from administration of omega-3/-6 fatty acid combinations.

lem isn't food-related.

A word of caution here. Many pet food companies have begun making lamb-based dog foods, claiming that they are good for the skin. This is just not true. There's nothing magical about lamb. Dogs get just as allergic when fed lamb as they do with beef. The reason we often select lamb is because North American consumers once rarely fed lamb to their dogs. If dogs were never exposed to lamb, they couldn't be allergic to it. That is now changing as more and more people feed these lamb-based diets.

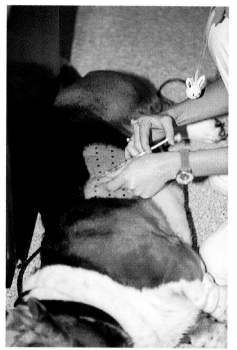

Performing intradermal allergy testing.

easily accomplished if you have done a proper food trial. At the end of the trial, if there has been significant improvement, your veterinarian will have you reintroduce food ingredients one at a time every week or so. On the first week, you might add small amounts of chicken each day to the hypoallergenic diet. If this doesn't cause a problem, you know chicken is OK and you begin challenging with a new ingredient. Eventually, you will have a list of those food ingredients that are well tolerated and those that aren't. Then, go to the pet supply shop and match your list with the pet food labels.

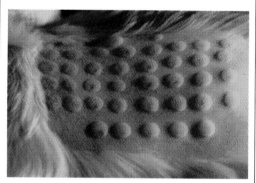

Results of intradermal allergy testing.

Another word of caution. Several laboratories have begun selling blood tests to identify adverse food reactions. Be aware that these tests are not reliable and only correctly predict food allergies about ten percent of the time. This isn't surprising when you consider that not all food allergies are associated with the antibodies measured in these tests and that these tests *never* determine food intolerance. Blood tests should never replace dietary trials when trying to make a proper diagnosis.

The best way to manage an adverse food reaction is to stop feeding the ingredient that is causing the problem. For example, if the dog is allergic to beef, feed a diet that is based on another protein source such as chicken, pork or soy. This is

You can effectively select a commercial pet food that is hypoallergenic for your particular dog. Feeding a commercial hypoallergenic diet is effective about 80% of the time, but is usually much more expensive and there are fewer choices.

AUTOIMMUNE SKIN DISEASES

Autoimmune skin diseases are an exciting group of disorders in which the body targets part of the skin as foreign and sets out to attack it. In very simple terms, it is sometimes described as the dog being allergic to itself, but this is really an oversimplification. What really happens is that abnormal antibodies are produced in the blood which latch onto specific regions of the skin and cause tissue destruction.

There are many different types of autoimmune skin disease, but only the most common will be discussed here. What they all have in common is the production of abnormal antibodies. Otherwise, they are quite a diverse collection of diseases.

Clinical flea bite hypersensitivity (FBH) in a dog.

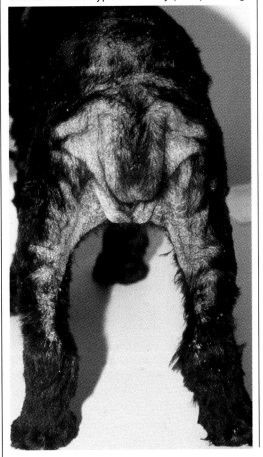

Lupus Erythematosus

Lupus erythematosus or lupus, as it is commonly known, is a collection of immune-mediated diseases that target various tissues. Systemic lupus erythematosus is the most dangerous, because it often involves many body systems. For example, an affected dog may have anemia, kidney disease, and a variety of skin disorders. In people, lupus is often referred to as the great impersonator because it has so many different ways of presenting. The same is true in dogs.

Systemic lupus erythematosus is the most dangerous variant of lupus and is potentially life-threatening. Diagnosis is made by identifying that the various clinical conditions are part of one syndrome, with several common patterns. Antinuclear antibody tests are positive about 75% of the time, and Lupus erythematosus preparations (LE prep) are positive in about 60% of cases. Routine blood tests and biopsies for histopathology are important tools in arriving at a correct diagnosis. This is a very serious disease, and many dogs die of complications of both the disease and its treatment. The most common forms of treatment are powerful drugs like corticosteroids, azathioprine and chlorambucil that suppress the immune system. Unfortunately, they suppress the good aspects of the immune system as well as the undesirable ones. Therapy must be carefully individualized for each animal so few generalizations can be made.

Discoid lupus erythematosus,

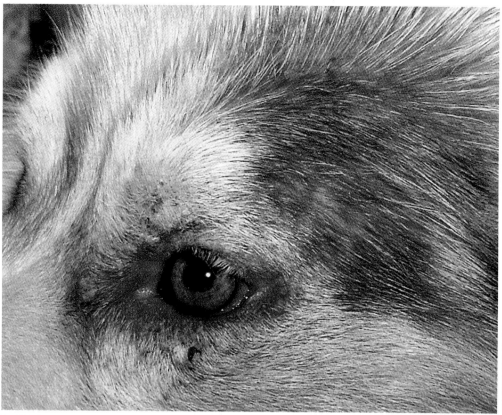

Red, itchy facial rash associated with an adverse food reaction.

also known as cutaneous lupus erythematosus, is a benign variant of systemic lupus in which none of the internal organs are involved. It is an immune-mediated disease strictly limited to the skin. It is also the more common form of lupus seen in animals. The most common presentation is scaling or an ulcerating rash on the face, although the ears, feet and other body parts can be involved. Often the first sign is a loss of pigment on the nostrils; the black tissue there starts showing blotches of pink. In time, the areas expand and there is scaling, erosion and eventual crusting. Many cases were once known as Collie nose and Collies, Shetland Sheepdogs, Siberian Huskies and Alaskan Malamutes are the breeds most affected.

The diagnosis of discoid lupus can be confirmed by biopsies, but often the clinical picture is very suggestive. In most cases, the treatment needn't be so aggressive because this is more a cosmetic disease than a medical emergency. Avoiding direct sunlight is important, not because it causes lupus, but because it aggravates the already sensitive skin affected by lupus. Sunblocks and sunscreens can also be used. Vitamin E is often prescribed to help lessen the amount of scarring associated with the disorder. A new form of treatment combines the B vitamin, niacinamide, with tetracycline. This seems to be effective in about two-thirds of cases. Topical corticosteroids are also helpful but it is important not to use powerful fluorinated products for too long or internal problems can result. In very resistant cases, some of the treatments used for systemic lupus can be used but this is very undesirable because of the potential side effects.

Pemphigus and Pemphigoid

Pemphigus and pemphigoid are similar autoimmune diseases in which the abnormal antibodies target the thin layer of epidermis di-

Cutaneous or discoid lupus erythematosus.

rectly. Pemphigus targets material that surrounds the epidermal cells, while pemphigoid antibodies target the thin basement membrane zone that divides the epidermis from the dermis below. In people, this results in blisters (pemphigus means blister) but this is rarely seen in dogs. Most dogs with either pemphigus or pemphigoid have erosions, ulcers, crusts and scales. Crops of pimples are sometimes seen, depending on the variant.

We talk about pemphigus and pemphigoid like two disorders, but each actually has different variants, just like lupus. There are four pemphigus variants with pemphigus foliaceus being the most common in dogs. It usually presents as scaling, crusting and ulcers that start on the face and/or feet and become more generalized. Pemphigoid has two variants: bullous pemphigoid is an ulcerative disease that can affect most body parts, while cicatricial pemphigoid most often affects the mouth and the lining of the eyelids.

Both pemphigus and pemphigoid are diagnosed the same way, by sending biopsy samples to a pathologist for evaluation. There are no specific blood tests for pemphigus in dogs (there are for people), and routine hematology and biochemistry tests are usually normal. The treatment for pemphigus and pemphigoid are also similar, although there is quite a bit of variability, depending on the variant and how aggressive it is. Most treatments start with prednisone, but less than half of the cases can be sustained with

this type of therapy. Additional drugs, such as azathioprine (Imuran) and chloram-bucil (Leukeran) are usually added to the regimen. In some cases, treatment with gold salts (chrysotherapy) can be helpful, and this is one of the best options for long-term management.

ADDITIONAL READING

Ackerman, L: Guide to Skin and Haircoat Problems in Dogs. Alpine Publications, Loveland, Colorado, 1994, 182 pp.

Ackerman, L: Hypersensitivity disorders. In Handbook of Small Animal Practice, 2nd edition. R. Morgan (ed.). Churchill Livingstone, New York, 1992, 996-999.

Ackerman, L: Autoimmune disorders. Handbook of Small Animal Practice, 2nd edition. R. Morgan (ed.). Churchill Livingstone, New York, 1992, 991-996.

Ackerman, L: Adverse reactions to foods. Journal of Veterinary Allergy and Clinical Immunology, 1993; 1(1): 18-22.

Ackerman, L: Medical and immunotherapeutic options for treating atopic dogs. Veterinary Medicine, 1988; 83: 790-797.

DeBoer, DJ: Canine staphylococcal pyoderma: Newer knowledge and therapeutic advances. Veterinary Medicine Report, 1990; 2: 254-266.

Miller, Jr., WH: Topical management of seborrhea in dogs. Veterinary Medicine, 1990; 85: 122-131.

Your local pet shop can supply medications which may be helpful. Consult your veterinarian for all persistent health problems. Photograph courtesy of Hagen.

Facing page: Pemphigus foliaceus produces a crusting skin condition that often first affects the face.

Dr. Patricia White received her Doctor of Veterinary Medicine degree from Tuskegee Uniiversity's School of Veterinary Medicine in 1983, then pursued and completed a small animal internship at Michigan State University in 1984. She then returned to Tuskegee where she served on the faculty for three years. Dr. White then completed a dermatology residency program at the Ohio State University as well as a Master of Science degree. A board-certified veterinary dermatologist, Dr. White currently operates the Atlanta Veterinary Skin and Allergy Clinic, which she founded in 1992.

Understanding Medications

By Patricia White, DVM
Diplomate, American College of
   Veterinary Dermatology
Atlanta Veterinary Skin & Allergy
   Clinic, P.C.
33 Avondale Plaza North
Avondale Estates, GA 30002

As pet owners, we take on a huge responsibility when caring for our dependent friends. When an injury or illness occurs, we employ our knowledge of first aid to encourage the healing process, or we seek the advice of a veterinarian. Most people have at least one over-the-counter (OTC) oral analgesic (aspirin, ibuprofen, etc.) and one topical anti-itch or antibacterial cream or lotion in the medicine cabinet. Whether a home remedy or a prescription drug, it is important to know and understand some basic concepts of classes of medications, how they work, and when they should be used or avoided.

HORMONAL THERAPY

Glucocorticoids

Cortisol is an extremely potent hormone, is vital to normal bodily functions and affects every cell in the body. It is required for carbohydrate, protein, and fat metabolism, influences water and sodium balance, and affects glucose synthesis. Normal (physiologic) amounts of cortisol are made by the adrenal gland located in the abdomen next to the kidney. The amount of cortisol made by the adrenal gland is held in delicate balance by the release of a hormone called ACTH. ACTH comes from a gland in the brain called the pituitary gland. The ACTH hormone stimulates the adrenal gland to make more cortisol when blood levels drop below a predetermined level, then a "feedback process" tells the pituitary gland to stop making ACTH when cortisol is back to normal. Administration of cortisone for therapeutic purposes can upset this delicate balance and will adversely affect immune function, normal tissue metabolism, and may suppress both adrenal and pituitary gland function. The impact brought about by a single dose may continue for weeks to months.

Synthetic glucocorticoid (corticosteroid) hormones, also referred to as steroids, cortisone, prednisone, or allergy shots/pills, are the most common group of drugs prescribed for pruritic (itching) skin conditions. They are also the most used and

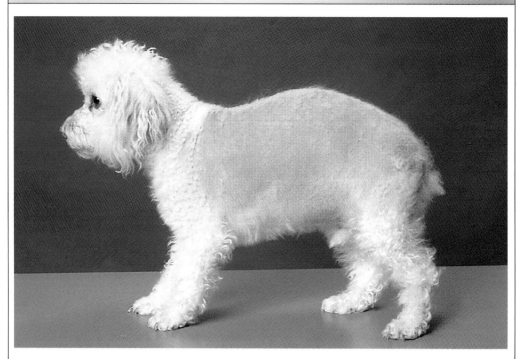

Profound hair loss (alopecia) in a dog with gluco-corticoid excess. Overproduction or over-supplemenation of glucocorticoids is often referred to as Cushing's syndrome or hyperadrenocorticism.

abused class of drug in dermatology. The medication may be injected, administered orally, or applied topically. The effect on the body is related to the amount given, the potency of the drug, and how long the effects last. Short-acting cortisone (hydrocortisone, prednisone, prednisolone) is prescribed to reduce itching, redness, and swelling. It is invaluable in treating hypersensitivity reactions (flea allergy, pollen allergies) and "hot spots", and to relieve the discomfort in areas of self-inflicted trauma. Longer-acting more potent steroid medications (triamcinolone, dexametha-sone) suppress differ-

ent parts of the immune system and are a vital part of therapy in diseases such as lupus erythematosus and cancer.

Problems can occur when these powerful drugs are given indiscriminately. Increased water intake, increased frequency of urination, increased appetite, aggressive behavior, and weight gain are common side effects of even short-term cortisone therapy. Evidence of cortisone excess includes the development of fat deposits over the lower back, a pot-bellied appearance to the abdomen, decreased tolerance to exercise, and panting. Dermatologic changes associated with cortisone excess include hair loss, thin skin, development of comedones (blackheads) on poorly haired skin, and the development of bruising in areas of minor trauma. Systemic effects

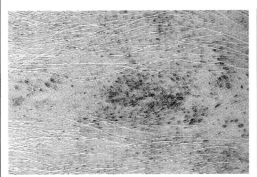

Comedones (blackheads) on the belly is another common sign of glucocorticoid excess.

of cortisone excess may include stomach ulcers, pancreatitis, and diabetes.

Most people understand that excessive amounts of cortisone can cause severe damage to tissues and the immune system. A guide to using cortisone safely is to be sure that the smallest dose of the weakest formulation possible is given as infrequently as possible to bring about the desired effect. Anti-inflammatory doses are administered daily for five to seven days, then the dose is reduced to every other day. Alternate-day therapy allows adrenal gland activity to continue uninterrupted and ensures the availability of physiologic cortisone if needed.

Thyroid Hormones

Hypothyroidism (low levels of thyroid hormones) is a common endocrine disorder in dogs but may be over-diagnosed in animals with conditions of hair loss and darkening of the skin (hyperpigmentation). Hyperpigmentation (darkening of the skin) is more common as a sequel to itchy skin conditions rather than hormone imbalance. Thyroid hormone is required for initiation and maintenance of hair growth and for normal glandular secretions, so a dog with non-thyroid related skin disease may experience a mild transient increase in the growth rate of the hair when given thyroid hormone. Assessment six weeks after starting therapy will reveal a condition not much changed over that seen prior to replacement therapy. A dog with inadequate thyroid hormone will show dramatic improvement in the skin condition after a six-week therapeutic trial.

Antihistamines

Glucocorticoids are very effective in controlling itch, but the side effects associated with prolonged use have prompted the evaluation of other safer drugs to control itch. Antihistamines are a group of drugs that have proven to be quite helpful, especially in controlling signs of atopy (inhalant allergy, hay fever). Antihistamines are H-1 blockers. This means that they reduce itching

Diphenhydramine (Benadryl®) and chlorpheniramine (Chlor-Trimeton®) are two commonly used antihistamines that are available without a prescription.

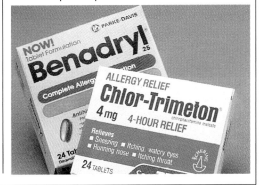

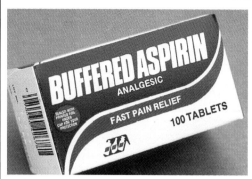

Buffered aspirin is the most common non-steroidal anti-inflammatory agent (NSAID) used in dogs. Check with your veterinarian before use to make sure it can be safely given to your dog.

by preventing histamine, a promoter of inflammation, from attaching to specific histamine receptors present on inflammatory cells. Although the antihistaminic effects play a role in the animal's response, these drugs also cause drowsiness (sedation). It is the sedative effects that can be especially beneficial to the chronically itchy pet because it allows the pet (and owner) to rest.

There are seven classes of antihistamines; many are available only with a prescription. Individuals respond to antihistamines differently, so a therapeutic two-week course of each of three different drugs given individually will allow selection of one that will work the best on your pet. Two OTC antihistamines, diphenhydramine (Benadryl – 2 mg/kg of body weight every eight to 12 hours) and chlorpheniramine maleate (Chlor-trimeton® – 4-8 mg total dose every 12 hours) are commonly used in dogs. Clemastine is also popular and may be the most effective antihistamine to use for dogs. Antihistamines rarely eliminate pruritus (itchiness), but most allow a marked reduction in the amount of cortisone needed to control itching. Occasionally, antihistamines will cause an increase in itching, trembling, excitation, and marked sedation. Discontinuing the drug will eliminate these adverse effects. Female dogs should not be bred while on antihistamines since these drugs have been associated with birth defects.

NON-STEROIDAL ANTI-INFLAMMATORY DRUGS (NSAIDS)

This group of drugs covers a wide range of pharmacologically diverse compounds. Most NSAIDs are available OTC and many are hidden in topical and oral medications. It is important for an owner to read all drug labels, to know which NSAIDs are safe to use, and to recognize signs indicating toxicity.

NSAIDs are present in both over-the-counter and prescription drugs and are used to reduce inflammation and swelling caused by prostaglandins and thromboxanes. Prostaglandins and thromboxanes are chemicals made by tissues after an injury, infection, or adverse immunologic reaction. Their presence in tissue contributes to the pain, redness, and swelling experienced at the site of an injury. A possible indication for an NSAID in a dog with a skin problem is to relieve redness and itching experienced with allergic reactions, or when antihistamine or steroid (prednisone, cortisone) therapy has been discontinued in order to perform a medical procedure.

Aspirin is the most commonly used anti-inflammatory drug (next to cortisone) in companion animal medicine. It is used to relieve muscle and joint pain, to help with vascular (blood vesssel) complications following treatment for heartworm disease. It may also reduce pain and swelling associated with chronic self trauma (licking, chewing, biting). The recommended dosage in dogs is 10-20 mg/kg (½ tablet for a 25-30 pound dog) of a buffered aspirin every 12 hours. Toxic side effects include nausea, vomiting blood, abdominal pain, seizures, and coma. Old dogs, puppies, and dogs with kidney or liver disease should not be given aspirin.

Other common OTC NSAIDs are ibuprofen, naproxen, and acetaminophen. They are excreted by the kidney very slowly by dogs and should be use with extreme caution. Side effects include vomiting, gastrointestinal bleeding, abdominal pain, and acute kidney failure. Acetaminophen is especially toxic to the kidney and should not be use in dogs. The safest way to use NSAIDs is to ask your veterinarian first to be sure that there are no reasons not to use them in your pet.

FATTY ACID NUTRITIONAL SUPPLEMENTS

Linoleic acid and arachidonic acid are polyunsaturated fatty acids that are essential components of healthy skin. When these key elements are lacking in the diet, the hair coat becomes dull and the skin dry and scaly. Luckily the source of these essential fatty acids is vegetable oil. One teaspoon of safflower oil added to the diet daily often will correct the problem.

Fatty acids also play a fundamental role in the formation of prostaglandins and leukotrienes during periods of inflammation. Eicosapentaenoic acid (EPA-derived from marine fish oil) and gamma-linolenic acid (GLA-derived from evening primrose oil or borage oil) are specific dietary fatty acids that have been shown to reduce inflammatory prostaglandins and leukotrienes. These fatty acids have been proven effective in reducing pruritus and dermatitis in allergic pets. In addition, when fatty acids are combined with an antihistamine, glucocorticoids often can be eliminated from the treatment regime.

PSYCHOTHERAPEUTIC MEDICATIONS

A lot of public attention has been given to the use of several human antidepressant drugs such and amitriptyline HCl (Elavil®) and Fluoxetine HCl (Prozac®). They have been used with variable success for behavioral abnormalities and lick granulomas. Due to the popularity of these kinds of drugs, they have become the number one cause of drug overdose in humans. As a consequence, accidental overdoses are a possibility for pets as well.

Here are some facts:
* There is a very narrow margin of safety between therapeutic and toxic or lethal doses. None of these drugs should be used on your pet without specific veterinary supervision.

- They should *never* be prescribed or used routinely for any dermatologic condition.
- Amitripytiline and Doxepin are two tricyclic antidepressant drugs having potent antihistaminic effects as well. These drugs may be prescribed for the seasonally allergic dog when other antihistamines have not been helpful in reducing itching. Dosage instructions should be followed to the letter.
- Additional appropriate use may be for repetitive behavioral abnormalities (tail chasing, lick granuloma) where all non-behavioral causes of the activity have been investigated and eliminated, and for which other approved drugs have been tried and failed.
- A pet placed on one of these medications should be monitored closely by the owner and the veterinarian. Bizarre changes in behavior, appetite, or activity should be noted.

Acral lick dermatitis or lick granuloma is a sore created by a dog repeatedly licking at one area.

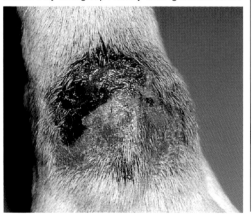

TOPICAL MEDICATIONS

General Principles

The skin is a protective barrier between internal structures and the environment. The outer layers of skin, called the stratum corneum, together with the hair coat and oily glandular secretions, provide a carefully balanced physical, chemical and immunologic defense against all sorts of worldly microbes and toxins. When the skin is washed or when medications are applied, some of the protective oils and secretions are removed along with these pathogens.

Most early skin problems are characterized as red, swollen, and warm to the touch; this is the classic description for inflammation. An acute lesion such as a hot spot will also be moist to the touch. Topical therapy is directed at reducing all of these signs. The formulation of medication (lotion, cream, ointment, etc.) can be as important to the efficacy of therapy as the actual drug because the form may determine how rapidly and efficiently the medication can traverse the outside defenses in order to be absorbed.

Lotions are the mildest formulation in that they tend to be water-based liquids in which medications have been suspended. The liquid phase will evaporate after application leaving behind a thin film of the active ingredient to be absorbed into the skin. Lotions are non-occlusive, non-oily, somewhat drying, and the best form for moist lesions. Calamine lotion is a classic example of a lotion.

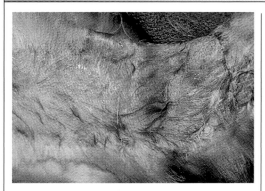

Acute moist dermatitis, also known as a "hot spot". This is not a specific diagnosis but is a common sequel to flea hypersensitivity, allergies, ear infections, and anal sac problems.

Creams and ointments usually contain some mixture of oil, water, and the suspended medication. Creams are a little heavier than lotions, may have an oil base, may take longer to be absorbed, but stay on the skin longer than lotions. They are excellent for softening mild crusting lesions. When applied after cleaning a wound, they can create an oil barrier between the skin and outside world. The effect is to extend the time the medication is in contact with the skin. Ointments are heavy, tend to stay on even when water is applied, and are occlusive by nature. The best example of an ointment is petrolatum. Ointments should not be used on hot spots but are excellent for conditions where the skin is thickened and hard.

Occasionally, one or more ingredients in topical creams or lotions can cause an allergic or irritant contact dermatitis. This is evident by increased redness, swelling, scaling, blistering, or itching after applying the product. Should this hap-pen, discontinue use and wash the area with fresh water and a mild soap to remove the medication.

Medications

For the most part, topical medications (creams, ointments,and lotions) have limited use on our pets because they tend to lick every bit off as soon as it is applied. This point is an important one because seemingly harmless topical preparations may be quite dangerous if ingested. Fortunately, a large amount of the medication must be ingested for most drugs to be toxic. It is important to know which items in our own medicine chests are appropriate and safe to use on our pets. There are literally thousands of OTC topical medications with endless numbers of active and supposedly inert ingredients. Their advantages include ease of application, rapid response, and relative benign effects on the patient overall.

Most skin conditions causing itch are generalized. Home remedies in the form of soothing soaks (colloidal oatmeal) and rinses are available and will provide temporary relief until you can get to the vet's office. A ten to 15 minute soak in cool water can be helpful. The cooling effect competitively inhibits itch providing temporary relief that may last for one to two hours. If the itching is due to a dry skin condition, then oils or humectants added to the water will help alleviate the dryness. The addition of colloidal oatmeal (Aveeno®—Rydell Laboratories:

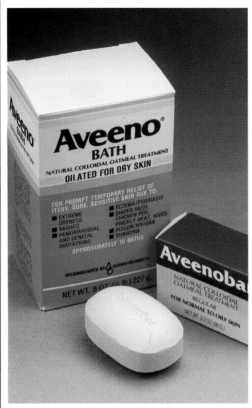

Colloidal oatmeal products are often very soothing for the skin and help reduce itch.

Episoothe®—Allerderm/Virbac) to the water may extend the soothing and anti-itch effects for several hours to one to two days.

Aluminum acetate powder added to water is an astringent, helps dry moist lesions, and reduces itching for several hours to one to two days. It is especially effective for hot spots, areas that the pet has made raw by excessive licking, and moist inflamed ear conditions. It has no antimicrobial effects so the area should be gently cleansed first. One packet of powder is mixed in 1 pint of cool water and the solution applied as a compress for ten minutes twice daily for three to four days.

Once the affected area is dried, its use may be discontinued.

Camphor (Campho-phenique®) and menthol (Gold Bond® Powder) are added to topical lotions and sprays because of their cooling effects. Topical anesthetics (lidocaine, benzocaine) and antihistamines (Bendaryl®, Caladryl®) are also added to products and may provide temporary relief to localized lesions. Zinc oxide and calamine are mild astringents, antipruritic products present in many topical OTC products.

Topical corticosteroids are available as creams, lotions, ointments, or sprays and are used abundantly for both human and veterinary dermatologic conditions. The reduction in redness and itching after application is dramatic and almost immediate, but significant amounts of the drug may be absorbed systemically when applied to inflamed skin. Hydrocortisone (0.5% or 1.0%) is the safest form and is available alone or in combination with antibiotics in numerous OTC products. More potent corticosteroids are available only with a prescription. Local side effects include aggravation of an existing infection and thinning of the skin. Systemic effects have been observed with long-term use and are the same as those described for excessive systemic use described above. You should use a cotton ball to apply the medication to minimize the possibility of absorbing the medications through your skin.

Benzoyl peroxide is a potent antimicrobial product that also has "follicular flushing", degreasing, and anti-itch properties. Benzoyl peroxide is present in many veterinary shampoos but is also available as a cream or gel for treatment of local lesions. As a cleaner, it is very effective in breaking down and removing dried tissue exudate and greasy glandular secretions. Its potent antimicrobial effects and ability to open plugged hair follicles make it the treatment of choice for chin and muzzle acne. The disadvantage of benzoyl peroxide is that it can be a potent skin irritant and may cause redness, swelling, and occasionally blisters if left on too long. It also may bleach the skin, hair coat, as well as fabric. There are several OTC products containing benzoyl peroxide, but the concentration (usually 10%) is too strong for our pet's skin. Veterinary products containing 3-5% benzoyl peroxide are safest and may be applied one to two times a day.

The most common OTC antibiotic products (Polysporin®, Neosporin®,

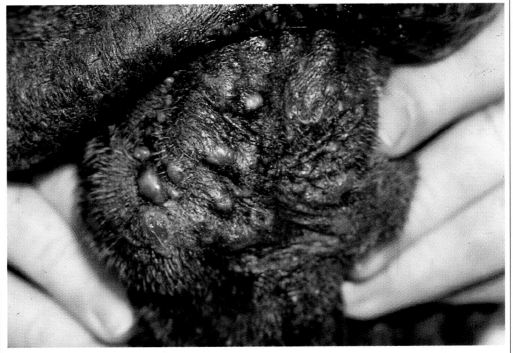

Chin acne in a Boxer. Benzoyl peroxide is often the treatment of choice because it helps clean out the follicles (pores).

Panolog®) contain a combination of bacitracin, neomycin sulfate, and polymyxin B sulfate. If the pet leaves the application on long enough, then the medication will diffuse through the upper layers of skin. Occasionally, a contact allergic reaction is seen from these triple antibiotic medications and are attributed most frequently to the neomycin. An adverse reaction to the medication should be suspected if the wound improves for the first few days after

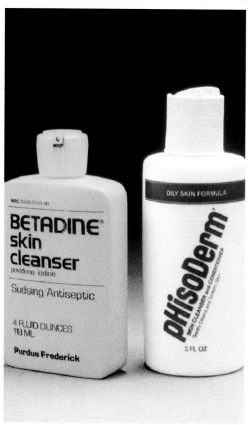

Gentle skin cleansers are very helpful in controlling microbes on the surface of the skin.

the medication is applied then suddenly gets worse.

Topical medications are best suited for small, localized lesions. The first rule of thumb when applying a topical medication is if it is wet (e.g., hot spots, feline eosinophilic plaques), dry it, if it is dry (scaling disorders), rehydrate or moisten it. All wounds should be cleansed before using a topical medication to ensure that no dirt or bacteria is trapped under the medication. The more hydrated the skin is, the more rapidly the medication will diffuse into the skin. My preference in treating mildly infected superficial wounds is first to clip away any hair around the wound. The second step is to gently cleanse the skin with an antimicrobial cleanser (e.g., Physoderm®, Betadine®). Thoroughly rinse and dry the area making sure that *all* the cleanser has been removed. Then apply a small amount of non-occluding antibacterial lotion or cream. These steps should be repeated once or twice daily for seven to ten days. If the problem persists or worsens, seek the advice of a veterinarian.

EAR MEDICATIONS

Infections involving the external ear canal accompany allergic conditions in dogs and tend to become chronic problems requiring constant attention. There are endless numbers of ear medications. Most contain a combination of antifungal (miconozole or clotrimizole), antibacterial (neomycin, polymyxin), anti-inflammatory (hydrocortisone, triamcinolone, or betamethasone), and parasiticidal (thiabendazole) drugs. In fact several are multipurpose drugs and are also used for skin abnormalities. However, not every red ear is infected and not all ear medications are created equal. Your veterinarian should examine the ear canal and ear drum before the medication is applied, since some antibiotics (gentamicin, neomycin) may cause hearing loss if the ear drum is ruptured. Like all chronic conditions, the cause of the ear problem should be identified specifically to maximize the potential for cure.

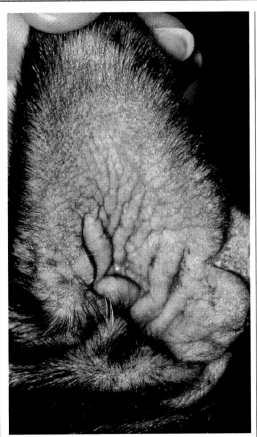

Ear problems (otitis) can be chronic, and proper management requires detecting the underlying cause as well as using appropriate medications.

Two principles are important when treating ear problems:

1) If it is moist, dry it out.

2) If it is dirty, clean it out.

No medication should be put in a dirty ear. For maintenance purposes, an owner should know how to clean the pet's ear, including plucking or trimming excess hair. Most ear cleaners contain a ceruminolytic (wax-dissolving) agent and may have an antimicro-bial agent as well. These are excellent to have on hand at home. Some cleaners contain alcohol or acetic acid; these should not be used in an inflamed ear because they will aggravate an already painful condition. When in doubt, ask your veterinarian!

SUMMARY

Owners are confronted on a daily basis with information about medications. This chapter should help you to determine when a drug is warranted, the properties of that drug, and side effects that might be anticipated. Do not give any drug to your pet unless your veterinarian has approved its use and you fully understand the purpose for giving the drug and any adverse effects that might result.

ADDITIONAL READING

Ackerman, L: Guide to Skin and Haircoat Problems in Dogs. Alpine Publications, Loveland Colorado, 1994, 182 pp.

Codner, EC; Thatcher, CD: Nutritional management of skin disease. *Compendium on Continuing Education for the Practicing Veterinarian*, 1993; 15(3): 411-423.

DeBoer, DJ: Canine staphylococcal pyoderma: Newer knowledge and therapeutic advances. *Veterinary Medicine Reports*, 1990; 2:254-266.

Rosser, EJ Jr.: Antipruritic drugs. *Veterinary Clinics of North America, Small Animal Practice*, 11988; 18: 1093-1099.

Dr. Duclos graduated Cum Laude from the Washington State University College of Veterinary Medicine in 1978. He was as a general practitioner until 1988 and then received his post-graduate training in Veterinary Dermatology at the University of Pennsylvania from 1988–1991. Dr. Duclos is a board-certified veterinary dermatologist and is a member of the American College of Veterinary Dermatology and the American Academy of Veterinary Dermatology. He has lectured to professional veterinary groups around the United States, and has published scientific papers in both veterinary medicine and human dermatology journals. He owns and is the clinical dermatologist at the Animal Skin and Allergy Clinic in Lynnwood, Washington (near Seattle).

Shampoos and Moisturizers

By David Duclos, DVM,
Diplomate, American College of
   Veterinary Dermatology
Animal Skin and Allergy Clinic
16418 7th Place West
Lynnwood, WA 98037

INTRODUCTION

There are so many shampoos available today that selection is not always a simple matter. I find in my dermatologic practice that there are three questions that clients ask most often regarding shampoo use on dogs. These are: "What shampoo to use?"; "How often to bathe the pet?"; and "Are human shampoos suitable for use on dogs?". We'll take a look at each of these questions in turn as soon as we review some shampoo basics.

PRINCIPLES OF SHAMPOO USE

Shampoo is used for two general purposes. One is for the dog with a normal skin and haircoat, the other is as a delivery system for medication in skin diseases. In the dog with normal skin and hair, shampoo is used for hygiene. Bathing should be done when an odor is detected. This indicates that there is a overgrowth of the normal skin microbes which produce the odor or that the skin and hair are dirty and need to be cleaned. You can't bathe your dog too often. A dog's hair coat is exposed to the lawn, the floor, the carpet, the roadway, and dirt. If your hair came into physical contact daily with these areas what do you think it would look like, feel like, or smell like? Your dog's haircoat is no different; in fact, dogs have more oily and waxy secretions from their skin onto their hair than humans so it is impossible to over bathe your dog . Some dogs can become sensitive to an ingredient in shampoos or detergents. This is a rare occurrence but can happen.

The frequency of bathing for the normal dog will be dependent on where the dog lives and on personal preferences of the dog's owner. As mentioned already, you can't bathe your pet too often. Some people like to bathe their pet often because they like their dog to smell and feel clean. Some people like to bathe dogs once per week, others every two weeks and some only bathe once per month or less. It is important that you decide on a frequency that keeps your dog's skin clean and free of dirt and odors so that the pet is pleasing to be around. If you set up a normal routine, your pet will look forward to its routine.

Which shampoo is best for normal skin and hair coat is really a matter of personal preference. You can use a general shampoo from your veterinarian such as D-Basic, HyLyt, or Allergroom. There are also many shampoos available at pet stores, groomers, and dog shows that are fine. One has to try them out and use the one that seems best for the individual animal. Creme rinses may be useful for dogs with long hair that mats easily. These rinses add lanolin, protein, and oils to the hair to make it comb and brush out easier. In general, dog shampoos are preferable but as we will discuss later, human shampoos can also be used.

HOW TO BATHE YOUR PET

Step 1. Before shampooing, comb out matted hair, clipping mats off if indicated.

Step 2. Protect eyes with sterile eye lubricant, if recommended by your veterinarian. Eye lubricant is available from your local veterinarian or pharmacy.

Step 3. Start with water that is body temperature and thoroughly wet the animal's hair down to the skin.

Step 4. Then, beginning at the head and being careful around the eyes, apply shampoo and add more water as needed to work up a vigorous lather. Be sure to follow recommendations from your veterinary dermatologist or general practitioner and also read the shampoo bottle for additional bathing tips and instructions. A second shampooing may be necessary if your pet is excessively dirty, oily or greasy.

Bathing your dog regularly is beneficial to his coat and makes him a more pleasant and presentable family pet. Photograph by Isabelle Francais.

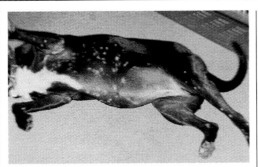

Dog with multiple circular spots of hair loss. Need to find out the cause of this problem.

Step 5. Rinse until the coat rinses clear. On long-haired dogs, squeeze the hair so that the shampoo and water thoroughly penetrate into the skin. Be prepared for your dog's shaking. You can prevent shaking until you are done if you keep your hands on the head and neck whenever you feel the dog prepare to shake.

Step 6. When finished, let the dog shake off the excess water and then towel dry and, if you like, you can use a hand-held hair dryer for the final drying process.

Additional Tips: Pets are bathed easiest if you use the shower spray method; use a hose or sprayer

Dog with bloody sores; severe itch is present. Shampoos will soothe, but must find the cause of the sores and treat them to get a cure.

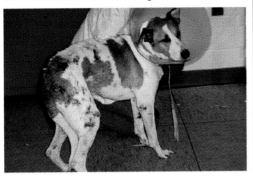

attachment for your shower. Rinsing thoroughly is important. Unrinsed shampoo can be irritating to your pet's skin but more importantly are the effects of water on the skin. Water is as important as the shampoo because of its hydrating (adding water to the skin) and soothing effects on the skin.

ARE HUMAN SHAMPOOS ACCEPTABLE FOR USE ON PETS?

Much has been written comparing the dog's skin to human skin and dog shampoo to human shampoo. Dog's skin is slightly thinner

Many top-quality shampoos are available at pet shops. Photograph courtesy of Hagen.

than human skin, and the pH of dog's skin is slightly different than human skin. The major difference is the quantity of hair and the large surface area of haired skin on the dog. Also, dogs have sweat glands in their skin that are very different from human skin. This has led to the development of shampoos that address these differences. In dogs we need shampoos that lather well and are able to cover large areas in an economical and effective fashion. You can use human shampoos on your dog, but most people find

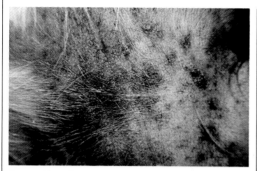

Dog with skin disease, red areas, black spots, dandruff, crusts, hair loss, and itch. Many things can cause this, and we need to find the cause to help this dog.

that shampoos made for dogs are preferable over human shampoo.

SHAMPOO USE ON DOGS WITH SKIN DISORDERS

If your dog has a skin disorder, special prescription shampoos and rinses are very important in treatment though they are rarely the only mode of therapy. For skin disease, treatment and diagnostic tests to improve or correct the underlying cause for the disease are important in addition to bathing . As a dermatologist, this is where I find it is best for the pet owner to seek out a specialist. Dermatologists are

Dog with dandruff, thickened skin, crusts—needs a combination of several shampoos.

trained to recognize readily not only which shampoo therapy is needed but also, just by looking at the dog, which medicines to use with the shampoos. Diagnosing the problem correctly is critical.

GENERAL PRINCIPLES FOR SELECTING MEDICATED SHAMPOOS

If your dog has what looks like dry skin, you should feel the skin and hair. If you get an oily to waxy feel on your hands, this is evidence that the skin is not dry but is in fact producing more oil than

For small dogs with tearing eyes, tear stain removing products can wipe away the problem. Photograph courtesy of Four Paws.

normal and needs frequent bathing to remove the excess oil and the increased skin secretions. If you pet your dog and your hands do not get oily and the hair feels brittle and dry or both and there is excessive scale, then special moisturizers along with shampooing are needed. Adequate contact time is needed for the ingredients in medicated shampoos to percolate into the pores of the skin and down along the hair shafts. One must remember that medicated shampoos are not just shampoo, the shampoo is used because it has been found to be the best vehicle to carry medication to the skin.

Some medicated shampoos do not lather up well because of the medications in them. In these cases you will be directed to use a combination of two shampoos. The first shampoo will be a gentle cleansing shampoo such as D-Basic, Allergroom or HyLyt . There are other over-the-counter products that are also useful for this first bathing, but the above shampoos are the ones I am most familiar with and use in my clinical practice. These

Antifungal, antibacterial shampoos can be prescribed and purchased from your veterinarian. Photo courtesy of Virbac.

shampoos have more emulsifying agents (the things that make shampoo breakdown oils and develop a lather) so they will enable more efficient removal of dirt and oils. The second bathing is then with the appropriate medicated shampoo. Since this second shampoo contains medication, adequate contact time is necessary to allow the medication to get into the skin and hair; most medicated shampoos need five to ten minutes to achieve this. You may find that a timer is a useful aid for you to know when the shampoo has had long enough contact on the

Dog with crust and dandruff may look dry but is actually oily and needs frequent bathing.

skin. Since you have cleaned the dog with a regular shampoo first, you will not need as much of the medicated (more expensive) shampoo. It is not important that the medicated shampoo lather up as much as regular shampoos.

SHAMPOOING CAUSES MY PET TO ITCH

Often, when a dog's skin becomes diseased, it will gradually worsen to a point when anything that you do to the skin, even petting the dog, will induce an exaggerated sensation of itch. This is known as pathologic (diseased) itch. It is caused by a change in the nerves of the skin which send signals to the brain. The same nerves which sense touch, pain, hot and cold also sense

Dog with greasy, waxy, scaling and oily skin.

Dog with a "hot spot", due to severe itch at this site. This caused the dog to chew at the site until it was moist, raw and very sore. Needs anti-itch shampoos, drying agents and treatment of the cause of the severe itch.

itch. Under normal circumstances the brain sorts out the sensations. However, when the skin is diseased the normal sensations of itch, or touch, or pain can not be readily distinguished as separate sensations by the brain. Many of these sensations are perceived by the brain as itch. When this malfunction of the nerves of the skin occurs, you will see your pet itching frequently. If you bathe the dog at this point, he will scratch excessively afterwards. This is because of the hypersensitive state. This diseased state of the skin can be caused by conditions such as allergy, infections, parasite

Dog with a bacterial skin infection.

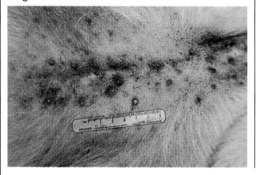

infestations or combinations of these. Pet owners often feel it is the shampoo that induced this severe itching. Some think their groomer must not have rinsed off the shampoo completely or used the wrong shampoo on their pet, or their pet is allergic to the shampoo.

I find in my clinical practice, pet owners are very confused by this severe disease-induced itching that they see after bathing. I hear their false impressions that their dog "can't be bathed with any sham-

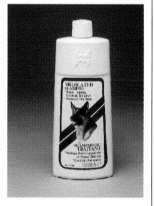

Medicated shampoos bring cleanliness as well as itch relief. Photograph courtesy of Hagen.

poo." "All topical products make my pet itch, even flea dips or sprays." Additionally, friends, or pet owners with dogs of the same breed have advised them that they must be bathing their pet too often, or they are using an inferior product. Clients frequently come in with a whole bagful of shampoos, flea products, and anti-itch medications they have purchased at various places to show what shampoos and topicals they have tried and feel can't be used on their pet. The truth is, dogs with skin disease really need frequent shampoo therapy. However, it is important that the right shampoo is chosen. Next, let's look at the various types of medicated shampoos and how they work.

SHAMPOOS FOR BACTERIAL INFECTIONS

The most common canine skin disorder seen by both veterinary dermatologists and general practitioners is a skin infection with bacteria. Antibacterial shampoos have become a consistent part of our treatment of these infections. The best antibacterial shampoos contain either benzoyl peroxide,

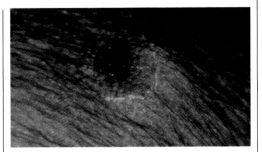

Dog with a bacterial skin infection.

Your veterinarian can recommend an antibacterial shampoo best suited to your dog. Photograph courtesy of Virbac.

chlorhexidine, or ethyl lactate. One of these would be used for the initial treatment of skin infections. Other antibacterial ingredients found in shampoos are triclosan and iodine. Iodine-containing shampoos have a problem of staining light-colored hair and is a contact sensitizer so some animals (or more often their owners) can develop contact-sensitivity reactions to iodine. Because of this I don't recommend iodine-based shampoos. Triclosan is a mild antibacterial and is used in shampoos for use after the bacterial infection

has been cleared by the first-line of treatment with shampoo and medicine. Shampoos with triclosan or any of the first line shampoo ingredients such as ethyl lactate, chlorhexidine, or benzoyl peroxide can serve as preventative shampoos agent against future recurrence of bacterial infections. In our dermatology specialty practice, the shampoos we most frequently dispense contain either benzoyl peroxide, chlorhexidine, or ethyl lactate. Along with shampoos we have to use medications to correct or prevent the cause of the underlying disorder. Such as allergy vaccinations for allergic dogs, thorough flea prevention for flea-allergic dogs, and most often a combination of these.

Dog with dry skin and hair, severe dandruff, hair loss. Needs anti-dandruff shampoos and moisturizers.

SHAMPOOS TO HELP STOP ITCHING

Just the physical process of bathing is helpful in the therapy of skin disease. Not only are the cleansing and medicating effect of the shampoo important but also the water applied to the skin has tremendous benefit in adding moisture back into the diseased skin. All of these contribute to help relieve itching. This is particularly true if contact time with the water is ten to 15 minutes. Therefore, thorough rinsing between shampoos serves two purposes. It

Specially designed shampoos relieve itching in dogs and contain hydrocortisone. Photography courtesy of Virbac.

removes potentially irritating shampoo ingredients and it allows the skin to absorb water. Too short a bath can have the reverse effect; it can remove the skin moisture and have a drying effect on the skin. After bathing and soaking the skin adequately with water, creme rinses have ingredients in them that bind this water to the skin and keep the moisture in the skin longer.

There have been several shampoos recently developed with anti-itch agents in them. These agents consist of colloidal oatmeal, tar, and pramoxine (a topical local anesthetic

Dog with heavy crusts and scale—a tar shampoo may be indicated here.

agent). Topical anesthetics act like novocaine by blocking the nerves that feel the itch. Most topical anesthetics like novocaine are not safe to use on the skin of pets; pramoxine is the only one that is safe for frequent use on the dog's skin. Again, these agents alone will rarely stop itching but often, when used together with other agents aimed at the primary disease, will help. The other agents needed will depend on the cause of the itch. If it is allergy, treatment will include either allergen-extract injections or avoidance of the allergen if it is fleas or food. The simple act of bathing and removal of dirt and oils, adding moisture to the skin and the cooling

Dog with severe crusting, a tar shampoo is needed here.

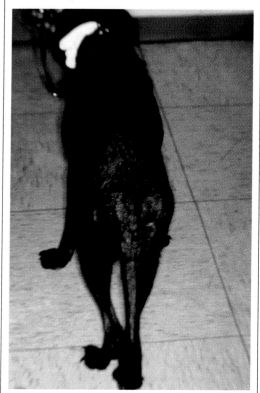

Dog with hair loss on tail and rump, due to severe itching caused by an allergic reaction to the flea bite.

effect of bathing has a soothing effect. There are also many hypoallergenic, moisturizing shampoos and moisturizing rinses that

Dog with dry skin, thin hair, poor hair coat needs moisturizing shampoos and moisturizers, oils, and creme rinses.

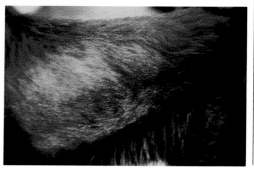

cool and soothe the skin. These are most useful when they are used for added relief with treatment for the primary cause of the itch.

SHAMPOOS FOR DANDRUFF

Other uses for shampoo are to remove scale (dandruff) and crusts (scabs). The active ingredients in most of the anti-dandruff shampoos are sulfur and salicylic acid. Examples of these are SeboRx, SebaLyt, and Sebolux . There are actually no major differences between the major brands except the

Sulfur and salicylic acid are common ingredients in dandruff shampoos for pets. Photo courtesy of Virbac.

way they lather, feel, and smell. It is simply a personal preference as to which one you want to use.

Tar shampoos are the more potent scale and crust removers. Tar is indicated in cases of severe dandruff and crusting. Tar has several effects on the skin: it has anti-itch effects, crust breakdown, and restoration of injured skin. Since tar has an offensive odor, and there are many other shampoos that perform the same function without the offensive odor, it is reserved for those conditions where there is severe crusting that needs the stronger properties of tar. Many other shampoos will deal with the scale and crust very adequately so tar shampoo is one of the least-prescribed shampoos. Most tar shampoos have sulfur and salicylic acid in them to add to the anti-dandruff effects. Most of the time one of the plain sulfur and salicylic acid shampoos are very effective. Again, if your dog has dandruff and crust, shampoo alone will not solve the problem. Your veterinary dermatologist or general practice veterinarian will need to determine the cause of the problem and treat with additional medications in conjunction with a shampoo.

FLEA SHAMPOOS

What about bathing for flea control? Does it work? Some clients use flea shampoo as their sole method of flea control. Flea shampoos are good to clean up the pet, remove the flea eggs, and the dried blood which the fleas leave all over your pet. Flea shampoos are the safest way to control fleas on nursing puppies. The problem with using flea shampoo as the only means of flea control is that once the flea shampoo is rinsed off there is no pesticide activity left on the pet. This means that new fleas in the environment can immediately repopulate the pet. This can happen to the pet after returning home from the groomer, kennel or veterinary clinic. If the pet is brought back to a home where fleas are waiting for the pet's return, the pet is quickly re-infested with fleas. The pet's owner is often unaware that this re-infestation came from

his own house. Most people erroneously feel that the fleas came from the groomer, kennel or veterinary clinic.

MOISTURIZERS AND CREME RINSES

Moisturizers and creme rinses are used after bathing to prolong the moisturizing effects of the water on the skin. Some creme rinses consist of just moisturizers, while some have colloidal oatmeal, or a combination of oatmeal and the topical anesthetic agent pramoxine to act as anti-itch agents as well as the moisturizer action. Some creme rinses have insecticides added to them to allow the addition of an insecticide and a moisturizer to your pet's skin. Moisturizers are grouped into two types: oils and non-oils. The oil types of moisturizers have oils, such as olive, cottonseed, corn, almond, peanut, or coconut, to add oil to dry skin. If your pet's skin is already oily, these may make the skin too oily. The moisturizers also have essential nutrients which help restore nutrient loss in damaged skin. The non-oily moisturizers have non-oily moisturizing factors such as lactic acid or carboxylic acid which act by binding the water which was absorbed by the skin during bathing. For best results, all of these moisturizing agents should be used after the skin has been adequately hydrated (water added) by thorough bathing or soaking in water prior to use. In other words, if water is absorbed by the skin during bathing, then this is sealed in by the creme rinse or moisturizer.

SUMMARY

In conclusion, for pets with normal skin and hair, then bathing with any regular dog shampoo which is pleasing to both you and your pet is fine. This, together with a routine bathing schedule, is an important way to help keep your pet a desirable family member.

Bathing with a medicated shampoo is a very beneficial part of the treatment of every pet with skin disease. In order for shampooing to achieve maximum benefit, the shampoo must contain the appropriate ingredients for the disorder, and every effort to correct the underlying cause of the skin disorder must be made. In some cases, your veterinary dermatologist or regular veterinarian may recommend a moisturizing conditioner or creme rinse after treatment with the medicated shampoo.

ADDITIONAL READING

Ackerman, L: Guide to Skin and Haircoat Problems in Dogs. Alpine Publishing, Loveland, Colorado, 1994, 182 pp.

Bukowski, J: Real and potential occupational health risks associated with insecticide use. *Compendium on Continuing Education for the Practicing Veterinarian*, 1990; 12(11): 1617-1626.

Muller, GH; Kirk, RW; Scott, DW: Small Animal Dermatology. W. B. Saunders Company, Philadelphia, 1989, 1007 pp.

Shampoos are helpful in the therapy of skin disease. Photograph courtesy of Hagen.

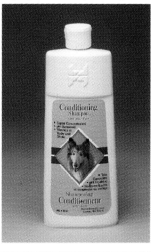

After-shampoo conditioners leave the dog feeling and smelling great. Photograph courtesy of Hagen.

Dr. Dunbar Gram received his undergraduate degree from Wesleyan University in Middletown, Connecticut and his Doctor of Veterinary Medicine degree (with high honors) from the College of Veterinary Medicine at Auburn University. Following veterinary school, he completed a one-year internship in small-animal medicine and surgery at the University of Illinois. Dr. Gram then completed a residency in veterinary dermatology at North Carolina State University's College of Veterinary Medicine. He also served on staff there as a clinical instructor in dermatology. Dr. Gram is currently practicing his specialty in Virginia Beach, and Richmond, Virginia.

Soothing the Itchy Dog

By Dunbar Gram, DVM,
Diplomate, American College of
  Veterinary Dermatology
Animal Allergy and Dermatology
5265 Providence Road, #300
Virginia Beach, VA 23464

INTRODUCTION

Itching has been defined as a sensation that provokes the desire to scratch. An itchy dog may also lick, rub or chew excessively. Sometimes, the symptoms can be so severe that the skin may become irritated, sore and infected. Many diseases that cause these symptoms are chronic and frustrating in nature.

The single most important aspect of controlling the itching sensation is to identify and treat the underlying problem. This is especially true in severe or chronic cases. Evaluation by a veterinarian or a veterinary dermatologist should be one of the first steps to help identify contributing factors and begin treatment to soothe an itchy dog. Some causes of itching respond quickly to treatment, while others do not. Often, several contributing factors may be present in a single pet.

Potential causes of itching include parasites (fleas and mites), allergies (food, inhalant, contact and flea), infections (bacterial and fungal) and other less common but potentially life threatening diseases. This chapter will include a brief overview of each of these conditions as well as various therapies.

PARASITES

Fleas

The most common parasite that causes itching is the flea. Most fleas that infest dogs are actually the cat flea (*Ctneocephalidies felis*). Although some dogs may harbor large number of fleas without any apparent discomfort, the presence of fleas and their associated flea bites alone will cause most dogs to exhibit some degree of itching. In these cases, dogs may lick, chew or rub their tail, back, "rump" or thighs. Other diseases can have similar symptoms. A significant percentage of dogs will also be allergic to the flea saliva. In this case, a single flea and its associated flea bites can make a pet miserable. Flea allergy dermatitis is one of the most itchy dermatologic diseases affecting dogs.

Many people are under the false impression that if fleas or flea bites do not affect humans, fleas are not a problem for their pet. Most fleas prefer dogs and cats instead of humans. Mild to moderate flea infesta-

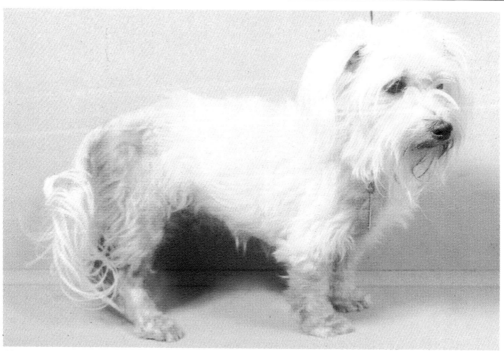

Above: A patient suffering from itching and licking of all four paws and the rump region. Intradermal allergy testing documented reactions to inhalants and fleas.

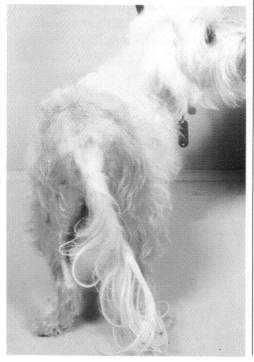

tions may not actually result in a problem for the humans in the house, but a relatively few number of fleas can cause a significant problem for the animals in the house. Devices called "flea traps" are extremely useful for illustrating the presence of fleas in the indoor environment and emphasizing the need for environmental control of fleas. Unfortunately, they are not effective as a sole means of eliminating fleas in the house. Although fleas were once very difficult to control, the advent of insect growth regulators (for use both on and off the pet) and boric acid derivatives (for use in the indoor environment) have dramatically improved our methods for controlling this pest. Consultation

Left: Note the patient's loss of fur and color change over the rump.

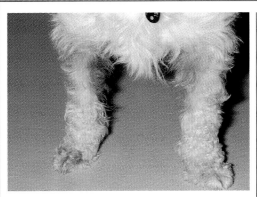

Itching of the armpits and feet is common with most forms of allergy.

with a veterinarian concerning potential toxicities and effectiveness is strongly recommended when implementing any flea control program.

If adequate flea control is not effective in controlling itching, other possible causes should be considered. In many cases, fleas complicate the task of identifying other causes of itching. Often, a pet's itching may be due to a combination of fleas and other factors. Without adequate flea control, it can be difficult to determine how much a pet would itch if only the factors unrelated to fleas were present. The clinical signs of allergic inhalant dermatitis, food allergy and even some hormonal diseases can be very similar to symptoms associated with flea associated dermatitis.

Mites

Most mites are so small that their presence can only be confirmed through the use of a microscope. The two most common mites seen in dogs include Demodex and Sarcoptes. Dogs exhibiting disease associated with either of these mites are said to have "mange". Other mites such as ear mites, Cheyletiella mites and other less common mites can also be associated with itching in dogs.

An infestation with sarcoptid mites (*Sarcoptes scabiei*), also called scabies mange, is one of the most itchy diseases seen in dogs. It is potentially highly contagious, but not all animals that are exposed to the affected pet will become affected themselves. Some dogs may actually harbor the mites on their bodies but not show any symptoms. Typical clinical signs include extreme itching and crusts on the margins of the ear, elbows and sternum. However, some animals will be affected in different areas or may only show signs of itching without any crusts, redness or hair loss. The mites have also been known to temporarily cause problems in humans. If you suspect this, you are advised to seek an evaluation by a physician dermatologist. The human scabies mite is different than the dog scabies mite and is generally believed not to be transmissible from humans to dogs. Microscopic diagnosis of scabies mange can be difficult to confirm because of the small number of mites required to cause clinical signs. Often, response to appropriate therapy is the method used to make the diagnosis of this mite infestation.

Demodex mites usually do not cause itching. These mites are actually found on normal dogs and are not considered contagious. Transmission of mites occurs before pup-

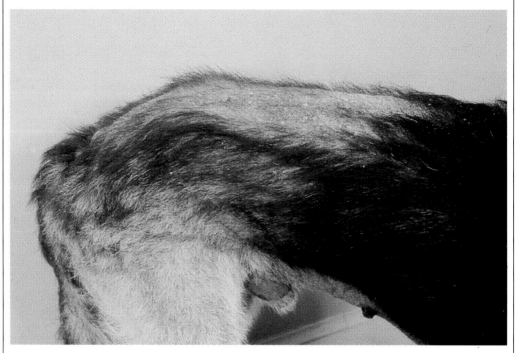

Chewing of the rump region, suggestive of flea bite hypersensitivity. However, flea allergy can also result in scratching, chewing or licking of other areas of the body.

pies are a few days old while they are nursing their mother. Occasionally, dogs may show clinical signs associated with the presence of these mites such as patchy hair loss on the face and feet without itching. Rarely, other areas are affected or itching may be present. Mild cases affecting a single or a few areas of skin are referred to as having localized demodicosis. More severe cases that affect several areas or even the whole body are referred to as having generalized demodicosis.

Localized demodicosis is often self limiting and will go away on its own. This is the most common type of demodicois seen in young dogs. The generalized disease is treated differ-ently than the localized disease and is considered to have a genetic basis. Therefore, dogs that have had generalized demodicosis should not be bred because they may pass the tendency for acquiring this disease to future generations. For this reason, cases of localized demodicosis should not be treated in the same manner as cases of generalized demodicosis. Treatment of a localized case of demodicosis with the same regimen used to treat a generalized case of demodicosis may artificially prevent an animal from developing a genetic disease. This could result in inadvertently passing the tendency for this disease to future generations.

It is important to note that while all cases of generalized demodicosis start as localized cases, the vast majority of localized cases do not progress to the more severe form and therefore do not have the genetic predilection for the generalized disease. Indiscriminate treatment of cases of localized demodicosis with the same treatment as that used for generalized demodicosis would result in the inability to determine which dogs carry the genetic tendency for generalized demodicosis. It is imperative that we do our best to prevent the breeding of dogs that harbor the genetic predilection for generalized demodicosis.

Above: Two unrelated but allergic West Highland White Terriers.
Below: Allergic Westies viewed from the rear.

ALLERGIES

The two most common types of allergies seen in dogs include flea allergy and inhalant allergy (similar to hay fever in humans). Food allergy is much more rare. Contact allergy is significantly less common than food allergy. The hallmark clinical sign of allergies is itching. Often these different types of allergies may have symptoms that look alike with only subtle differences in history, distribution of clinical signs or response to therapy. Flea and mite infestations may also mimic the clinical signs of allergies. The basic physiologic aspect of the different types of allergies is similar. The allergy-causing substance gains entrance into the body either through the skin, lungs or digestive tract. In normal animals, these substances (called allergens) do not cause the individual any problems. In affected animals, the allergens cause an exaggerated immune response resulting in various clinical signs. These clinical signs will be discussed individually with each allergy.

Flea Allergy

Flea allergy is the most common allergy seen in dogs and it is one of the most itchy diseases encountered. A majority of flea-allergic dogs will also suffer from inhalant allergies. In contrast to a non-flea-allergic dog that itches when exposed to several fleas, a flea-allergic dog can suffer from extreme discomfort associated with a single flea. The flea-allergy reaction occurs when a flea bites a flea-allergic dog and exposes the dog's immune system to flea saliva. The ensuing allergic reaction can occur very quickly and may also last for many days. Clinical signs

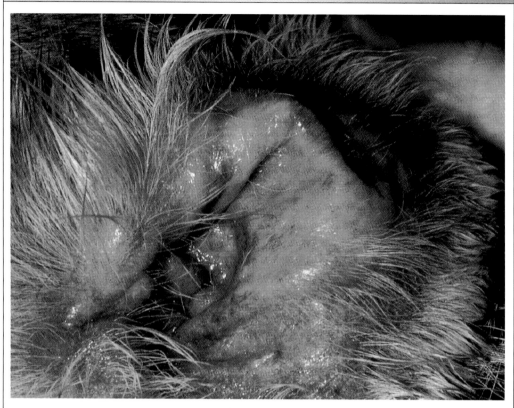

Inflammation in the ear is common in many dogs with allergies. Secondary infections with bacteria and yeast are not unexpected. This contributes to the foul odor that is often associated with the condition.

are often more severe near the area of the flea bite but can also occur in distant locations. Itching, redness, small bumps and self-induced trauma result. As with flea infestation, the most severely affected area is often on or near the rump region, where flea numbers are usually at their greatest. Excessive licking or chewing of both the front and rear legs and paws can be seen with flea allergy as well as other allergies. Conversely, other allergies can also cause clinical signs affecting the skin of the rump region.

Eradication of fleas is the most important aspect of relieving a flea-allergic dog. Flea-control measures that kill fleas by requiring them to be exposed to a toxin only after biting the dog and ingesting the dog's blood are not very helpful in treating a flea-allergic dog. They may help reduce the total number of fleas. However, before the flea dies, they must bite the pet, thus initiating the allergic reaction. The use of flea shampoos are also not very helpful because they do not offer significant residual repellant action. The shampoo kills the fleas on the pet, but fleas from the environment quickly jump back on and the itching continues. Environmental control, the use of insect growth regulating hormones and topical application of products with residual repellant action are imperative components of stringent flea control for a flea-allergic dog. Consultation with a veterinarian concerning potential toxicities and effectiveness is strongly recommended when implementing any flea-control program.

Allergic Inhalant Dermatitis

Allergic inhalant dermatitis is also called atopy. This disease involves allergic reactions to various pollens (grasses, trees, molds and weeds) as well as other substances with microscopic allergens that can be inhaled such as dust and dust mites. These substances interact with the dog's immune system primarily through the lungs. Humans with inhalant allergies generally suffer from symptoms such as runny noses, irritated eyes and sneezing. Dogs manifest this type of allergy by scratching, rubbing, licking and biting themselves. The feet, forearms, armpits, abdominal region, face, ears and occasionally the rump may become red and irritated. Many dogs may only be affected in one or two of these areas. Some dogs may seem to itch all over their body. The symptoms often start sometime between the age of one to three years and initially cause problems during a particular season. With time, the clinical signs become more severe and may last all year long. Bacterial infections take advantage of the abnormal skin and are a common secondary problem.

Although controlling exposure to the allergens that cause flea, food and contact allergy is often pos-sible, it is very difficult to control exposure to substances in the air. If the clinical signs cause the pet to be uncomfortable, medical therapy may be necessary. If the symptoms do not adequately respond to medical therapy or side effects of the drugs occur, allergy testing should be considered.

Currently, two different methods for allergy testing exist. Skin testing for allergies involves the intradermal injection of small amounts of various types of diluted purified al-

Inhalant allergies and excessive licking of the front paws and forearm in this patient have resulted in an early stage of lick granuloma. Significant face rubbing and scratching were also present. A properly performed hypoallergenic diet trial showed that food allergy was not the problem.

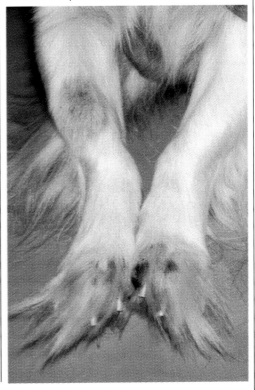

lergen extracts and monitoring for a wheal (a localized reaction that looks like a hive or welt). Skin testing, or intradermal skin testing as it is also known, is similar to the human allergy test that most people are familiar with. Blood testing is a relatively new type of test which involves obtaining a sample of blood and submitting it to a laboratory that performs the specialized testing. After the positive reactions identified with the allergy test are correlated with the history, the immunotherapy solution (allergy extract) can be formulated. This solution contains a mixture of specific allergens. The exact mix of allergens is different for each patient and is based upon the pet's history, positive allergy test results, the veterinarian's (and/or the laboratory's) clinical experience in treating allergies and other considerations. Injections of immunotherapy solution of allergy extract are also referred to as allergy shots. This type of allergy shot should not be confused with steroid or cortisone injections, which are quite different.

The treatment of allergies is complicated and the likelihood of success with immunotherapy (or allergy shots) can be affected by a number of factors. The allergy tests themselves can be technically complicated and are best interpreted by a veterinarian who has received specialized training in the treatment of allergic skin diseases. The most precise results are obtained with the use of individual allergens rather than groups of allergens. The disadvantage of using groups of mixed allergens becomes apparent while considering the results of the test. When a group of mixed allergens has a negative test, all allergens in the group or mix are considered to be negative. This is unfortunate because if the allergens were tested individually, one of the allergens could actually show a true positive test result. Conversely, a group of mixed allergens that test positive may actually contain an individual allergen that would truly test negative if individual testing were performed.

The less accurate nature of using groups or mixes for allergy testing complicates the formulation of the immunotherapy solution and may inadvertently lead to omission of an important allergen in the allergy extract. Additionally the practice of using groups or mixes could lead to the inclusion of allergens which are not relevant thereby diluting the concentration of the important allergens. Both situations are likely to reduce the efficacy of the treatment. Studies indicate that the highest success rate with immunotherapy is achieved through the use of the most precise testing and the highest concentration of immunotherapy solution. Grouping of allergens should be avoided in either type of allergy test and the highest concentration of immunotherapy solution that can safely be used should be administered as an allergy shot.

An additional complicating factor in testing for allergies is the presence of two different immunoglobulins (products of the immune system) which are important in aller-

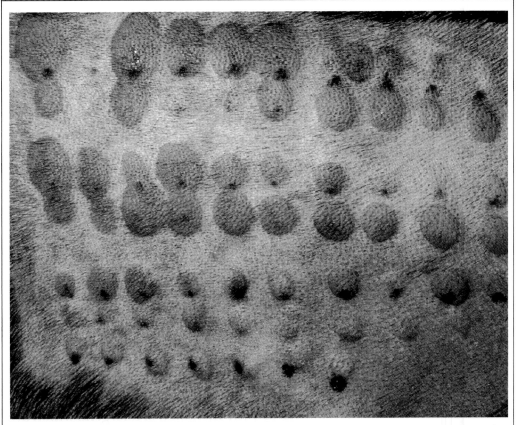

Intradermal allergy testing is very important in the diagnostic process. This dog had reactions to many inhalants as well as fleas.

gies and allergy testing. These immunoglobulins are known as IgE and IgGd. Tests that rely solely on measuring IgE have an inherent disadvantage when compared to other tests that utilize both IgE and IgGd as indicators of allergies. IgE is found in the bloodstream and the skin. IgGd is found in the skin. Thus, some falsely negative reactions may be seen when such tests are performed on animals which have normal levels of IgE but itch because of IgGd associated allergies. Additionally, falsely positive reactions may be seen when an animal has elevated blood levels of IgE due to internal parasites (such as worms) or external parasites (such as fleas). These parasites can result in very high levels of non-allergy-related IgE in the blood and may cause falsely positive reactions.

Skin testing allows for relatively inexpensive identification of individual allergens and is able to take into account both of the important allergy-associated immunoglobulins (IgE and IgGd). Commercial blood tests for allergies measure only IgE and do not measure IgGd. Many blood tests are also at an additional disadvantage because they test for groups or mixes of allergens. Although it is possible to utilize groups or mixes of allergens with skin test-

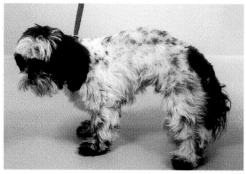

Above: This dog had demodectic mange involving its feet. The problem was caused by overuse of corticosteroid drugs that weakened the immune response. The corticosteroids were originally prescribed to treat the itching of inhalant allergies.
Below: Closeup look at the feet of dog with demodectic mange.

ing, most allergens are tested for individually. The concentration of the immunotherapy (allergy extract) solution can also vary with the type of test performed and as previously discussed can affect the success rate. Skin testing has numerous advantages over blood testing, but is complicated to perform and interpret. Both types of test are best performed under the guidance of a veterinarian with training in allergic skin diseases. In summary, intradermal skin testing is the historical standard and the preferred method for allergy testing. Some veterinary dermatologists find the combined use of both tests to be useful.

Food Allergy

Food allergy is a relatively rare disease and generally overemphasized by many pet food companies as a cause of itching. The clinical signs may be sudden in onset and are virtually indistinguishable from those seen in allergic inhalant dermatitis. The symptoms are not usually associated with a change in diet. They may start at any age and do not vary with the time of year or season. Many food-allergic dogs also have inhalant allergies and therefore may exhibit some degree of seasonality.

Various tests are available for assistance in diagnosing food allergy. However, neither blood tests or the skin tests are very helpful in confirming the diagnosis. While positive reactions are often seen, they are usually not clinically important. Falsely positive reactions may lead to the incorrect belief that a pet is very food-allergic. Negative reactions offer slightly more useful information and indicate that a pet can likely tolerate a specific food substance. Most veterinary dermatologists do not recommend blood tests or skin tests for the diagnosis of food allergy. The best way to diagnose a food allergy is with the proper use of a hypoallergenic diet. This diet should have undergone clinical trials which verify its hypoallergenic nature. Manufacturer claims that a diet contains certain substances does not indi-

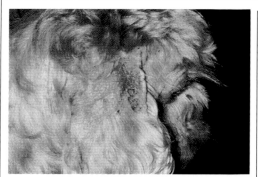

Above: This Cocker Spaniel had suffered from moderate itching for years, associated with its allergies. Recently the itching became severe, especially on the ear flaps. Skin scrapings revealed that a new problem had arisen—sarcoptic mange. The parasite was contracted from another dog that had recently visited. Treatment of the sarcoptic mange was successful, but the moderate itching from the allergies persisted. **Below:** Note the redness and inflammation involving the chest, abdomen and elbows.

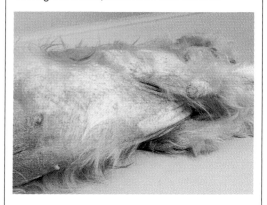

cate that the diet is truly hypoallergenic.

In order for an animal to be allergic to a food substance, the animal must have been exposed to the substance before. Lamb is a good example. There is absolutely nothing magic about lamb and food allergy. Simply, most dogs have not eaten lamb before and therefore cannot be allergic to it. A dog that has eaten lamb as part of its normal diet may actually be allergic to lamb. For

years lamb has been recommended by veterinarians as alternative to beef or chicken as a protein source in the diet of dogs suspected of having food allergy. Unfortunately, the indiscriminate use of lamb in many dog foods has further complicated the necessary steps required to diagnose food allergy.

Before initiating a hypoallergenic diet, a pet owner must understand that it is a true diagnostic test and should not be undertaken without conviction. Many times a hypoallergenic dietary trial is not strictly followed and the pet is allowed continued exposure to table scraps or flavored treats, rawhides and chew toys. Vitamin supplements and medications such as heartworm preventatives that contain meat flavorings should be substituted with a comparable product that does not contain these potential allergens. Failure to observe these requirements invalidates the test and results in unnecessarily exposing the pet to another potentially allergenic substance, such as lamb. This unnecessary exposure may preclude the use of such substances from being utilized in the future when a more strictly followed hypoallergenic diet is considered.

In summary, a properly performed hypoallergenic dietary trial is the most appropriate test for diagnosing food allergy. An improperly, performed hypoallergenic dietary trial may actually do more harm than good because it may complicate future attempts at diagnosing food allergy. Diets containing certain substances such as lamb are not

Cocker Spaniel with scabies and a secondary bacterial infection. The symptoms are also consistent with food or inhalant allergies, but scabies is particularly itchy. Proper testing was critical in arriving at the correct diagnosis and initiating the proper treatment. Cocker Spaniels are no more common victims of scabies than other breeds; these parasites do not discriminate—they affect all breeds without preference.

necessarily hypoallergenic. Only diets which have undergone clinical trials confirming their hypoallergenic nature should be used during the testing period. Unfortunately, an extremely small number of diets have undergone these trials. The hypoallergenic diet should be continued until the dog improves or for a duration of eight to ten weeks. If a pet improves while eating a hypoallergenic diet, the original diet should be reintroduced and the pet monitored for the return of itching within seven to 14 days. Sometimes the itching may return within a matter of hours. This reintroduction of the original diet is a critical part of the test and helps prove that the improvement was due to the food and not due to coincidence. Once a food allergy is confirmed in this manner, the patient should be placed back on the successful hypoallergenic diet until the itching is no longer present. The dog may be maintained on this diet (provided it is well balanced and complete) or placed on another diet and monitored for recurrence of itching. It is at this time that the use of diets, which have not undergone true clinical trials proving their hypoallergenic nature, may be considered for the individual pet. Introduction of potential allergenic substances may also be added individually to the proven hypoallergenic diet. This protocol allows for more precise identification of the offending food substance.

INFECTIONS

A bacterial or fungal infection may sometimes cause a dog to itch. Bacterial infections are especially common and are often associated with an underlying problem such as an allergy or hormonal imbalance. The most common bacterial agent identified in superficial skin infections is *Staphylococcus intermedius*. The most-well-known fungal infection is called "ringworm". The use of the word "worm" is confusing because worms have nothing to do with this disease. Yeast infections affecting the skin are increasingly being recognized.

Although itching is not often present, hair loss can be seen with any of these infections. Most pets with circular areas of hair loss actually have a bacterial infection rather than ringworm. Rashes or a bad odor can also exist with bacteria as well as yeast. If a dog suffers recurrent infections of any type, the possibility of an underlying cause should be investigated. The use of steroids can make a pet more susceptible to infections. Inflamed skin associated with allergies or other diseases also predispose a dog to infections.

Most of these organisms are not contagious. However, ringworm can be transmitted among pets and people. Some animals, especially cats, can be inapparent carriers of the ringworm-causing organism. This means that they do not show any symptoms of an infection, but are capable of passing it along to other animals or people. Children, the elderly and people with an immunodeficiency are more susceptible to this disease, but anyone can catch it. The organism may even be transmitted by inanimate objects such as bedding materials, towels or brushes.

TREATMENT FOR THE ITCHY DOG

If the underlying reason for an itch cannot be identified, various means of decreasing the sensation should be considered. It is important to remember that more than

Above: A young and very itchy stray puppy affected with sarcoptic mange.
Below: Note the dandruff on the puppy's coat. This is not typical of scabies but is sometimes seen. Dandruff is more often associated with a different type of mange, known as cheyletiellosis.

one disease may be contributing to itching. If identification and treatment for one of the causes do not result in adequate improvement, other causes should also be considered. Sometimes, the treatment of a specific disease may require some time until becoming effective. In these situations, or in cases involving an unidentified cause, non-specific treatment for itching should be considered. Both topical therapy (shampoos, sprays, lotions and creams) and systemic therapy (medications given by mouth) can be useful.

Topical Therapy

Topical therapy is most helpful in mildly itchy pets. For localized areas, sprays, lotions and creams are most appropriate. If the itching involves many areas, shampoos are the most appropriate. Colloidal oatmeal can be found in virtually all forms of topical therapy. In some cases, it is very beneficial, but its duration of effect is usually less than two days. Topical antihistamines may be found alone or in combination with other ingredients. They have not been shown to have a beneficial effect and with prolonged use may result in a contact reaction. Because of this and the additional cost associated with products containing antihistamines, veterinary dermatologists seldom recommend topical antihistamines. Topical anesthetics may offer a very short duration of effect and in some cases can also cause a contact reaction. Antibacterial shampoos help control bacterial infections that cause itching. However, some antibacterial shampoos such and those containing benzoyl peroxide or iodine can cause increased itching.

Topical steroids are probably the most useful topical medication. However, they are not without their risks. If used excessively, they can cause localized and systemic side effects. Hydrocortisone is the mildest and most common topical steroid. Stronger steroids are usually more effective, and expensive, have more side effects, and are not available without a prescription. Some topical steroid medications also contain other ingredients, such as alco-

Over-the-counter products may offer the benefit of decreasing incidence of fur biting as well as furniture chewing. The manufacturer states these sprays and gels are both safe and non-toxic. Photograph courtesy of Four Paws.

hol, which can irritate already irritated skin. In some animals, the application of any substance, including water, can result in an increased level of itch. The use of topical medications are best performed under the guidance of a veterinarian. Inappropriate use of medications can worsen the skin problem and may delay the initiation of appropriate therapy.

Systemic Therapy

Steroids are the most well-known drug used to control itching. They are also known as cortisone, prednisone, triamcinolone or Vetalog® and may be administered in pill form or by injection. This group of drugs is effective in controlling most itchy dogs but have significant long-term and not always obvious side effects. Short-term side effects include aggressive behavior, increased water consumption, increased urination ("accidents" in the house), increased appetite, pancreatitis and sometimes panting. Long-term side effects are many and varied. Basically, the steroids we give act to inhibit the body from producing its own steroids. This upsets the normal hormonal balance. Other effects include weight gain, behavior changes, liver damage, poor hair coat, demodectic mange, thin skin and hair loss. The body's defenses are compromised, and bladder or skin infections are common. The effects can occur slowly over time and may make the dog appear as if premature aging is occurring.

To help decrease potential side effects with long-term use, daily administration of steroids such as prednisone should be avoided. Triamcinolone, or Vetalog®, remains in the body slightly longer than prednisone and should not be given more frequently than every three days if chronic use is required. The days without medication give the body a chance to recover and return to normal. For this reason, long-term steroid injections (such as Depo Medrol® or betamethasone) which help reduce itching for several weeks should be avoided. Itching may ac-

tually return before the injectable steroid has entirely worked its way out of the dog's system.

Long-term side effects are more likely with injections than pills. However, chronic use of steroid pills can also lead to serious side effects. Another advantage of the pill formulation is that if your pet gets sick and should not be given any more steroids, most pill formulations will be out of the dog's system after a day or two. Once a long-term injection of a steroid is administered, the

Many professional groomers state that warm-oil treatments are effective to help relieve dry skin and hair. Photograph courtesy of Hagen.

drug remains in the body for a long time and cannot be removed. Steroids do provide a very important form of therapy. If used wisely, they are usually safe. Short-term use seldom causes serious problems. If steroids are needed for months or years, other options should be considered. As always, it is best to identify the underlying reason for chronic itching than to use non-specific medical control to suppress the symptoms.

Options to steroids include other medications such as antihistamines and fatty acids. In order to understand how medical therapy is effective, it helps to think of three separate and individual pathways that lead to inflammation and itching. Steroids block all three pathways, but, because of their side effects, drugs that help block the individual pathways should be considered.

Antihistamines include drugs such as hydroxyzine, diphenhydramine, chlorpheniramine, Seldane® and Tavist®. They help block only one of the three main pathways that lead to inflammation and itching. Antihistamines work better as a preventative, but they can be used on an as-needed basis if the itching has not become severe. Although generally safe, this group of drugs can have side effects and should not be used without consulting a veterinarian.

Fatty acids are available in powder, liquid and capsule formulations. They help block another of the individual pathways that lead to inflammation but may require six to eight weeks of use until maximum effect may be observed. Fatty acids work better as a preventative rather than stopping the inflammation once it has become a problem. They also help control dry or flaky skin which can also cause itching. There are many different brand names of this type of drug available. The optimum ratio of specific ingredients has yet to be determined. Label claims of greater quantity of important ingredients do not necessarily correlate with a greater success rate. The use of formulations which have undergone clinical trials proving their efficacy is recommended.

Drugs with psychological actions can also be helpful in controlling itch. Amitriptyline (Elevil®), a drug used as an antidepressant in humans, has rather potent antihistaminic actions in dogs and has been used to treat severe itchiness in dogs. Prozac® has also been used successfully in treating some dogs with a syndrome known as acral lick dermatitis or lick granuloma. Diazepam (Valium®) has also been beneficial in some cases. At this time, however, these mood-altering drugs have few advantages over more conventional therapies (e.g., antihistamines) and the potential for more side effects. In addition, these products are not licensed for use in dogs and so must be used at the owner's own risk.

The use of drugs other than steroids to control itching is less convenient but reduces the potential for serious side effects. If these other drugs are not totally effective in controlling clinical signs, they often help reduce the amount of steroids that is necessary to decrease itching. The costs of antihistamines and fatty acids are usually greater than the costs of steroids. However, the costs of side effects and diseases associated with excessive steroid use can be substantial in both monetary and health-related terms. The importance of identifying the underlying cause for itching can not be over-emphasized.

SUMMARY

Dogs can be itchy for a lot of different reasons. The best success in treating the itchy dog is to determine the specific cause for the itchiness and institute corrective measures. In the interim, or in those cases when a cause is not determined, non-specific therapy can greatly alleviate the discomfort of itching. This can be as simple as a cool-water bath or an over-the-counter antihistamine or fatty acid. However, whenever possible, the treatment should be specific for the underlying cause.

ADDITIONAL READING

Ackerman, L: Guide to Skin and Haircoat Problems in Dogs. Alpine Publications, Loveland Colorado, 1994, 182pp.

Ackerman, L: Pet Skin and Haircoat problems. Veterinary Learning Systems, Trenton New Jersey, 1993, 216 pp.

Anderson, RK: The diagnosis of atopic disease- intradermal or in vitro testing. *Journal of Veterinary Allergy and Clinical Immunology*, 1993; 1(1): 23-28.

Halliwell, REW: Comparative aspects of food intolerance. *Veterinary Medicine*, 1992; September: 893-899.

Children and puppies can be the best of friends, but health and safety precautions are in order for the happiness of both. Photograph by Isabelle Francais.

Dr. Jean Swingle Greek is a board-certified veterinary dermatologist practicing at the Dermatology & Allergy Clinic for Animals in Overland Park, Kansas, just south of Kansas City. She divides her time between her practice, writing articles and lecturing. Dr. Greek graduated from the University of Wisconsin School of Veterinary Medicine, completed her internship at the University of Tennessee and her dermatology residency at the University of Pennsylvania.

Safe Use of Insecticides for Dogs

By Jean Swingle Greek, DVM,
Diplomate, American College of
  Veterinary Dermatology
Dermatology and Allergy Clinic
10333 Metcalf Avenue
Overland Park, KS 66212

INTRODUCTION

As pet owners, veterinarians, veterinary technicians and groomers, we are concerned with keeping our pets comfortable and parasite free. In most environments, this mandates that we will treat both our animals and our homes with insecticides (better termed parasiticides because some parasites we treat aren't insects). The purpose of this chapter is to provide guidelines to help you to do this safely for both you and your pet(s).

Safety is dependent on a combination of factors. The active ingredients, the carrier solution, the formulation and interaction of multiple ingredients all merge to determine the ultimate safety of parasiticides. Difference in tolerance to ingredients is also important. Some pets may be sensitive to ingredients that are generally safe for other members of their species. This is true for people as well.

Most of the emphasis of toxicology reports involves acute toxicity and this information is usually well established. Signs of bad reactions that occur immediately after exposure are well described. Unfortunately for those of us who are likely to be exposed repeatedly, the long-term effects are not as well understood. The potential of insecticides to cause cancer and birth defects has not been consistently evaluated. Therefore, it is mandatory that we minimize our exposure to these agents and we make every effort to use the least toxic products.

PRODUCT SELECTION

Polyborates (Borax)

Tremendous strides in creating less-toxic environmental treatments are being made. One of the most exciting is the use of inert substances such as polyborates for environmental flea control. These products have essentially no toxicity for people or their pets. In the government-mandated studies required of all insecticides, the toxicity proved to be less than the toxicity of table salt. The tiny particles are impregnated in the furniture and carpets and act as desiccants to fleas. That is, they cause the fleas' outer shells to be disrupted

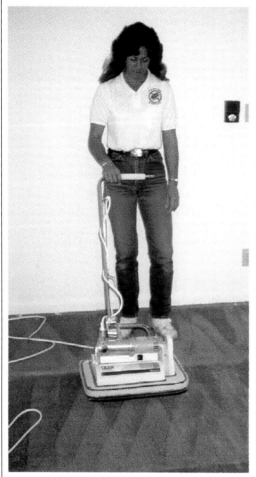

A technician applies Rx for Fleas Powder™, a form of polyborate. Photo courtesy of Rx for Fleas.

and the fleas die from dehydration. Additionally, the flea larvae eat the substance and die. The other advantage to this tremendously effective product is that it only needs to be applied once yearly. The most widely used version of the product is distributed by Fleabusters™ as Rx for Fleas™ powder. This is an extremely safe product. I feel that it is the house treatment of choice for pet owners who have fish, exotic pets or small children. It is also

ideal for people who are concerned about the effects of traditional parasiticides on their health and on our planet. This product is so safe that animals and people need not leave the house during treatment. Some dust may be noticed during the application process and for up to three days afterward. Particularly sensitive individuals may find this irritating, but it has not been reported to be a health hazard. This seems to be most noticeable in cases where the carpet fibers are short, such as Berber carpets. Long-term studies conducted on the people who mine borates, the basic ingredient, have not found any ill-effects on health or reproduction.

Numerous similar products are becoming available. These are available for over- the-counter sales and may be applied by the homeowner. The disadvantages of these over-the-counter products are that they have not yet undergone the rigorous safety testing performed on the Rx for Fleas™ product. Also, achieving penetration of the carpet fibers may be less effective when done by the non-professional, as they lack the applicator. Rx for Fleas™ powder is the only borate-based product licensed in California. This is the only product that has met all the rigorous testing demands of that state. A disadvantage to all polyborate products is that they are inactivated when wet. Carpets can not be steam-cleaned.

Insect Growth Regulators

Another important advance has been the development of insect growth regulators (IGRs). These products mimic naturally occurring hormones in fleas. This prevents fleas from developing to the adult stage. These products are very low in toxicity. They are available as products for both on-animal use and use in the inside environment. The toxicity of methoprene is extremely low. In some less-developed countries, it is routinely added to drinking water supplies to inhibit mosquitoes. The two IGRs currently available are fenoxycarb and methoprene. Fenoxycarb is the more stable of the two. It may last in the environment for up to six months. Fenoxycarb has been formulated in products for outdoor use. Methoprene degrades in sun and therefore is to be used only indoors.

The beneficial nematode, *Steinernema carpocapsae*, is an active ingredient in the product Interrupt™. Photo courtesy of Biosys.

The increased stability of fenoxycarb allows you to treat the environment less frequently. Unfortunately, neither of these products kill adult fleas. Therefore, they must be combined with a more traditional adult-flea-killing insecticide. Adulticides (insecticides that kill the adult parasite) are, as a group, much more likely to be toxic. Adulticides combined with IGRs include chlorpyrifos, an organophosphate combined with fenoxycarb in Basus™ (Ciba-Geigy). Ovitrol™ (VetKem) contains methoprene combined with pyrethrins. The toxicity of these adulticidal insecticides is worthy of discussion.

Microencapsulation

Another important advance leading to increased safety is a process known as microencapsulation. A slowly dissolving capsule made of polyurea coats the insecticide. The

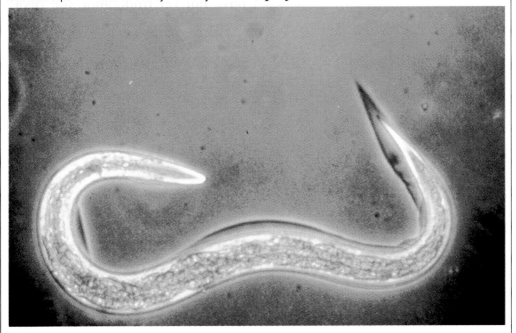

capsule allows the insecticide to slowly permeate outwards but is resistant to outside forces. The capsule breaks down gradually. Since the insecticide is delivered slowly and consistently over a longer period of time, it not only lasts longer, but is also more safe. Duritrol™ (Merck Ag Vet) is a microencapsulated chlorpyrifos for indoor and outdoor use. Sectrol™ (Merck Ag Vet) is a microencapsulated pyrethrin spray for use on both pets and premises.

Beneficial Nematodes

Beneficial nematodes are naturally occurring worms. One type, *Steinernema carpocapsae*, is unique in that it feeds on only flea pupae and larvae. It is now being sold for outdoor flea control as Interrupt™ (Veterinary Products Laboratories) and Bio Flea Halt™ (Biosys). The product is applied to the yard with a tank or hose sprayer. The worms eat exclusively flea larvae and pupae. The worms die as soon as all the immature fleas are eaten. Unfortunately, the worms may also die when temperatures drop too low or rise too high. They also require watering. The nematodes do not kill adult fleas. This product is safe for animals and people.

Organophosphates and Carbamates

Organophosphates and carbamates are common small-animal insecticides. The most common examples are fenthion, malathion, chlorpyrifos and carbaryl. They are available in dips, sprays powders, collars and foggers. Fenthion is sold as Pro-Spot™ (Haver) for spot-on use in dogs. Most cases of pesticide poisonings in both humans and animals are caused by organophosphates; the next-most-toxic products are carbamates. One study in California found that 50% of groomers using organophosphate dips had experienced some symptoms of toxicity.

Organophosphates can be recognized by reading the label for instructions in case of toxicity. On products containing organophosphates, the drug 2-PAM will be mentioned as an antidote. On products containing carbamates, atropine should be listed as the antidote.

Acute poisoning causes your eyes to blur because your pupils become narrow. You may salivate, tear, wheeze, have muscle cramps, vomit, have diarrhea and feel weak. In severe cases, death occurs from either heart block or from paralysis that leads to suffocation.

There are specific antidotes for this class of insecticide so medical help should be sought immediately. As with all toxic exposures that occur from topical applications, the animal or person should be washed to prevent any further absorption.

Organophosphates can also cause long-term adverse effects from chronic exposure. Most of the long-term negative effects involve loss of nerve function. More subtle effects have included memory loss, decreased alertness, sleep disorders and psychotic reactions.

Dichlorvos and carbaryl are thought to cause cancer with long-term exposure. Malathion and chlorpyrifos are suspected of causing birth defects.

Organochlorines

This class of insecticides contains some potentially toxic compounds. However, methoxychlor is the only one commonly used on small animals. Side-effects are uncommon. Depression, weakness and diarrhea have occurred in cases of overdose. Animal studies have suggested that methoxychlor does not cause cancer or birth defects.

Pyrethrins and Synthetic Pyrethroids

Pyrethrins are very commonly employed as on-animal treatments. They are derived from natural products and therefore have a reputation for safety. However, animals can convulse and die from very high doses. Most cases of human toxicity have involved ingestion of these products by small children. Despite the fact that pyrethrins are extremely safe, some people can develop contact dermatitis rashes after repeated exposures to pyrethrins. Occasionally, pyrethrins can cause asthmatic attacks and rarely may cause severe, potentially deadly allergic reactions known as anaphylaxis. Pyrethrin cross-reacts with ragweed and may be more problematic to people and animals that are allergic to ragweed. Animals which are allergic to pyrethrins may develop hives. This happens after a sensitive animal has been treated repeatedly. True allergic reactions require previous exposure. Thus, although pyrethrins are extremely safe, owners should still take the same precautions they would with more-toxic insecticides; people with asthma and ragweed allergies should probably leave handling of the product to someone else in the household.

Blockade™ (Hartz Mountain) is a combination of the pyrethroid fenvalerate and an insect repellent called N,N-diethyl-m-toluamide (DEET). Although the toxicity of each of these ingredients is quite low, there have been problems with the combination. Both cats and dogs have died after being treated with this product. The signs of toxicity include tremors, salivation and death. Respiratory failure caused the deaths. Although adverse reactions are rare, people applying the product should follow the manufacturer's directions closely.

Permethrins are another man-made pyrethrin. They are very stable, and therefore they last longer. In low concentrations, they may be used on cats. Higher concentrations, which are safe for dogs, may be toxic to cats. Preventic Spray™ (Virbac) is safe, long-lasting and highly effective in dogs. It is toxic to cats.

AMITRAZ

Amitraz is most commonly used as a dip (Mitaban®:Upjohn) for killing *Demodex* mites in dogs. It is also available as a collar (Preventic™: Virbac) to prevent tick attachment. Side effects are rare but are most commonly reported in very small dogs. The most common side effects are depression and vomiting. There is also a specific antidote for this toxicity so veterinary attention should be sought immediately. Amitraz should not be applied by diabetic people or to diabetic animals. It causes blood sugar to rise. This is only a problem in diabetics. Use amitraz with great caution, if at all, in cats.

IVERMECTIN

Ivermectin is used for a wide variety of parasites in small animals. It is usually given orally or by injection under the skin. The only federally approved use of ivermectin in dogs and cats is for once-per-month heartworm prevention. Many practitioners routinely use more than 60 times the approved dose to treat a variety of mite infestations. This should not be done in Collies, Shetland Sheepdogs (Shelties), Old English Sheepdogs, Australian Shepherds or related breeds. About 25% of Collies are extremely sensitive to ivermectin. Although, this problem occurs most in these breeds, toxicity can happen in any breed.

Signs of ivermectin toxicosis are related to the nervous system. Animals may wobble or appear drunk. In severe cases, the animal may become comatose or die. Signs of ivermectin toxicosis may develop in four to 12 hours after administration.

I have primarily seen ivermectin toxicosis when owners attempted to use the cattle form of this drug on their pets. The large-animal ivermectins are extremely concentrated, making it easy to overdose your pet.

ALTERNATIVE METHODS OF FLEA CONTROL

There are many supposedly safe alternatives to parasiticidal products. Garlic, sulfur, thiamin and yeast are fed to pets to prevent fleas. Ultrasonic collars and light traps are touted to drive fleas away or catch them. Avon Skin-So-Soft™ is used by some as an insect repellent. These products do not appear to be unsafe. Unfortunately, they have never proved to be effective in clinical studies. The ingredients in Skin-So-Soft™ are a well-kept industry secret. Therefore, the safety of this product when used on animals for insect control has not been evaluated.

One safe, completely non-toxic method of removing fleas is the use of a flea comb. This very fine-toothed comb has at least 31 teeth to one inch. This allows fleas to be manually removed. I prefer to use a flea comb on flea-infested puppies and kittens. Unfortunately, fleas must be removed before the pet comes in to infest your house. This technique will not adequately protect flea-allergic animals that can not tolerate any flea bites.

METHOD OF DELIVERY

The formula for pesticide delivery is important in determining the overall risk of contacting the product. On-animal products, that are packaged to be used as is, are generally less toxic than products that must be diluted prior to use. Products that do not require dilution include shampoos, sprays and powders. Dips are the most-common form of concentrate. Great care must be taken in measuring so that the proper dilution is obtained. General guidelines would include the wearing of gloves and protective clothing and eyewear while applying dips and sprays. Any of your skin that contacts the product should be thoroughly washed with soap and water. Dips should be applied in well-ventilated areas. In my practice, we never dip cats. Even dips that have been labeled as appropriate for cats have caused deaths. Dogs that are dipped frequently should be thoroughly shampooed prior to dipping. This will eliminate any residual parasiticide still present on the dog from the last dip. Also, bathing prior to dipping allows the dip to penetrate the coat more thoroughly and less product will be required.

Powders are generally less effective than sprays. This may be because the powder does not adhere to fur as well as sprays. It is not uncommon for pets treated with powders to leave small powder spots on furniture and carpets. I prefer formulations that adhere to the pet. Powders may also be irritating to pet owners or animals with breathing problems, especially during application.

Products sold as systemic spot-ons are very concentrated. These should be handled with great care and gloves should be worn. The product must be allowed to completely dry prior to handling the dog. These products are also too toxic for cats. Groomers have become seriously ill from handling a highly concentrated fenthion product.

Sprays are an effective and safe form of delivery. Many animals who object to the sound of the sprayer can be effectively treated by spraying the product on a cloth. The cloth is then rubbed on the animal. A hollow brush that delivers insecticide through holes at the end of the bristles is also an effective way to apply spray to pets that resist being sprayed directly. The product is sold through veterinarians and pet supply houses as a "brushette". Some sprays con-

---

Symptoms that require immediate medical attention. Not all signs will be present. If one or more are seen, see your doctor. Excessive salivation in cats is common after applying flea sprays. This may not require veterinary attention if it is the only sign present.

- excess tearing
- sweating
- difficulty breathing
- facial twitching
- blue tint to the gums
- "sawhorse" stance

- pinpoint pupils
- hyperactivity
- vomiting or diarrhea
- weakness
- abdominal cramping
- seizures

tain alcohol. The alcohol will kill fleas extremely fast. Unfortunately, it will dry your pet's skin. Also, the alcohol is painful for pets that have scratched until their skin is broken. I do not use alcohol-based sprays in my practice.

Some clients are disturbed by the impression that fleas are not killed by their choice of flea spray. If you spray a flea directly with a pyrethrin-based flea spray without any alcohol, it does not die immediately. It will however ultimately die; true resistance is rare. The impression of resistance occurs because of the slower kill time of the newer, less-toxic flea products.

More-recent developments in carriers include the formulation of insecticidal "mousse". The insecticide, usually a pyrethrin, is in a formulation similar to hair mousse. Cats who object to the "hiss" of a spray bottle may be especially amenable to this formulation. Ectofoam™ by Virbac is an example of a mousse which is labeled for use even in very young animals.

Flea collars rarely cause toxicity problems. Unfortunately, they are not generally effective. Cats have died from organophosphate impregnated collars. Dogs are more likely to develop allergic-type reactions to the collar itself.

However the product is delivered, care must be taken around the pet's eyes. Dips or sprays should be sponged on with a cloth instead of applied directly on the face. In years past, we routinely put bland eye ointment in animals' eyes before bathing. I no longer recommend this. If insecticide is splashed in the pet's eye, there is evidence that the ointment causes it to stay in the eye longer. Ointment will inhibit flushing out the eye. Animals have developed very painful ulcers on the surface of their eyes because of this practice. Should insecticide be splashed in your or your pet's eyes, flush it thoroughly with saline solution. This is sold over-the-counter for contact lens wearers. Medical or veterinary advice should be sought immediately. It is very difficult to determine if the eye has been damaged without special procedures.

Technicians and groomers who dip frequently should be discouraged from wearing contacts at work. There are two reasons for this. First, should they be splashed in the eye, the contact may hold the parasiticide against their eye. This may cause more damage. Secondly, soft contacts may absorb fumes from concentrated products, even when none of the solution gets directly in the eye. This has been reported to cause eye irritation or damage to the eye's surface.

Delivery method is also important in environmental treatments. If the ingredients are identical, premise sprays are less toxic than foggers. Premise sprays may be applied directly to problem areas of furniture and carpet. Insecticide from foggers is disseminated in a fine mist in a perfect circle around the can. Foggers allow insecticide to settle on everything in the room, including your bedding, your children's toys, the table where you eat, and so on. Cooking utensils and surfaces must be covered and cleaned. Additionally, these products are less effective than the premise sprays as "flea-friendly" areas such as under beds, corners and closets are not adequately treated. This lower efficacy leads to increased exposure as the environment needs to be retreated more often. When either form of environmental insecticide is used, remove all animals from the house. Do not allow children and pets to return until the carpets are thoroughly dried. In my house, after using a premise spray, this takes about an hour. The actual time may vary. It depends on how heavy your application is, the temperature and the product used. If foggers are used, leave the house for two to three hours. Then open the windows and allow the house to air out for several hours. In my practice, people with respiratory difficulties, such as asthma, seem to be bothered more by the residual odor of foggers than that of premise sprays. Check the label prior to using any type of premise sprayer or fogger. Follow the instructions of the manufacturer. Most of these products are extremely toxic to birds and fish.

SUMMARY

The point of this chapter is not to frighten you or to discourage use of insecticides. It is meant to emphasize the real and potential problems with their use. To summarize:

- Always follow the manufacturer's and your veterinarian's instructions. Most toxic reactions are due to applying higher concentrations or more-frequent applications than recommended. This is one time where more is definitely not better!
- Be mindful of delayed toxicity as well as acute problems. In many ways, the long-term effects are more worrisome.
- Err on the side of caution. If you think you or your pet may be having a reaction, seek professional medical attention immediately! Take the product with you so your medical professional can see the ingredients.
- Pick products with low toxicities. Be especially careful of using multiple products with the same toxicities. Do not use two organophosphates or carbamates together. Pyrethrins may be safely used with these products.
- Do not use flea-control products on sick or pregnant animals. Do not use flea-control products on puppies or kittens less than eight weeks of age without consulting your veterinarian.
- Do not induce vomiting unless instructed to do so. Depressed individuals may drown in their vomit.
- Remember, your veterinarian is trained to help you select the appropriate combination of insecticides for both your home and pets.

ADDITIONAL READING

Bukowski J: Real and potential occupational health risks associated with insecticide use. *The Compendium for Continuing Education in Small Animal Medicine* Vol. 12, No 11, 1990, pp. 1617-1623.

Greek JS and KA Moriello: Treatment of common parasiticidal toxicities in small animals. *Feline Practice* Vol. 19, No. 4, 1991, pp. 11-18.

Greek JS: Environmental flea control: General guidelines and recent advances. *Veterinary Medicine*: Aug. 1994, pp. 763-769.

Murphy M: Toxin exposures in dogs and cats: Pesticides and biotoxins. *Journal of the American Veterinary Medical Association*, Vol. 205, No. 3, 1994, pp. 414-421.

Collies have been found to have an extreme sensitivity to ivermectin, used in heartworm preventatives. About 25% of Collies have suffered reactions from the drug. Photograph by Karen Taylor.

Where to Find Help

By Lowell Ackerman, DVM
Diplomate, ACVD
8901 East Altadena Ave.
Scottsdale, AZ 85260

INTRODUCTION

When your pet has a skin problem, you have a lot of options these days. Your veterinarian is still the best resource to contact first because he or she can do an initial assessment and decide whether the condition warrants referral to a specialist. Groomers are also important and are especially useful when a pet has a non-medical problem, such as mats, poor condition of the fur, dandruff, and some external parasites (such as fleas and ticks). Many groomers have also been trained in the safe use of insecticides and can properly and safely apply these preparations to your pet.

Veterinarians and pet paraprofessionals are gaining more and more skills when it comes to recognizing and managing pet skin and hair-coat problems. Dermatology is recognized as a specialty discipline by the American Veterinary Medical Association and board-certified "Diplomates" of the American College of Veterinary Dermatology are entitled to refer to themselves as veterinary dermatologists. Of course, there are many veterinarians with a special interest in dermatology, but the board-certified dermatologists have completed recognized specialty residency programs and passed the stringent examinations of the American College of Veterinary Dermatology.

The grooming situation is also not static. At present there aren't too many restrictions on who can call themselves a groomer, and so talents and training are quite variable. In some states, groomers must pass examinations on the safe use of insecticides, but this is not true everywhere. Groomers are in the process of trying to regulate themselves, and this will help the public determine who has appropriate credentials and who doesn't.

VETERINARY DERMATOLOGY

The American College of Veterinary Dermatology (ACVD) is an official specialty board organization, accredited by the American Veterinary Medical Association and charged with maintenance of high standards of postgraduate training in veterinary dermatology. The ACVD is empowered to examine qualifying candidates and confer Diplomate status in the College. Board certification in the ACVD has been achieved by 82 veterinarians in the United States, Canada, and Australia since its creation in 1978.

The ACVD's functions are diverse, ranging from regulation of residency training programs in veterinary dermatology and conferring of Diplomate status to active participation in continuing education, and annual meeting and scientific program, and funding of research grants.

The ACVD established criteria for approval of residency programs to maintain high standards of training. Most dermatology residency programs are conducted at veterinary schools. However, alternative residency programs are available, whereby trainees gain the bulk of their required practice experience working under an ACVD Diplomate in private practice.

One of the major functions of the College is to grant Diplomate status to trained veterinary dermatologists. The process of board certification begins with the applicants submission of credentials: verification of training in an approved program, scientific publications, letters of evaluation, and written case reports. Each applicant's credentials are reviewed carefully. If accepted, the applicant become eligible to take the certification examination.

The College co-sponsors a four-day scientific program held each spring. The annual meeting is an opportunity for presentation of pre-publication research studies and case reports, as well as review sessions and guest speakers addressing a variety of topics.

The ACVD sponsors several programs to disseminate knowledge and improve the level of training of general veterinary practitioners in dermatology. General practitioner-level review courses are offered at the annual meeting. The ACVD is co-sponsor of the World Congress on Veterinary Dermatology held every three years or so. The 1992 meeting was held in Montreal, Canada in May; the 1996 meeting will be in Edinburgh, Scotland.

A limited number of research grants are offered by the ACVD annually on a competitive proposal basis. Many of these grants have been used to fund research activities that lead to new diagnostic procedures and treatments for your pet's skin problems. The majority of the research sponsorship is from drug companies. However, you too can help by making a donation to the ACVD Research Fund.

ACVD DIPLOMATES
(as of March, 1995)
(Compiled by Lowell Ackerman, DVM, Diplomate, ACVD)

Ackerman, Lowell
Arizona, Scottsdale
Arizona, Mesa
Ontario, Thornhill

Anderson, Richard
Massachusetts, Boston

Angarano, Donna
Alabama, Auburn

Atlee, Barbara
California, Fairfield
   (Cordelia)
California, Walnut Creek

Austin, Victor
California, Westlake
   Village

Baker, Benjamin
Washington, Pullman

Barbet, Joy
Florida, Archer

Beale, Karin
Texas, Houston
Texas, San Antonio

Bevier, Diane
North Carolina, Raleigh

Blakemore, James
Indiana, West Lafayette

Breen, Patrick
Kentucky, Louisville
Ohio, Cincinnati
Ohio, Columbus
Ohio, Richfield Village

Brignac, Michele
Florida, Ft. Walton Beach

Buerger, Robert
Maryland, Baltimore

Caciolo, Paul
Missouri, St. Louis

Campbell, Karen
Illinois, Urbana

Cayette, Suzanne
Florida, Largo

Chalmers, Stephanie
California, Santa Rosa
California, Walnut Creek

Charach, Mike
British Columbia,
   Coquitlam
British Columbia,
   Kelowna
British Columbia,
   Nanaimo
British Columbia,
   Richmond
British Columbia, Victoria

Chester, David
Texas, College Station

Conroy, James (Pathologist)
Arizona, Prescott

DeBoer, Douglas
Wisconsin, Madison

Delger, Julie
South Carolina, Columbia

Doering, George
California, Walnut Creek

Duclos, David
Washington, Lynnwood

Evans, Anne
Massachusetts, North
   Grafton

Fadok, Valerie
Texas, College Station

Foil, Carol
Louisiana, Baton Rouge

Frank, Linda
Tennessee, Knoxville

Garfield, Reid
Oklahoma, Tulsa
Texas, Dallas
Texas, Ft. Worth
Texas, Tyler

Gilbert, Patricia
California, Rancho Santa Fe

Globus, Helen
Minnesota, Apple Valley
Minnesota, Golden Valley

Gordon, John
Ohio, Columbus

Gram, Dunbar
Virginia, Virginia Beach
Virginia, Richmond

Greek, Jean
Kansas, Overland Park

Griffin, Craig
Alaska, Anchorage
Alaska, Fairbanks
California, Alta Loma
California, Bakersfield
California, Garden Grove
California, Los Gatos
California, San Diego

California, Scotts Valley
Hawaii, Honolulu
Hawaii, Kamuela
Hawaii, Kaneohe
Hawaii, Kona
Hawaii, Wahiawa
Hawaii, Waipahu
Nevada, Las Vegas

Hall, Jan
Illinois, Urbana

Halliwell, Richard
Scotland, Edinburgh

Hansen, Bruce
Virginia, Springfield

Hillier, Andrew
Australia, Perth

Ihrke, Peter
California, Davis

Jeffers, James
Maryland, Gaithersburg

Jeromin, Alice
Ohio, Brecksville
Ohio, Toledo
Pennsylvania, Wexford

Kalaher, Kathleen
Maryland, Baltimore

Kirk, Robert W.
New York, Ithaca

Kuhl, Karen
Illinois, Downers Grove

Kunkle, Gail
Florida, Gainesville

Kwochka, Kenneth
Ohio, Columbus

Lewis, Diane
Florida, Gainesville

Lewis, Thomas
Arizona, Mesa
Arizona, Tucson
New Mexico,
    Albuquerque
New Mexico, Santa Teresa
Utah, Salt Lake City

Logas, Dawn
Florida, Gainesville

MacDonald, John
Alabama, Auburn

Manning, Thomas
North Carolina, Raleigh

McKeever, Patrick
Minnesota, St. Paul

Medleau, Linda
Georgia, Athens

Merchant, Sandra
Louisiana, Baton Rouge

Messinger, Linda
Florida, Winter Park

Miller, Wiilliam
New York, Ithaca

Moriello, Karen
Wisconsin, Madison

Mueller, Ralf
Australia, Victoria

Muller, George
California, Walnut Creek

Mundell, Alan
Washington, Seattle

Nesbitt, Gene
Maine, Standish
New Jersey, West
    Caldwell
New York, Coram

Panic, Rada
New Jersey, Tinton Falls
New York, Burnt Hills
New York, Mineola

Paradis, Manon
Quebec, St. Hyacinthe

Phillips, Margaret
Tennessee, Nashville

Plant, Jon
California, Santa Monica
California, Ventura
California, Woodland
    Hills

Power, Helen
California, Los Gatos

Rachofsky, Marc
Texas, Dallas

Reedy, Lloyd
Texas, Dallas
Texas, Fort Worth
Texas, Plano
Texas, Tyler

Reinke, Susan
California, Corte Madera

Helton-Rhodes, Karen
New York, New York

Rosenkrantz, Wayne S.
Alaska, Anchorage
Alaska, Fairbanks
California, Alta Loma
California, Bakersfield
California, Garden Grove
California, Los Gatos
California, San Diego
California, Scotts Valley
Hawaii, Honolulu
Hawaii, Kamuela
Hawaii, Kaneohe
Hawaii, Kona
Hawaii, Wahiawa

Hawaii, Waipahu
Nevada, Las Vegas

Rosser, Edmund
Michigan, East Lansing

Scheidt, Vicki
New Hampshire, Lyme

Schick, Robert
Georgia, Augusta
Georgia, Riverdale
Georgia, Roswell

Schmeitzel, Lynn
Tennessee, Knoxville

Schwartzman, Robert
Pennsylvania,
   Philadelphia

Scott, Danny
New York, Ithaca

Shanley, Kevin
Delaware, Newark
Pennsylvania, Valley Forge

Shoulberg, Nina
New York, Katonah
New York, Yonkers

Small, Erwin
Illinois, Urbana

Sousa, Candace
California, Sacramento

**Stannard, Anthony (Patholo-
   gist)**
California, Davis

Stewart, Laurie
Massachusetts, North
   Grafton

Torres, Sheila
Minnesota, St. Paul

Werner, Alexander
California, Camarillo
California, Los
   Angeles
California, Studio City
Nevada, Reno

White, Patricia
Georgia, Avondale
Georgia, Marietta

White, Stephen
Colorado, Fort Collins

Locations of Veterinary
Dermatology Referral Centers
Compiled by Lowell Ackerman, DVM, Diplomate, ACVD

ALASKA
Northern Lights Animal
   Clinic
Dr. Craig Griffin
Dr. Wayne Rosenkrantz
2002 W. Benson
Anchorage, AK 99517
(907) 276-2340
(Visits twice yearly)

Aurora Animal Clinic
Dr. Craig Griffin
Dr. Wayne Rosenkrantz
1651 College Rd.
Fairbanks, AK 99507
(907) 452-6055
(Visits approximately
   twice yearly)

ALABAMA
Auburn University

Dr. Donna Walton
   Angarano
College of Veterinary
   Medicine
Auburn, AL 36849
(205) 844-4690

Auburn University
Dr. John M. MacDonald
College of Veterinary
   Medicine
Auburn, AL 36849
(205) 844-4000

ARIZONA
Mesa Veterinary Hospital,
   Ltd.
Dr. Lowell J. Ackerman
Dr. Thomas P. Lewis II
858 N. Country Club
   Drive

Mesa, AZ 85201
(602) 833-7330

Southwest Veterinary
   Specialist
Dr. Thomas P. Lewis II
141 East Ft. Lowell
   Road
Tucson, AZ 85705
(602) 888-4498

CALIFORNIA
Animal Dermatology &
   Allergy Center
Dr. Barbara A. Atlee
Encinna Veterinary
   Hospital
2803 Ygnacio Valley
   Road
Walnut Creek, CA 94598
(510) 937-5008

Animal Dermatology &
Allergy Center
Dr. Barbara A. Atlee
Solano Pet Emergency
Clinic
4437 Central Place
Fairfield (Cordelia), CA
94585
(707) 864-3742

Animal Dermatology
Center
Dr. Stephanie A.
Chalmers
4900 Sonoma Hwy.
Santa Rosa, CA 95409
(707) 538-4643

Veterinary Dermatology
Service
Dr. Stephanie A.
Chalmers
Dr. George G. Doering
1411 Treat Blvd.
Walnut Creek, CA 94596
(510) 934-8051

Veterinary Specialty
Hospital
Dr. Patricia Gilbert
6525 Calle Del Nido, Box
9727
Rancho Santa Fe, CA
92067
(619) 759-1777

Animal Dermatology
Clinic
Dr. Craig Griffin
Dr. Wayne Rosenkrantz
13132 Garden Grove
Blvd.
Garden Grove, CA 92643
(714) 971-6211

Animal Dermatology
Clinic
Dr. Craig Griffin
Dr. Wayne Rosenkrantz

13240 Evening Creek
Drive, #302
San Diego, CA 92128
(619) 486-4600

Baseline Animal Hospital
Dr. Craig Griffin
Dr. Wayne Rosenkrantz
9350 Baseline Rd.,
Suite A
Alta Loma, CA 91701
(714) 486-4600
(Monthly visits)

Valley Oak Veterinary
Clinic
Dr. Craig Griffin
Dr. Wayne Rosenkrantz
4650 Scotts Valley Drive
Scotts Valley, CA 95060
(408) 438-6546
(Visits approximately
twice yearly)

Oak Meadow Veterinary
Hospital
Dr. Craig Griffin
Dr. Wayne Rosenkrantz
641 University Avenue
Los Gatos, CA 95030
(408) 354-0838
(Visits approximately
twice yearly)

Bakersfield Veterinary
Clinic
Dr. Craig Griffin
Dr. Wayne Rosenkrantz
4410 Wible Rd.
Bakersfield, CA 93313
(805) 834-6005
(Visits approximately
twice yearly)

University of California
Dr. Peter Ihrke
School of Veterinary
Medicine
Department of Medicine

Davis, Ca 95616
(916) 752-1355

Animal Dermatology
Specialty Clinic
Dr. Jon D. Plant
1304 Wilshire Blvd.
Santa Monica, CA 90403
(310) 394-6982

Animal Dermatology
Specialty Clinic
Dr. Jon D. Plant
23015 S. Victoria Ave.
Ventura, CA 93003
(310) 394-6982
(800) 606-ADSC

Animal Dermatology
Specialty Clinic
Dr. Jon D. Plant
20037 Ventura Blvd.,
Suite 105
Woodland Hills, CA
91364
(310) 394-6982
(800) 606-ADSC

Dermatology for Animals
Dr. Helen T. Power
17480 Shelburne Way
Los Gatos, CA 95030
(408) 354-1840

Madera Pet Hospital
Dr. Susan I. Reinke
5796 Paradise Drive
Corte Madera, CA 94925
(415) 924-1271

Animal Dermatology
Clinic
Dr. Candace Sousa
5701 H Street
Sacramento, CA 95819
(916) 451-6445

University of California
Dr. Anthony Stannard

School of Veterinary
   Medicine
Department of Medicine
Davis, CA 95616
(916) 752-1363

Valley Veterinary
   Specialty Services
Dr. Alexander Werner
Animal Dermatology
   Centers
13125 Ventura Blvd.
Studio City, CA 91604
(818) 981-8877
(800) 781-8877

Animal Dermatology
   Centers
Dr. Alexander Werner
1221-B Avenida Acaso
Camarillo, CA 93012
(818) 981-8877

Animal Dermatology
   Centers
Dr. Alexander Werner
4254 Eagle Rock Blvd.
Los Angeles, CA 90065
(818) 981-8877

Animal Dermatology
   Centers
Dr. Alexander Werner
1736 S. Sepulveda Blvd.,
Ste C
Los Angeles, CA 90025
(818) 981-8877

COLORADO
Colorado State University
Dr. Stephen D. White
College of Veterinary
   Medicine
Dept. of Clinical Studies
Fort Collins, CO 80523
(303) 221-4535

DELAWARE
Newark Animal Hospital

Dr. Kevin J. Shanley
245 E. Cleveland Avenue
Newark, DE 19711
(302) 737-8100
(800) 394-3874

FLORIDA
Friendship Veterinary
   Clinic
Dr. Michele Brignac
623 Beal Parkway
Ft. Walton Beach, FL
   32548
(904) 862-9813

Tampa Bay Veterinary
   Referral
Dr. Suzanne M. Cayatte
1501-A Belcher Road
   South
Largo, FL 34641
(813) 539-7990

University of Florida
Dr. Gail A. Kunkle
Dr. Diane T. Lewis
College of Veterinary
   Medicine
Box 100126
Gainesville, FL 32610-
   0126
(904) 392-4700

University of Florida
Dr. Dawn Logas
College of Veterinary
   Medicine
Box J-126
Gainesville, FL 32688-
   0126
(904) 392-4700

Animal Eye & Skin
   Associates
Dr. Linda Messinger
843 South Orlando
   Avenue
Winter Park, FL 32789
(407) 629-0044

GEORGIA
University of Georgia
Dr. Linda Medleau
College of Veterinary
   Medicine
Department of Small
   Animal Medicine
Athens, GA 30602
(706) 542-3221

Atlanta Animal Allergy
   and
   Dermatology
Dr. Robert O. Schick
280 S. Atlanta Street
Roswell, GA 30075
(404) 642-9800

Atlanta Animal Allergy
   and
   Dermatology
Dr. Robert O. Schick
6607 Powers Street
Riverdale, GA 30274
(404) 642-9800

Atlanta Animal Allergy
   and Dermatology
Dr. Robert O. Schick
Animal Emergency Clinic
   of Augusta
2401-B Washington Road
Augusta, GA 30904
(404) 642-9800

Atlanta Veterinary Skin
   and Allergy Clinic
Dr. Patricia D. White
33 Avondale Plaza North
Avondale Estates, GA
   30002
(404) 294-0580

Atlanta Veterinary Skin
   and Allergy Clinic
Dr. Patricia D. White
828 Cobb Parkway
Marietta, GA 30062
(404) 294-0580

HAWAII
Aloha Animal Hospital
    Associates
Dr. Craig Griffin
Dr. Wayne Rosenkrantz
4224 Wailae Avenue
Honolulu, HI 96816
(808) 734-2242
(Visits approximately
    twice yearly)

Animal Clinic Waipahu
Dr. Craig Griffin
Dr. Wayne Rosenkrantz
94-806 Moloalo Street
Waipahu, HI 96797
(808) 671-1751
(Visits approximately
    twice yearly)

Honolulu Pet Clinic
Dr. Craig Griffin
Dr. Wayne Rosenkrantz
1115 Young Street
Honolulu, HI 96814
(808) 537-5336
(Visits approximately
    twice yearly)

Kaneohe Veterinary
    Clinic
Dr. Craig Griffin
Dr. Wayne Rosenkrantz
45-480 Kaneohe Bay
    Drive
Kaneohe, HI 96744
(808) 235-3634
(Visits approximately
    twice yearly)

Kilani Pet Clinic
Dr. Craig Griffin
Dr. Wayne Rosenkrantz
810 Kilani Avenue
Wahiawa, HI 96786
(808) 622-2607
(Visits approximately
    twice yearly)

Kona Coast Veterinary
    Hospital
Dr. Craig Griffin
Dr. Wayne Rosenkrantz
P.O. Box 730
Kealakekua
Kona, HI 96750
(808) 322-3469
(Visits approximately
    twice yearly)
Veterinary Associates
Dr. Craig Griffin
Dr. Wayne Rosenkrantz
P.O. Box 839
Kamuela, HI 96743
(808) 885-7941
(Visits approximately
    twice yearly)

ILLINOIS
University of Illinois
Dr. Karen L. Campbell
Dept. of Veterinary
    Clinical Medicine
1008 West Hazelwood
    Drive
Urbana, IL 61801
(217) 333-5300

University of Illinois
Dr. Jan Andrea Hall
National Animal Poison
    Control Center
1220 VMBSB
College of Veterinary
    Medicine
2001 South Lincoln
Urbana, IL 61801
(217) 333-2053

Animal Allergy and
    Dermatology
Arboretum View Specialty
    Services
Dr. Karen A. Kuhl
2551 Warrenville Road
Downers Grove, IL 60515
(708) 934-6056

INDIANA
Purdue University
Dr. James C. Blakemore
School of Veterinary
    Medicine
Lynn Hall 1248
West Lafayette, IN 47907-
    1248
(317) 494-1107

KANSAS
Dermatology and Allergy
    Clinic
Dr. Jean S. Greek
10333 Metcalf Avenue
Overland Park, KS 66212
(913) 381-3937

KENTUCKY
Louisville Veterinary
    Dermatology Services
Dr. Patrick T. Breen
10466 Shelbyville Road
Louisville, KY 40223
(502) 245-7863

LOUISIANA
Veterinary Teaching
    Hospital and Clinics
Dr. Carol S. Foil
Dr. Sandra R. Merchant
Louisiana State
    University
Baton Rouge, LA 70803
(504) 346-3333

MAINE
Animal Dermatology
    Consultants
Dr. Gene H. Nesbitt
42 Highland Road (mail
    only)
Standish, ME 04084
(207) 893-0058

MARYLAND
Veterinary Dermatology
    Center

Dr. Robert G. Buerger
32 Mellor Avenue
Baltimore, MD 21228
(410) 788-8130

Dr. James Jeffers
9039 Gaither Rd.
Gaithersburg, MD 20877
(301) 977-9169

MASSACHUSETTS
Angell Memorial Animal
    Hospital
Dr. Richard K. Anderson
350 South Huntington
    Avenue
Boston, MA 02130
(617) 522-7282

Tufts University
Dr. Laurie J. Stewart
School of Veterinary
    Medicine
200 Westboro Rd.
North Grafton, MA 01536
(508) 839-5302

MICHIGAN
Michigan State
    University
Dr. Edmund J. Rosser,
    Jr.
Dept. of Small Animal
    Clinical Studies
Veterinary Medical Center
    D-208
East Lansing, MI 48824-
    1314
(517) 355-7721

MINNESOTA
Veterinary Dermatology
    Service
Dr. Helen Globus
South Metro Animal
    Emergency Care
14520 Pennock Avenue
Apple Valley, MN 55124
(612) 928-8097

Veterinary Dermatology
    Service
Dr. Helen Globus
Affiliated Emergency
    Veterinary Services
4708 Olson Memorial
    Highway
Golden Valley, MN
    55422
(612) 928-8097

University of Minnesota
Dr. Patrick J. McKeever
Dr. Sheila Torres
Dept. of Small Animal
    Clinical Sciences
1352 Boyd Avenue
St. Paul, MN 55108
(612) 625-9229

MISSOURI
The Animal Skin Clinic
Dr. Paul Caciolo
11148 Olive Blvd.
St. Louis, MO 63141
(314) 997-0920

NEVADA
Tropicana Veterinary
    Clinic
Dr. Craig Griffin
Dr. Wayne Rosenkrantz
2385 E. Tropicana
Las Vegas, NV 89109
(702) 736-4944
(Monthly Visits)

Animal Dermatology
    Centers
Dr. Alexander Werner
855 E. Peckham Lane
Reno, NV 89502
(818) 981-8877

NEW HAMPSHIRE
Animal Dermatology
    Service
Dr. Vicki J. Scheidt
6 Montview Drive

Lyme, NH 03768
(603) 448-3534

NEW JERSEY
West Caldwell Animal
    Hospital
Dr. Gene H. Nesbitt
706 Bloomfield Avenue
West Caldwell, NJ 07006
(201) 226-3727

Garden State Veterinary
    Specialists
Dr. Rada Panic
1 Pine Street
Tinton Falls, NJ 07753
(908) 922-0011

NEW MEXICO
Dermatology Clinic for
    Animals
Dr. Thomas P. Lewis II
Albuquerque Animal
    Emergency Clinic
50055 Prospect Avenue
    NE
Albuquerque, NM 87110
(505) 881-7205

El Abrigado Animal Clinic
Dr. Thomas P. Lewis II
900 Country Club Road
Santa Teresa, NM 88008
(505) 589-1818

NEW YORK
The Animal Medical
    Center
Dr. Karen Helton Rhodes
510 E. 62nd Street
New York, NY 10021
(212) 838-8100 Ext 233

Cornell University
Dr. William H. Miller, Jr.
College of Veterinary
    Medicine
Department of Clinical
    Sciences

Ithaca, NY 14853
(607) 253-3029

Animal Emergency
  Service
Dr. Gene H. Nesbitt
485 Middle Country
  Road
Coram, NY 11727
(516) 698-2225

Burnt Hills Veterinary
  Hospital
Dr. Rada Panic
145 Goode Street
Burnt Hills, NY 12027
(518) 399-5213

Veterinary Dermatology
  Consulting Service
Dr. Rada Panic
UltraVet Diagnostics
220 E. Jericho
  Turnpike
Mineola, NY 11501
(516) 294-6680

Cornell University
Dr. Danny W. Scott
College of Veterinary
  Medicine
Department of Clinical
  Sciences
Ithaca, NY 14853
(607) 253-3029

Katonah Veterinary
  Group
Dr. Nina Shoulberg
120 Bedford Road
Katonah, NY 10536
(914) 232-1800

County Animal Clinic
Dr. Nina Shoulberg
1574 Central Park
  Avenue
Yonkers, NY 10710
(914) 779-5000

NORTH CAROLINA
North Carolina State
  University
Dr. Diane E. Bevier
College of Veterinary
  Medicine
4700 Hillsborough
  Street
Raleigh, NC 27606
(919) 829-4495

North Carolina State
  University
Dr. Thomas O. Manning
College of Veterinary
  Medicine
4700 Hillsborough Street
Raleigh, NC 27606
(919) 821-9500

OHIO
Veterinary Dermatology
  Services
Dr. Patrick T. Breen
4725 Cornell Road
Cincinnati, OH 45241
(513) 489-4644
(800) 476-9461

Cleveland Veterinary
  Dermatology Services
Dr. Patrick T. Breen
4050 Broadview Road
Richfield Village, OH
  44286
(216) 659-4169

Columbus Veterinary
  Dermatology Services
Dr. Patrick T. Breen
5747 Cleveland Avenue
Columbus, OH 43231
(614) 891-2070

Med Vet
Dr. John G. Gordon
5747 Cleveland Avenue
Columbus, OH 43231
(614) 891-2070

Veterinary Allergy &
  Dermatology, Inc.
Dr. Alice Jeromin
8979 Brecksville Rd.
Brecksville, OH 44141
(216) 278-2446

Veterinary Allergy &
  Dermatology, Inc.
Dr. Alice Jeromin
2785 W. Central Avenue
Toledo, OH 43606
(419) 473-0328

The Ohio State
  University
Dr. Kenneth W. Kwochka
College of Veterinary
  Medicine
601 Vernon L. Tharp
  Street
Columbus, OH 43210
(614) 292-3551

OKLAHOMA
Animal Emergency
  Center
Dr. Lloyd M. Reedy
Dr. Reid A. Garfield
7220 E. 41st.
Tulsa, OK 74145-4504
(214) 241-6266

PENNSYLVANIA
Veterinary Allergy &
  Dermatology, Inc.
Dr. Alice Jeromin
10309 Perry Hwy.
Wexford, PA 15090
(412) 935-5912

Metropolitan Veterinary
  Associates
Dr. Kevin J. Shanley
Box 881, 915 Trooper
  Road
Valley Forge, PA 19482
(610) 650-0747
(610) 666-1050

SOUTH CAROLINA
South Carolina
    Dermatology Referral
    Service
Dr. Julie M. Delger
124 Stonemark Lane
Columbia, SC 29210
(803) 798-0803

TENNESSEE
The University of
    Tennessee
Dr. Linda A. Frank
College of Veterinary
    Medicine
Department of Urban
    Practice
P.O. Box 1071
Knoxville, TN 37901-1071
(615) 974-8387

Animal Allergy and
    Dermatology Referral
    Service
Dr. Margaret K. Phillips
5814 Nolensville Rd.,
    Suite 107
Nashville, TN 37211-
    6521
(615) 831-2898

The University of
    Tennessee
Dr. Lynn P. Schmeitzel
College of Veterinary
    Medicine
Department of Urban
    Practice
P.O. Box 1071
Knoxville, TN 37901-1071
(615) 974-8387

TEXAS
Gulf Coast Veterinary
    Specialists
Dr. Karin Beale
5255 Beechnut
Houston, TX 77096
(713) 666-4414

Lincoln Heights Animal
    Hospital
Dr. Karin Beale
7510 Broadway
San Antonio, TX 78209
(210) 826-6100

Texas A&M University
Dr. David K. Chester
Dept. of Small Animal
    Medicine and Surgery
College of Veterinary
    Medicine
College Station, TX 77843
(409) 845-2351

Texas A&M University
Dr. Valerie A. Fadok
College of Veterinary
    Medicine
College Station, TX 77843
(409) 845-2351

Allergy & Dermatology
    Clinic for Animals
Dr. Marc A. Rachofsky
12101 Greenville
    Aveenue, #320
Dallas, TX 75243
(214) 680-0408

Animal Dermatology
    Referral Clinic
Dr. Lloyd M. Reedy
Dr. Reid A. Garfield
2353 Royal Lane
Dallas, TX 75229
(214) 241-6266

Western Hills Animal
    Hospital
Dr. Lloyd M. Reedy
Dr. Reid A. Garfield
3325 Phoenix
Fort Worth, TX 76116
(214) 241-6266

Emergency Clinic of
    Collin County

Dr. Lloyd M. Reedy
Dr. Reid A. Garfield
909 Spring Creek Pkwy.,
    Suite 410
Cross Creek Shopping
    Center
Plano, TX 75074
(214) 241-6266

Emergency Clinic
Dr. Lloyd M. Reedy
Dr. Reid A. Garfield
3326 South S.W. Loop
    323
Tyler, TX 75701
(214) 241-6266

UTAH
Eye Clinic for Animals
Dr. Thomas P. Lewis II
1892 E. Ft. Union Blvd.
Salt Lake City, UT 84121
(801) 942-3937

VIRGINIA
Animal Allergy &
    Dermatology
Dr. Dunbar Gram
3312 West Cary St.
Richmond, VA 23221
(804) 358-3376

Animal Allergy &
    Dermatology
5265 Providence Rd #300
Virginia Beach, VA 23464
(804) 467-3376

Dermatology and Allergy
    Services for Animals
Dr. Bruce L. Hansen
6651-F Backlick Rd.
Springfield, VA 22150
(703) 440-9206

WASHINGTON
Washington State
    University
Dr. Benjamin B. Baker

College of Veterinary
   Medicine
106 McCoy Hall
Pullman, WA 99163
(509) 335-0711

Animal Skin and Allergy
   Clinic
Dr. David D. Duclos
16418 7th Place West
Lynnwood, WA 98037
(206) 742-0342

Animal Dermatology
   Service
Dr. Alan C. Mundell
6525 15th Avenue NW
Seattle, WA 98117
(206) 789-2959

WISCONSIN
University of Wisconsin-
   Madison
Dr. Douglas J. Deboer
School of Veterinary
   Medicine
2015 Linden Drive West
Madison, WI 53706
(608) 263-8399

University of Wisconsin-
   Madison
Dr. Karen A. Moriello
School of Veterinary
   Medicine
2015 Linden Drive West
Madison, WI 53706
(608) 263-7600

AUSTRALIA
Animal Skin and Allergy
   Clinic
Dr. Andrew Hillier
597 Stirling Highway
Cottesloe, Perth, WA 6011
(9) 3841089
(9) 3841877

547 Dandenong Road
Dr. Ralf S. Mueller
Armadale, VIC 3143
(61) 3-5096477

CANADA
Doncaster Animal Clinic
Dr. Lowell J. Ackerman
99 Henderson Avenue
Thornhill, Ontario L3T 2K9
(905) 881-2922

Garden City Veterinary
   Hospital
Dr. Michael Charach
140-8040 Garden City Rd
Richmond, British
   Columbia V6X 2N9
(604) 270-6199

Fairfield Animal Hospital
Dr. Michael Charach
1987 Kirschner Road
Kelowna, British
   Columbia V1Y 4N7
(800) 3337-6838

Island Veterinary Hospital
Dr. Michael Charach
1621 Townsite Road

Nanaimo, British
   Columbia V9S 1N3
(800) 337-6838

Central Victoria
   Veterinary Hospital
Dr. Michael Charach
760 Roderick Street
Victoria, British Columbia
   V8X 2R3
(800) 337-6838

After Hours Pet
   Hospital
Dr. Michael Charach
963 Brunette Avenue
Coquitlam, British
   Columbia V3K 1E1
(604) 270-6199

Universite de Montreal
Dr. Manon Paradis
Faculte Medicine
   Veterinaire
CP5000
St. Hyacinthe, Quebec
   J2S 7C6
(514) 773-0162

GREAT BRITAIN
Royal School of
   Veterinary Studies
Dr. Richard E.W.
   Halliwell
Dept. of Veterinary
   Clinical Studies
Summerhall, Edinburgh
EH3 91Q Scotland
(44) 31 650 6149

The Professional Groomer

By Hazel Christiansen
President, American Grooming
   Shop Association
4575 Galley Road, Suite 400A
Colorado Springs, CO 80915

Hazel Christiansen has shown dogs in both conformation and obedience in the United States, Canada and Hong Kong. She is President of the American Grooming Shop Association, a national non-profit association, and has been grooming for 30 years. Hazel teaches pet education in the public school system, is a regular on local radio programs, and serves on the editorial board of Casamount Publications. She owns Blue Ribbon Pet Grooming in Lewiston, Idaho.

Although there are a lot of groomers out there, training and level of skill are not uniform. Some individuals refer to themselves as dog groomers, some as canine cosmetologists, and others as professional pet stylists. The profession is embarking on a course to provide testing procedures, training seminars, and networking for groomers and would-be groomers.

The International Society of Canine Cosmetologists has a three-stage program of advanced instruction and testing. It provides a validation process for qualified individuals. Level One is called DermaTech and it covers topical skin treatments, chemicals, ergonomics, and breed identification. Level Two, the Certified Master Pet Stylist, includes grooming Non-Sporting, Sporting, and Terrier breeds. After two years of pet styling experience, testing is available for the Master Canine Cosmetologist Program. Contact Pam Lauritzen & Co. at 2702 Covington Drive, Garland, TX 75040.

National Dog Groomers Association conducts testing and training seminars. Their testing format requires both written and hands-on grooming to be judged by a panel of judges. Individuals take a written test for Sporting, Non-Sporting, Terriers, and a final exam for National Certified Master Groomer.

Contact Jeff Reynolds, National Dog Groomers Association of America, Inc., P.O. Box 101, Clark, PA 16113.

Western World Pet Supply Association conducts training and testing for certification as a Companion Animal Hygienist. The course includes lectures and tapes covering theory. Those who complete all three sections of their course can receive certificates for CAH, Clipper and Scissor Technique, and The Grooming of Cats. Contact Western World Pet Supply Association, Inc., 818-447-2222.

The American Grooming Shop Association is a national non-profit trade association of shop owners and managers. It provides free consultation to its members for solving their business problems. Their educational programs are being formed to allow testing for the individual, and accreditation for the shop itself. AGSA also conducts two seminars per year on "buying, building and operating a successful grooming shop". These seminars cover location, design, business practices, hiring and firing properly, new shop equipment, and other subjects relevant to shop management and ownership. Contact AGSA at 4575 Galley Road, Suite 400-A, Colorado Springs, CO 80915.

International Professional Groomers also have a testing process that includes hands-on grooming and theory. It is a non-profit trade association. They test a groomer's technique on a dog from Sporting, Non-Sporting and Terrier Groups and have a Master's test as well. They can be contacted at 1108 Elk Grove, IL 60007.

State organizations for groomers are active in Illinois, California, Washington and others. While they may not have testing procedures, they do conduct grooming seminars.

Grooming seminars are held throughout the United States. These seminars often include breed demonstrations, suggestions on ways to increase client satisfaction and how to run a grooming business more efficiently. Some of the major seminars are:

- Atlanta Pet Fair, 4782 Jimmy Carter Blvd., Ste 2a, Norcross, GA 30093. (404) 925-9284.
- All American Midwest Dog Grooming Seminar, Jerry Schinberg, (708) 364-4547.
- Groom Expo, Barkleigh Publications, 6 State Road #13, Mechanicsburg, PA 17055.
- Intergroom, 250 E. 73rd St., Ste 4F, New York, NY, 10021, Shirlee Kalstone, (212) 628-3537.

Many trade shows and grooming seminars also have grooming contests, where pet stylists can have the opportunity to demonstrate their work. The dogs are groomed in front of the crowd, then a judge checks the work and awards prizes for the best-groomed dogs. There are different classes available, depending upon the breed of dog and the groomer's experience.

There are also contests for creative grooming, where the contestant thinks of a theme, grooms the dog to fit the theme, then decorates around the dog. Sometimes these contestants complete the image with music. It allows the creative and artistic ability of the individual to shine. Groomers usually pay an entrance fee, and cash awards are usually given as prizes.

Groomers winning the most points at shows across the U.S. may be selected for "Groom Team", and have an opportunity to represent their country in international competition.

Index

Page numbers in **boldface** refer to illustrations.